TWILIGHT OF AUTHORITY

TWILIGHT
OF
AUTHORITY

Robert Nisbet

NEW YORK   OXFORD UNIVERSITY PRESS   1975

PREFACE

PERIODICALLY in Western history twilight ages make their appearance. Processes of decline and erosion of institutions are more evident than those of genesis and development. Something like a vacuum obtains in the moral order for large numbers of people. Human loyalties, uprooted from accustomed soil, can be seen tumbling across the landscape with no scheme of larger purpose to fix them. Individualism reveals itself less as achievement and enterprise than as egoism and mere performance. Retreat from the major to the minor, from the noble to the trivial, the communal to the personal, and from the objective to the subjective is commonplace. There is a widely expressed sense of degradation of values and of corruption of culture. The sense of estrangement from community is strong.

Accompanying the decline of institutions and the decay of values in such ages is the cultivation of power that becomes increasingly military, or paramilitary, in shape. Such power exists in almost exact proportion to the decline of traditional social and moral authority. Representative and liberal institutions of government slip into patterns ever more imperial in character. Military symbols and constraints loom where civil values reigned before. The centralization and, increasingly, individualization of power is matched in the social and cultural spheres by a combined hedonism and egalitarianism, each in its way a reflection of the destructive impact of power on the hierarchy that is native to the social bond.

Over everything hangs the specter of war. Such war may be civil or foreign or both. War invariably has its expressed political, diplomatic, or economic objects, but no one can miss the degree to which it becomes increasingly an anodyne for internal torments and frustrations. As the way out of economic crisis, political division, and intolerable social disintegration, war, despite its consecration of force and violence, its raw disciplines, and its heavy blanket of regimentation upon a social order, becomes attractive to enlarging numbers.

A number of major twilight ages can be seen in the two and a half millennia of Western history. The post-Peloponnesian Athens in which the young Plato grew up is one; so is the period in the Greek world which just precedes the rise of Christianity; and Rome of the first century B.C. and again in the age of St. Augustine surely qualifies. In modern European history the period so inaccurately and widely referred to as the Renaissance—one so much better described, it seems to me, by Huizinga's phrase "the waning of the Middle Ages"—is surely one of the West's notable twilight epochs. All of the major stigmata—cultural and social decay, celebration of war and power, and intense, often morbid, subjectivism—are present in the Italy so brilliantly described by Burckhardt and a few of his greater successors.

So, I believe, is the twentieth century in the West a twilight age. That is largely what this book is about. It is not a study in comparative history, though I do not hesitate to draw from other ages in occasional stress of a point. My objective is that of seeking to light up the present, chiefly the American present, in the historical perspective of twilight. It is hard to think of any other useful perspective in which to set the combined phenomena of sense of cultural decay, erosion of institutions, progressive inflation of values in all spheres, economic included, and constantly increasing centralization—and militarization—of power. If there were no other indicator, the impact of war and of the military on the West, especially since about 1940, would be sufficient—that and the cognate spread of the kind of social equalitarianism which is bred less by the moral value of equality than by centralized power's leveling effects upon the natural hierarchies of all social institutions.

In the final chapter I seek to identify the essential social elements of an alternative to the twilight age we live in now. It is possible, as I suggest, that certain countervailing forces are already in evidence, leading at once to diminution of the state's power and to a greater degree of vitality in our social organization. What is clear is that the two processes, whenever and wherever they are to be found, are indissolubly linked. I know of no principle in history more often validated than that which tells us that social health and political power are inversely related. If, as this book suggests, social anemia is the necessary consequence of political hypertrophy, it is evident that renewal of strength in the social order demands a fundamental change in present uses of political power.

R.N.

New York
May 1975

ACKNOWLEDGMENTS

PARTS of this book have appeared, in very different forms and contexts, during the past half-dozen years in *The Public Interest, Commentary, Encounter, The Virginia Quarterly Review, Change, The New York Times,* and *The Montreal Star.* Needless to say, I am grateful to these journals for the opportunities provided for earliest formulation of some of the book's ideas. It is a pleasure to record here my gratitude to Joseph Epstein, editor of *The American Scholar,* for original encouragement to develop these ideas into a book. To Sheldon Meyer, vice president of Oxford University Press and friend of many years, I gladly acknowledge not only needed personal support but suggestions of content and style which have added greatly to whatever merit may lie in the book. Stephanie Golden, assistant editor at Oxford University Press, has provided detailed, often necessarily critical, invariably helpful advice that is embodied in literally every page. I thank her most warmly. Finally, to my wife Caroline I express loving appreciation of all that she has once again managed to do to make a book possible.

CONTENTS

TWILIGHT OF AUTHORITY

THE POLITICAL COMMUNITY AT BAY

I BELIEVE THE SINGLE most remarkable fact at the present time in the West is neither technological nor economic, but political: the waning of the historic political community, the widening sense of the obsolescence of politics as a civilized pursuit, even as a habit of mind. By political community I mean more than the legal state. I have in mind the whole fabric of rights, liberties, participations, and protections that has been, even above industrialism, I think, the dominant element of modernity in the West. To an astonishing degree modern Western society has been *political* society, and this has been made possible only by the growing sense of the state in modern times as being more than a structure of power, as being a cherished form of community.

In a very real sense the political community in the West has been the successor, certainly since the eighteenth century, of the church as the major arena of man's hopes, devotions, and aspirations. One would have to go to religion to find anything comparable to modern Western man's willingness to make sacrifices, of property and

life when necessary, in the name of political patriotism. Patriotism
through most of the nineteenth century and the first part of the
twentieth exercised every bit of the hold upon man's relation to
state that piety for so long had to church. Looking back, and reflecting on the innumerable centuries earlier when political government was the object of fear and distrust in so many areas, symbolized in popular consciousness by the policeman, soldier, or tax
collector, it is one of history's miracles that from the end of the
eighteenth century on in the West populations were willing to en-
trust so much of their economic, social, and moral life to the super-
vision of the political sphere. Without question, the political—
meaning not merely government and state but a whole way of life,
participation, and thought—has had man's trust to a degree no
other institution in modern times has had.

It no longer has. A variety of evidences, most of them by now
obvious to the layman, suggest that confidence and trust have been
replaced by opposite sentiments, that government, from being the
protector of the lives of its citizens, has become the greatest single
source of exploitation in the minds of a growing number of people.
Once political government in the United States signified some degree of austerity of life, of commitment to the public weal, of a
willingness to forego most of life's luxuries in the name of service
that was for a long time closely akin to what one found in the ranks
of clergy and teachers. Today, as scores of surveys and polls reveal, government is perceived by large numbers of citizens as the
domain of economic luxury, great personal power, high social status, all symbolized perfectly by the pomp and grandeur of public
architecture. It is also perceived, we learn from the same surveys
and polls, as being possessed of a degree of arrogance that no corporation could today get away with in the business world, that was
once regarded as the privilege of hereditary aristocracy.

A clerisy of power exists that in size and complexity is without
precedent since the height of the Roman Empire. This clerisy has
deep roots in modern European history, but never before, not even

in the post-Renaissance absolute monarchies, has it known the intellectual and economic affluence it knows at the present time. It is composed not only of those who occupy the top elective or appointive positions in our political society, and by their aides and subordinates, all alike preoccupied by the attributes of power, but also, and far from least, by the greater part of the intellectual, especially academic, class. For this class the political state has a sacredness that the church once possessed for its own clerisy. I shall have more to say about the clerisy of power later. Suffice it here to say that it is as vivid a reality in modern democracy as it ever was in any Renaissance monarchy; as vivid, and vastly larger.

We are nevertheless witnessing, as I write, a gathering revolt against this same political clerisy and against the whole structure of wealth, privilege, and power that the contemporary democratic state has come to represent. What we are also witnessing, and this tragically, is rising opposition to the central values of the political community as we have known them for the better part of the past two centuries: freedom, rights, due process, privacy, and welfare.

I say "tragically" advisedly. I find it hard to think that very much of the extraordinary burst of economic, social, and cultural growth we have known during the last two hundred years would have been possible apart from the structure of liberties and rights which were guaranteed by the political community. To lose, as I believe we are losing, this structure of values is surely among the more desolating facts in the present decline of the West. Nevertheless, looked at in historical terms, it would be remarkable if the present combination of political Leviathan and sense of helplessness and impotence in citizenry were not attended by disenchantment and rising hatred.

It would be comforting if the revolt were simply the result of Viet Nam and Watergate. But it cannot be so seen. In the first place the roots of revolt are deeper and older in this country. In the second place, precisely the same kind of revolt is to be seen in other Western countries, those which have known neither Viet Nam nor

Watergate. In West Germany, Italy, France, the Scandinavian countries, Holland, Belgium, and even—now especially—England, the reports of citizen unrest, citizen indifference, citizen alienation, and citizen hostility to government do not differ appreciably from what we are given in the United States.

Clearly, we are at the beginning of a new Reformation, this time, however, one that has the political state rather than the church as the central object of its force; a force that ranges from the slow drip of apathy to the more hurricane-like intensities of violence and terror. The first great Reformation, that of the sixteenth century, was also a period of twilight of authority in the West. It was terminated by the rise of the national state and the gradual retreat of church, kinship, guild, and hereditary class. Today we are present, I believe, at the commencement of the retreat of the state as we have known this institution for some five centuries, though what the consequences will be no one can be certain.

The new Reformation, it has to be said, was predicted clearly enough in the nineteenth century and also in the early part of our own century. True, little if any attention was paid these predictions at the time, or indeed in the decades following for the most part until just after World War II. But the predictions are there and remain fertile sources of insight into our present crisis. I have reference to those such as Burke, Lamennais, Tocqueville, Proudhon, Burckhardt, and Nietzsche, a wide enough variety surely, who early became aware of the potentialities for self-destruction which lay in the modernity that the new democratic state, above any other single institution, was generating. What these minds could see well in advance was the increasing massiveness of sheer political-military power coexisting with the crumbling of the pre-democratic strata of values and institutions which alone made political freedom possible, leaving in the end the centralized state of the masses.

Thus Edmund Burke, in his *Reflections on the Revolution in France* wrote of "a great crisis, not of the affairs of France alone, but of all

Europe, perhaps of more than Europe," and referred prophetically to "the hollow murmuring underground; a confused movement . . . that threatens a general earthquake in the political world." Nor did Burke fail to see the nature of the crisis that lay ahead: one compounded of atomized masses of citizens ruled by increasingly despotic, ever more militarized forms of government, all of them rooted in and consecrated to the masses.

Tocqueville thought that only in the occasional rise of a Napoleonic figure was future Western society likely to survive against the forces of bureaucracy, leveling, and endemic egoism which were being spawned by modernity. Of Napoleon he wrote: "The maintenance of order, the regular application of laws, the abolition of all unnecessary cruelty, even a certain taste for justice were characteristic of his government. Yet his suppression of free thought, the destruction of social responsibility together with the exaltation of martial courage were the main principles of that government." In our own time more and more people find themselves looking for precisely that kind of political figure.

A whole line of thinkers in the nineteenth century, one we have only really come to know in recent years, chiefly after World War II, took its envisagement of present and future from those observations by Tocqueville. Burckhardt, whose famous study of the Italian Renaissance had been constructed essentially around a fusion of the elements of hedonistic subjectivism, the arts of power, and novel uses of military despotism in the cultivation of welfare and the arts, wrote of the future:

"For a long time I have been aware that we are driving toward the alternative of complete democracy or absolute despotism without law or right. This despotic regime will not be practiced any longer by dynasties. They are too soft and kind-hearted. The new tyrannies will be in the hands of military commandos who will call themselves republican."

Among the greater sociologists of the late nineteenth and early twentieth centuries—Tönnies, Weber, Simmel, Durkheim foremost—there was common recognition of an accelerating atomization of morality and social order, with the ties of money and contract proving increasingly impotent in the maintenance of solidarity, and in the offing the prospect of a political power ever more centralized, bureaucratized, and leveling in its effects upon culture.

What Spengler called *The Decline of the West*—a work written before World War I, though not published until after—was only a restatement of the kinds of diagnosis and prophecy that had been present, though rarely recognized, in European writing since Tocqueville. Spengler, however, converted this diagnosis and prophecy into a law of history, one set forth in cyclical form and made applicable to each of the great civilizations of the past. Our Western civilization, Spengler wrote, like each of its forerunners in time, will succumb, has already begun to succumb, to the combined forces of loss of social authority and hierarchy, consequent creation of the faceless mass, and, rising above and giving domination to this mass, a new, harsh, and fundamentally barbaric military class that will govern with the rhetoric of humanitarian democracy. With Tocqueville, Burckhardt, Weber, and others before him, Spengler could see the early demise of genuinely democratic or republican forms of government, their place taken by a society so inherently atomized and unstable that military force alone would be able to give it cohesion and expression—through a constantly rising incidence of global warfare.

Has the West, in each of its nations, reached by now the condition prophesied by these and other minds of the past? There is much reason to believe so, and it would require a totally closed mind to be insensitive to the increase at the present time in forebodings of the future. Overwhelmingly these are political in character, anchored in the seeming incapacity of the political order any longer to sustain the lives and hopes of its citizens.

Strange specters hover over the land, none of them foreseen by any of us as recently as the 1930s in the United States or, for that matter, in any Western country.

There is the whole, spreading wave of unreason to be seen in both popular and philosophical writing, a recurrence of that "failure of nerve" Sir Gilbert Murray found in another of history's twilight ages, the age of social disintegration and militarism that followed the Peloponnesian Wars in ancient Greece and the consequent breakdown of the Athenian *polis*. Today, as then, the scene is filled with eruptions of the occult, the superstitious, and the antirational, of faith in blind fortune and chance, and of generalized retreat into the subjective recesses of consciousness. Salvation of the ego bids fair to replace the concern with the human community that was in a sense the mainspring of the birth of liberal democracy in the late eighteenth century.

There are other ways of perceiving the revolt against politics and the political community at the present time; no one of them crucial by itself but given extraordinary meaning by its association with other, related, phenomena. There is the all-too evident success of fundamentalist, pentecostal forms of religion, whose obvious impact—very destructive impact—upon the liberal and modernist forms of religions which had in so many instances forsaken religious for political creed should not blind us to the equally destructive impact these pentecostal forms of community have, or can easily have, upon the political habit of mind. For the war of these militant faiths is against all forms of belief which find in the political state or any other external structure of social order the possibility of redemption or salvation. The kinds of large audiences political orators attracted only a few decades ago in America are attracted today by the religious orators, revivalist and other, and there is much reason for suspecting that the gospel trail through Middle America has imposed itself on familiar political byways and avenues.

There is the upthrust of ethnicity—of what Michael Novak has brilliantly dealt with in a recent book as the "unmeltable ethnics"—with its only too clear implications for the American myth of the melting pot, yes, but also for the political bond itself which, after all, has justified itself during the past century or more largely on its capacity to divert loyalties from ancient tribalistic unities and to reunify these loyalties in the political community. We might have learned a general lesson from the profound change of black militants and intellectuals shortly after the civil rights revolution commenced in the late 1950s: a change of orientation or mission from the once-hallowed "integration" to something far more nationalistic, so far as blacks were concerned, and more pluralistic in thrust for America. Conceivably we could have sensed something coming even earlier from the renascence of the Jewish community, in so large degree generated by the holocaust in Germany but not the less important in sociological and political terms to the environing society. Ethnicity is, along with family, locality, and religion, among the most ancient and powerful of bonds for mankind. Only the political illusion could have caused us to forget this fact. We are re-learning it today.

There are other evidences of revolt against conventional political idols: the renewed search for neighborhood in city and town alike—a search for community in the larger sense, if we like, but one directly aimed at such vital matters as social welfare and education. The clamant appeal from blacks in the 1960s to become themselves responsible for the public school education of their children, to administer themselves the welfare funds released from Washington, with crises induced in respective bureaucracies the like of which America had never seen, has subsided somewhat in noise, but not, I would guess, in underlying intensity. In this fact too, as I shall later argue, there is some hope to be gleaned, but for the moment it is repercussion to political community alone that I am interested in.

There is the whole, remarkable movement, chiefly of youth, which began more or less with the so-called beatniks of the 1950s, which continued in the hippie culture, and which, in language, song, values, even mode of dress and hair-styling, has had such striking effect upon the larger population. Whatever else this move-

ment is, it is distinctly anti-political. If it is radical, it is a radicalism without direct interest in the kinds of things political radicals
have been concerned with for a couple of centuries, these being
chiefly the ends and means of power in the social order. One remembers even today the agitation of mind that seized the more militant intellectuals of the Old Left back in the 1950s when it became
apparent that their idols were not the idols of this then-emerging
group. Some, though not many, were to become the New Left of
the 1960s which itself had little but contempt for the Old Left. For
the most part, though, and this has become overwhelmingly true at
the present time, the group I refer to shows only a bare minimum
of interest in politics or its ends and instrumentalities.

There is far more interest among this group, and in many other
sectors of youth as well, in the contemporary commune. At the
moment it is impossible to be certain of the long-run influence of
this institution. There are approximately 10,000 such organizations,
rural and urban, today. Whether the number will rise or fall is anyone's guess. My own is that it will continue rising slowly. It is,
whether in fact or in aspiration, far closer to the heart of the *cultural* left than anything measurable in political terms, and there is
moreover the fact that the commune is close also to the general
ethos of recrudescent religion in our time.

I do not doubt that the ethnic, religious, and social phenomena I
describe have many sources. But surely a major one is repudiation
of the political state and of the whole pattern of thinking that has
been associated with the state for more than two centuries. Our age
is by no means unique in this respect. The breakdown of the Alexandrian Empire in ancient Greece was associated with the eruption
of numerous otherworldly, often frankly irrationalist, faiths. The
rise of Christianity itself has to be seen in circumstances of extraordinary political strain in the Mediterranean world. The beginnings
of Western monasticism in the Benedictine movement of the sixth
century lay in the conviction shared by Saint Benedict with others
that no further hope could be found in the established political

order of Rome. Throughout recorded history there is a high correlation between alienation of individual loyalties from dominant political institutions and the rise of new forms of community—ethnic,
religious, and other—which are at once renunciations of and challenges to these political institutions. It would be astonishing if the
number of such renunciations and challenges in our own day did
not increase markedly in the future.

But the revolt against the political community is far from being
limited to the internal intellectual, religious, ethnic, and social
forces I have just mentioned. There is the whole ominous international scene. I am not referring here to the rise to power of areas of
the Middle East which only yesterday were in effect pawns of
Western nations, though that fact is certainly far from insignificant. I am referring to the steady rise and spread of *new types of
economic enterprise;* those commonly called the multinational corporations. Only recently have we begun to appreciate the full significance of these powerful, worldwide organizations which, in the
very scope and diversity of their operations, in their decreasing
dependence upon the sovereignty and laws of any one nation, offer
additional challenge to the political community.

We have every reason to foresee a new feudalism in the kind of
economic pluralism that is now to be seen spreading through so
many parts of the world. Only now are we beginning to appreciate
how deeply national, how firmly rooted in the political state, was
the industrialism of the nineteenth and early twentieth centuries.
That there was colonialism, international trade, commerce reaching
all parts of the world that was generated by the West, all of this we
know. But linkage between state and economy was nevertheless a
close one, as indeed it had been since the Mercantilist era signalized
the dominance the political order would have, in whatever hands,
over manufacture, trade, and commerce.

But it is doubtful that any national state in the Western world at
the present time, not even the United States, is really capable of
restraining the huge conglomerates which, wherever they initiate,

reach out to invade dozens of countries for purposes of consumer-capture and, in the process, necessarily become like those feudal-military powers which by the sixth century in the West had made chaos of the once-sovereign Roman Empire in the West. The seeming incapacity of any national government to contain or restrain the huge multinational corporations is only in part, of course, the result of the potency of these economic leviathans. Far more does this incapacity result from the immensely diminished role of the political state, of government no matter in whose hands, to enlist any longer the confidence of substantial numbers of its citizens. And that is my principal concern in this book: that and the causes and consequences of this momentous decline of the political order and the political habit of mind.

DECLINE OF CREDIBILITY

In most ages of history some one institution—kinship, religion, economy, state—is ascendant in human loyalties. Other institutions, without being necessarily obliterated, retreat to the background in terms of function and authority. History is, basically, the account of the succession of institutional authorities; or rather we should say succession and repetition, for if we look at any given area long enough over a period of time we cannot help but be struck by the fact of recurrence. Now it is kinship, then state, then religion, then political state again, and so on. To look only at the area once occupied by Rome, now for the most part Western Europe, we see, over a three-thousand-year span, first the Roman family as the dominant social institution; then the state—gradually the imperial state of the Caesars; followed, in the period we call the early Middle (or Dark) Ages, by the recurrent ascendancy of kinship, with many other institutions taking their essential patterns from kinship. Then by the twelfth century the Christian church was in almost total authority in society, with state and family both weak by comparison. With the Reformation, however, we see the Church forced to recede, its place taken by the political arm.

When major institutions die or become weak, it is ultimately by virtue of their loss of power to command respect and allegiance. That loss of power is manifest today in the state. There are many evidences of this; the political surveys and polls revealing popular attitudes and sentiments which are steadily more hostile; the manifest decline of political parties as institutionalizations of will and purpose; the erosion of patriotism and its rituals; the decline of distinct political ideologies; and, ominously, the specter of lawlessness that hovers over all Western populations at the present time. I want to comment on each of these briefly; all of them are important as indicators. What they tell us is that large numbers of people, without any sure instinct yet as to what a feasible alternative would be, reveal a profound distrust of the political order, its politicians and its clerisy, the political intellectuals, and indeed of the whole political habit of mind that has been so ascendant in the West for several centuries now.

I know of no major poll that has not shown, over the past two decades, almost continuous decline in popular trust of government and its leaders, in expressed confidence in the political process, and in desire or willingness to participate directly in this political process. What the Gallup, Roper, and Harris polls reveal is shown also in research surveys by major university institutes and in detailed studies of voter apathy and alienation. The blunt fact is that a broad gulf between citizen and government exists in our time, a gulf broader, certainly, than any that has existed in the West since the period just prior to the American and French revolutions.

Louis Harris, one of the most respected of poll experts, in a study done specially for the Senate subcommittee on intergovernmental relations in late 1973, found that throughout America there is rising conviction that something "seriously wrong" exists in government; that political figures, whether appointed or elected, are in politics for their own enrichment in power or money, not for the welfare of the people they represent; and, finally, that despite the many billions spent on political and social projects of reform, the rich are richer, the poor poorer. Mr. Harris, in summarizing his study before the Senate subcommittee, stated: "Any objective analysis . . . can only conclude that a crisis of the most serious magnitude now exists in the response and assessment of the people to their government." There is a kind of gallows humor in Harris's further revelation to the subcommittee that a majority of governors and other high political figures in America do not themselves believe there is anything seriously wrong at the present time.

What begins in the political sphere spreads easily to other areas of institutional life. Alongside want of confidence in political leaders at every level is to be seen, as polls and surveys also make clear, comparable want of confidence in other spheres of society: predominantly, it is worth stressing, spheres which have become increasingly tinged by political action, or by some other relation to the political area, during the last half-century. The politicization of university, clergy, economy, and other sectors of society links their fate in rising degree to that of the political state itself. Leaders in these sectors must expect, in some measure at least, the same loss of esteem that is being suffered by political leaders. Ominously, only the military seems to have escaped the ravaged confidence we find in other areas.

We have placed, often with the best of intentions and under irresistible compulsion, a constantly growing burden of responsibility upon a single institution in society—the political state; and it would be no doubt strange if some kind of disillusionment with the political order were not all around us in the present age. Disillusionment cannot help but follow inflated expectations; and a large part of the history of modern Western thought is taken up with expectations of the blessedness that must prevail in all areas if we but seize properly upon the political state and extend its disciplines and beneficences widely in the social sphere, whether in the name of socialism, communism, social democracy, or ordinary planned economy. Only in religion, chiefly Christianity, is there comparable inflation of promise or expectation for what a single institution, properly understood, can do for mankind. The profound disillusionment in the Church that seized so many minds starting in the fifteenth century, if not earlier, resulted, as we know, in a remaking of Western Europe. Can we believe other than that analogous disillusionment with politics and the state in our time will prove to have major consequences, and perhaps deadly ones, for freedom and welfare alike?

GOVERNMENT AS DECEPTION

More and more it appears that the art of governing is the art of deceiving on a large scale. The consequence of this observation, when it is shared by enough people, can only be to destroy trust not only in political government but in society generally. David Wise, in his valuable *The Politics of Lying*, may exaggerate the case slightly, but he is utterly right, I believe, in his contention that any presidency with constantly enlarging staff and powers, with a self-protective passion for secrecy, and which is seized by the awareness of resolute opponents or enemies, is bound to create and then seek to reinforce what Wise calls the "system of institutionalized lying."

To be sure, how we ordinarily react to lying by the government, particularly by a president, seems to have depended during the past few decades pretty much on who was lying to whom about what. Ideological considerations can put quite different lights upon what is at bottom a straight lie. It can be one thing for a Roosevelt to lie about the real purposes of the Supreme Court reform bill and something else for an Eisenhower to lie about the U-2 plane over Russia. In the long run, though, lying can only destroy all trust.

Early critics of large-scale democracy foresaw a steady increase in deception, evasion, duplicity, and outright falsification in democratic governments the more widely and deeply the political process penetrated the social and economic sectors of life. Government, it was argued by such writers as Sir Henry Maine, James Fitzjames Stephens, Emile Faguet, and in this country Henry Adams, among others, has certain fixed power-objectives irrespective of its specific form—monarchical, oligarchic, or democratic—and such objectives demand means which are often repugnant to the moral sensibilities of the middle class. Democracy, with its tacit responsibility to the electorate, with its accountability in some degree to legislatures, press, and public, carries a larger potential for deception than is likely in other forms of government simply by virtue of this accountability.

Has organized, institutionalized lying in government increased measurably in this century? Everything suggests that it has. The vast expansion of bureaucracy, the vastly greater number of opportunities for embarrassing mistakes by administrative officials, the sheer number of such mistakes bound to occur, all put a premium upon concealment, ranging from ordinary failure to report the truth to outright lying—whether in routine reports or in public statements by high officials. Few persons today are under much illusion as to what the phrase "national security" can cover and has recently been shown to cover. Prior to World War II, the idea of national security as a cloak for domestic as well as foreign activities was hardly known.

Almost certainly the amount of direct lying to the people by American presidents has increased substantially in recent years. There are occasional instances earlier in the century now duly recorded in the history books, as when Woodrow Wilson, in the 1916 re-election campaign, denied explicitly that any preparation for American entry into the war in Europe had been made or that any understanding with Great Britain had been reached. The art of management of the truth improved visibly during the New Deal, and if "lying" is too strong a word for FDR's statements on the budget, the nature of the NRA, the Supreme Court "packing" bill, and, after about 1937, the American relationship once again with an England on the verge of war, there is no question but that deceptiveness and concealment reached new heights—all in the name, of course, of this or that domestic, or foreign, mission with high-minded ideological overtones.

Probably there was a distinct reduction in the amount of presidential lying in the period 1946–1960, though, as we have come to know, the Cold War created a good many agencies and missions in which the initial objective of deceiving the Communist countries passed insensibly into the added objective of deceiving the American people. Still, there was greater public outcry when Eisenhower was discovered to have lied about the U-2 incident than would be, I fear, the case today in any similar matter. Too much systematic deception has taken place, and been revealed, since.

The appearance in 1960 of the Kennedy administration, pledged to a "strong" presidency and to heroic stature, filled with intellectuals eager to demonstrate by whatever means their devotion both to Kennedy and to the heroic life, made an increase in governmental lying inevitable. From the point of view of the White House staff, America could be seen as alive with opponents of political, military, educational, and social progress. Full candor with such opponents could not be allowed. It is hardly a matter of surprise, in retrospect, that our entry as an armed power in Viet Nam should have been stage-managed with stealth, deception, and outright lying—lying that was solemnly rationalized at the time by a Kennedy aide.

Hannah Arendt has somewhere written that Eisenhower was the last President to believe that an act as important as the engagement of the United States in foreign war requires the prior consent of Congress. Certainly, as we know in rich detail today, the Kennedy administration did not believe this. There was no more Congressional authorization for the dispatch of nearly 16,000 uniformed, armed troops under a four-star general in 1963 than there was for the clandestine effort by Kennedy aides to unseat the South Vietnam government, thus inevitably committing this country morally to defense of that country. We were lied to from the beginning about Viet Nam.

As everyone knows, lying rose to even greater heights under Lyndon Johnson. The background of the Tonkin Gulf Resolution is surely without precedent in the history of the relationship between the executive and legislative departments of the American government. And the kind of deception that was greatest in military matters seems to have become an ever-enlarging element of strategy in purely domestic affairs. It is not necessary to idealize or romanticize earlier U.S. presidents; many of them, including Lincoln, added to the history of governmental delinquency or dereliction. But there was always the belief that in genuinely great matters, whether domestic or foreign, there must be consultation with Congress—a belief that was absent from the Kennedy and Johnson administrations.

With the election of Richard Nixon in 1968 there began, as is now widely known, the greatest single program of outright lying—in foreign and domestic matters—that any government of the United States had ever known. In respect of Viet Nam, the true extent of civil violence in America, the nature of the economic condition, and then Watergate and all that was connected with it, America was virtually deluged by official lying. Crescendo the Nixon administration assuredly is so far as systematic lying is concerned. But it is mere blindness not to recognize that the Nixon government's lying rested on a base American presidents had begun to build earlier—perhaps as early as 1916 when Wilson's re-election depended entirely on his denial that the slightest understanding existed between him and the Allied Powers.

Sober journalists have estimated that not more than about 50 percent of the American people will now believe any utterance from the White House, no matter who its occupant is, Republican or Democratic. That estimate may be high. For it is part of the decline of government's overall credibility that lying has come to be regarded as inherent in government's nature. On the European continent the recognition of a seemingly fixed relation between democratic government and official lying is much older than it is either here or in England. Only too clearly, though, this recognition is spreading rapidly in these countries, as well.

Of all passions, A. E. Housman once wrote, passion for the truth is the feeblest in man. Of course. Who will not lie to save himself? Neither the common law nor the American Constitution demands that any individual tell the truth when such an act would tend to incriminate him. Lying in behalf of self, of friends, of family, of military allies: all of this is as old, surely, as mankind. Casuistical nuances in matters of truth and falsehood are a part of the fabric of traditional law and morality.

It is different, however, in the great mass-societies we call democracies when habitual, institutionalized lying comes to be considered a part of the governmental process. A fateful circular pattern develops: the more that credibility in government's capacity to do all that it arrogates to itself drops, the greater is the amount of lying necessary by bureaucracies and officials; and the greater the amount of lying, the faster the decline in governmental credibility.

THE WEAKENING OF POLITICAL PARTY

Let me turn now to another, and in certain respects an even more fundamental, indication of the waning of the political community in the West. This is the rapid decay of political party. Few if any of the eighteenth-century architects of the political community foresaw the vital importance of party in modern liberal democracy; some indeed, as the famous tenth Federalist Paper suggests, actually feared parties, or factions as they were called. In fact, as history has shown, the all-important element of *participation* in the political community would never have become what it has become had it not been for the institutionalizations of ideology, the structurings of popular sentiment, which are what parties are about.

No matter how skeptical the Founding Fathers may have been about "factions" in politics, it was not long in the history of democracy in the West before the importance of parties was realized for what it was—the development of intermediate organizations of an unofficial kind which could serve as barriers against atomization of popular opinion and also against the coming-into-being of some form of plebiscitary mass democracy with its inevitable attractions to the would-be Napoleon, the man on horseback. Tocqueville was lavish in his praise of the party principle as he saw it working in America when he visited this country during Jackson's presidency. So, later, was Bryce, though also in awareness of the corruptions which had grown.

Nothing could be more inimical to the kind of free, representative government we have for the most part known in our history than the view—expressed more often on the left than the right—that parties obtrude themselves in the true democratic process, that they are in fact not representations but subversions of the people's will. Periodically in American history this view has erupted, generally in the context of one or other of the populisms which stretch down to our own time, and heretofore we have been able to count on luck and on the common sense of the majority (not to mention sheer habit and custom) for protection against the destructive political consequences of that kind of political atomism with its inevitable implication of a Caesarian or Napoleonic figure towering above.

Today, though, it is only too evident that parties are weaker as forces in American political life than they have ever been. As I write, memory is only too fresh of the efforts which flowed in 1972 from the Nixon campaign organization to sabotage and permanently cripple the Democratic Party and of the consequences that abortive effort had on the Republican Party as well. If the problem of our political parties could be rooted solely in the Watergate mentality, we should shortly be out in the clear. Unhappily the erosion of the political parties has been going on for some time now. Whereas for a century and a half the party was a proving ground for issues and candidates, it is evident that parties today are attacked by the same forces of distrust, disillusion, boredom, and intimations in the electorate of corruption which attack the idea of the political community. For a long time now, studies of what is called voter alienation have shown the steady increase in the numbers of those who either refuse to be identified with any political position whatsoever or else take refuge in the still respectable label "independent." The number of those categorizing themselves as independents is large and increasing, a fact that must strike dismay in the hearts of political party officials.

In contemporary political life, being an independent is less likely to bespeak personal autonomy of personal interest than personal disaffection and personal indifference. In 1971 a quarter of the American people described themselves as "independent"—the largest proportion since the Democratic and Republican parties became fixed elements of American political life. Far more indicative, however, of the significance of this phenomenon is the fact that *half* the younger vote so described itself. Add to this the disinclination on the part of a very large segment of the young, newly enfranchised in 1972, to so much as register—much less vote—and the potential long-run impact upon the two parties can be seen as fairly devastating. Nor should the present tendency of affiliation of newly enfranchised blacks be overlooked. Democratic preference is still to be seen, but in diminishing degree. Among blacks as among whites the category of independent enlarges steadily.

If there were some new party, however small or specialized, waiting in the wings, possessed even of the kind of energy and promise that existed, say, in the Progressive Party at the beginning of the century, or in the Socialist Party in the 1920s and 1930s, or in the La Follette or the Farmer-Labor movements of a few decades ago, we might take some comfort. At least the possibility would

exist of seeds of renewal in party structure amid the decaying husks
of present reality.

No such party or beginning of party is to be seen at the present
time; probably the first time in American history that such a statement can be made. All we see are enlarging aggregates of atom-like
individuals whose disenchantment with politics and party has become translated into massive indifference, always a dangerous cir-
cumstance in a democracy. David Broder, one of Washington's
most respected journalists, does not exaggerate when he writes, in
his excellent book *The Party's Over:*

> The level of frustration in the country is terribly high—dangerously
> high. I do not think we can just assume that people will bide their
> time and wait for relief to arrive from some new party, or some
> rearrangement of constituents between the Democrats and the Repub-
> licans. There is clear danger that the frustrations will find expression
> in a political "solution" that sacrifices democratic freedoms for a de-
> gree of relief from the almost unbearable tensions and strains of to-
> day's metropolitan centers.

No one has ever seen more clearly the vital relation between political party and freedom in a democracy than did Tocqueville. His
analysis of the matter in *Democracy in America* has the great merit of
placing political party under the larger heading of voluntary associations, bodies which Tocqueville's insight told him were crucial to
any freedom worthy of the name in modern society.

> There are no countries in which associations are more needed to
> prevent despotism of faction or the arbitrary power of a prince than
> those which are democratically constituted. In aristocratic nations the
> body of the nobles and the wealthy are in themselves natural associa-
> tions which check the abuses of power. In countries where such asso-
> ciations do not exist, if private individuals cannot create an artificial
> and temporary substitute for them, I can see no permanent protection
> against the most galling tyranny; and a great people may be oppressed
> with impunity by a small faction or by a single individual.

Whether there was indeed, as has been charged, a plan that began to take form during Nixon's first term which would have had the effect of centralizing and militarizing American government, with the individual citizen brought closer to the power of the national state, we shall perhaps never know. But if such a plan did exist in the minds of Nixon and a few close aides, no better beginnings could possibly have been found than in the efforts to weaken severely both major parties which, as we now know, so nearly reached fruition in the establishment of the notorious Committee to Re-Elect the President.

No lesson seems to me clearer in Western history than that which tells us that political parties—or analogous organizations such as those existing in the medieval period when modern representative institutions were coming into existence—are powerful buffers to despotism and individual centralization of government, and that if such despotism or centralization be the objective, prior weakening and destruction of strong political parties is absolutely vital. There are many periods of history to draw from in illustration of this, but I can think of none more vivid than that which preceded the transition of the ancient Roman Republic to the emperorship under Augustus. That emperorship and the disastrous consequences which eventually ensued for Rome would never have been possible had not the Caesarian principle of power first arisen, in the hands of Julius Caesar, amid the ruins of party politics in the Age of Cicero.

Whether our own impotence of party and growing fragmentation of electorate in the West will lead to analogous consequences in the final years of this century, no one of course can be sure at this moment. Our institutions of government are still strong—remarkably strong, all things considered—and there is always the possibility of a genuine reinvigoration at the roots of these institutions. Prophecy is always hazardous in these matters. But it is hard to doubt that we are living in a time when the parties have, so to speak, become tired of themselves. Our age is strikingly like that which Tocqueville, in some notes on the period just preceding Napoleon's rise to power, so well described. "The parties themselves, decimated, apathetic, and weary, longed to rest for a time during a dictatorship of any kind, provided only that it was exercised by an outsider and that it weighed upon their rivals as much as on themselves. This feature completes the picture. When great political parties begin to cool in their attachments without softening their hatreds, and at last reach the point of wishing less to succeed than to prevent the success of their opponents, one should prepare for servitude—the master is near."

In a later chapter I shall emphasize the strategic role in the contemporary world that the military—whether that of the left or the right—plays in such circumstances. For the moment it is enough to observe that the problem is worse in Western countries than that described in Tocqueville's final sentence. For in the present each of the great parties seems to have become divided into internal groups, and each of these has reached "the point of wishing less to succeed than to prevent the success of their opponents"—opponents, that is, within the same party.

What seems likely at this moment is a future less dominated politically—at least for a time—by parties in the strict sense of that word than by transparty popular movements. I mean movements which become organized around some overriding personality that can seem all things to all persons, the kind of personality Caesar, Napoleon, and Hitler so plainly had. It is hard to miss the desire at the present time for some kind of redemptive crusade, under the banner of a powerful individual presence, in the name of the people, naturally, pledged to destroy or reduce to nullity all enemies of the people, aloof to, disdainful of, all ordinary political affiliations, dedicated to something in the nature of a Common Cause. A great many intellectuals would, of course, flock to such a crusade. The McGovern campaign, which was more in the nature of a social movement at times than a political party in process of seeking election, made that fact clear. But, as is now a matter of record,

McGovern had neither the personality nor the resources of money, skill, mind, and planning to carry it off. I am inclined to think it will be different the next time.

DEMOCRATIC ROYALISM

Still another sign of the moribundity of the political community and of the larger crisis of authority in society is the astonishing growth during the past several decades of what can only be called democratic royalism. I refer to the presidency and the White House as repositories of a pomp, power, and splendor better known in the European monarchies which came into being during the Renaissance than in the kind of republic the Founding Fathers had in mind. There are many faces of royalism, and I shall describe only a few here as they have become obvious in the White House.

First, though, something must be said about the concept of royalism. It is, and has always been in its historical eruptions, fundamentally populist in root—populist and military. Say all we will about "ancient" monarchies and emperorships, the evidence is clear that, at least in the societies best known to us from their historical records, the constitutive institutions of European peoples in early times were of republican or conciliar kind. Thus in Athens and Rome alike, we find bodies typified by the great Roman Senate during the Republic long before there are monarchs and emperors in the cast of an Alexander or Augustus. It was the literal breakdown of republican institutions under the burden of war and intolerable inflation that brought into being Rome's first true monarch or emperor, Augustus, himself a soldier. The matter had not been very different in the Greece that followed the Cleisthenean reforms and the age of Pericles. The rise of the tyrants occurred in the ashes of representative institutions. And in each instance what we observe is a closer and closer tie effected between people and monarch, to the corresponding devaluation of all intermediate institutions, and, with this, an immense increase in the luxury, the splendor, and the centralized power of the government. Between king and people in the ancient world there existed the same kind of bond, basically, that we find between a general and his army or between a political boss and his constituents—one of absolute personal power, but power set in the context of benefaction and of claim upon affection.

Precisely the same kind of transformation is to be seen in the Renaissance in modern Europe. Despite a mythology still common even among historians, this was an age of increase, not in republican or representative institutions, but in types of personal and absolute power which had destruction or subordination of such institutions their primary object. The whole republican principle of assemblies of freemen, of parliamentary bodies, of, in short, *representation*, was an outgrowth of the long medieval period that came into being with the final disappearance in the West of the Roman Empire. This principle and these assemblies and parliaments remained strong in Europe until they were quite literally destroyed, or rendered impotent, by the kind of kingship that developed in the Renaissance. Royalism, in all its components of pomp and power, is a recurrent, not a universal, thing in history, and its ebb and flow are to be seen invariably against a background of the strength or weakness of representative, republican, institutions which lie intermediate to government and populace. In the more powerful of the modern monarchs—Henry VIII and Louis XIV will serve as examples—the same kind of affinity between despot and people I described above with reference to Augustus is to be seen, never more so than in the sixteenth and seventeenth centuries.

We are witnessing at the present time in America and in other Western nations an upsurge once again of the royalist principle. The modern political community, born in the eighteenth century, was, especially in its American form, a triumph once again in the West of representative and republican forms—even where, as in

England, the monarchy was retained. Whether in monarchical England or republican United States, the great fear in the minds of the champions of representation and of republican liberties—such minds as Burke in England and Adams and Jefferson in this country—was of what Burke called, in a series of important addresses and papers, "arbitrary power" and, more particularly, power set directly in the passions and loyalties of the populace. Hence the emphasis in the American Constitution upon not only checks and balances and division of powers but, equally important, upon institutions which would mediate, which would serve as buffers between central government and the populace.

With this went, in America, a consecration to austerity and simplicity in all areas of government, commencing with the presidency itself. It is fair, I believe, to say that from the time of Washington, himself a man who took greatest pride in his personal austerity and economy of life, down through the White House of Herbert Hoover, this spirit of austerity tended to prevail. There were of course strong and assertive presidents; there were even, as under Lincoln in the Civil War, suspensions of certain rights. Wilson reached the point in World War I of wielding powers greater than any that had been known in any executive, any monarch, in perhaps two centuries. But these powers were one and all granted him by Congress and it has to be said that Wilson's conduct of the presidency, like his personal life in the White House, was exemplary in regard for convention and in austerity of day-to-day existence.

Present-day royalism really begins with the administration of Franklin D. Roosevelt, and it has developed steadily ever since, though with occasional slight lapses in this or that detail of royalism, as during the administrations of Truman and Eisenhower. From FDR to the White Houses of Kennedy, Johnson, and Nixon there is a direct line of increase in the actual, asserted powers of the presidency and also in some of the other familiar attributes of royalism: attributes which may be seen in Alexandrian Greece, the Rome of the Caesars, and the Renaissance-born divine right monarchies. Let me list a few of these with briefest description, giving entire emphasis of course to the past several decades in the United States.

There is the ever-growing centrality of the *image* of the President and, with this, the constantly augmenting attention to the President by public and press alike. Not only what the President thinks on a given public issue, but what he wears, whom he dines with, what major ball or banquet he may choose to give, and what his views are on the most trivial or cosmic of questions—all of this has grown exponentially in the regard lavished by press and lesser political figures upon the presidency during the past four decades. The first care of royalty, beginning if we like with Alexander and coming down to the absolute monarchs of the sixteenth and seventeenth centuries, coming down indeed now to our own day, is that of being constantly visible, and naturally in the best and most contrived possible light for the people.

Along with the increasing vividness and centrality of presidential image has gone a constant seeking of increase in direct presidential power—power that might be originally mandated by Congress but that comes to take on an autonomy of its own. Historians are fond of distinguishing between "strong" and "weak" Presidents in American history, using such figures as Jefferson, Jackson, Theodore Roosevelt from the past as examples of the former. But the strongest of nineteenth- and early twentieth-century Presidents was weak by comparison with the actual powers of any President, irrespective of personality or temperament, in today's White House. The huge centralization of political power in twentieth-century Washington, D.C., has contained, ever since FDR, an inner centralization of power that is nothing if not royal.

Royalism properly connotes luxury, extravagance, and splendor. How else can the image of the wielder of absolute power be lustrous? Here too it is fair to say that the luxurious presidency began under FDR, though only, it must be added, in rather small degree; small, certainly, by contemporary standards. There was a distinct increase in size of White House budget for entertaining and other ends, there was now for the first time an equivalent of Balmoral, say, in the existence of a Hyde Park, and there were the visits to one or other part of the country, or after World War II of the world, all of them in ascendingly regal manner. But true White House royalism, in the sense I am now using the word, begins with John Fitzgerald Kennedy. Of a sudden the White House became a palace in every sense of the word, and the actual life of the occupant from day to day was regarded and written about in terms which had previously been reserved for European monarchs. And not only did the Kennedys love it, from all we read, but so did an adoring press and entire intellectual class in America. Such words as "regal," "kingly," and "queenly" became more and more common in the press and in television documentary. Such pomp, luxury, and extravagance of style of life increased a great deal after Kennedy's tenure in the White House, though with far less approval by press. It will suffice to say here that in terms of sheer wealth, ostentation, and splendor of life, personal and official, private and public, no Renaissance monarch held a candle to the American President as he lives in today's White House. And such opulence necessarily extends to all those who directly serve him. I do not think there is any imaginable luxury or appurtenance of vast wealth and personal power not present on a day in, day out basis in the White House at the present time.

Luxury is not, however, the most important of the attributes of royalism. Very probably it is the carefully cultivated image of democratic, popular roots of power that is the greatest of royal attributes. The bond between monarch and the people, at the expense of all traditional or constitutional bodies in between, is what strikes any student of the life of an Augustus or a Henry VIII or Louis XIV. To the common people of Rome or of sixteenth-century England it was the monarch who would have been hailed as "democratic," if that word had in those times been available in current meaning.

There are two other attributes of contemporary royalism, each also with historic precedent, which must be noted, and both of these have become more and more striking during the past four decades. The first is the idea of national security, and the second is the rising use of personal retainers who are largely unreachable by legislative bodies.

National security at first sight may seem a normal, even indispensable concept, and no doubt it is in time of military crisis or threatening revolution. But as this concept has become part and parcel of contemporary American government, it takes on ominous overtones from time to time of that Renaissance political concept, *raison d'état*. There were moments during the Ervin committee's interrogation of White House aides when one expected to hear this very phrase in defense of illegal, corrupt, and unconstitutional actions which had been taken by Nixon or one of his aides. The phrase that was in fact widely used, and that continues to be widely used, is of course "national security." The day is long past when this phrase was restricted to what is required in actual war. As everyone knows, it has been, since World War II under FDR, a constantly widening cloak or umbrella for governmental actions of every conceivable degree of power, stealth, and cunning by an ever-expanding corps of government officials. As we now know in detail, the utilization of the FBI and other paramilitary agencies by Presidents and other high executive department officers for the purposes of eavesdropping, electronic bugging, and similarly intimate penetrations of individual privacy goes straight back to FDR, and the practice has only intensified and widened ever since. Naturally, all such royalist invasions have been justified, right down to Watergate, under the name of national security. The record is clear and detailed that national security cover-up has been a practice of each of the Presidents since FDR, and while this practice undoubtedly reached its height under Nixon, it would be fatuous to pretend that it was not a standard operating procedure under Kennedy and Johnson in almost equal degree.

Raison d'état was the justification in Renaissance times for assaults upon privacy, for direct uses of monarchical power, and for the constant increase in governmental power. It was a concept almost totally foreign to earlier legal and political thought, and it was one that the protagonists of republicanism fought the hardest in the eighteenth century. Nothing could have been more offensive to the Founding Fathers than the thought of use of this idea. Every possible constitutional means was taken to prevent its appearance. But the blunt, unhappy fact remains: under the name of national security, commencing with FDR and increasing steadily to the present moment, the idea of *raison d'état*, with all its royalist overtones, has become a major element of the political world we live in and one more symptom of the disease which today has overtaken the historic political community.

Closely related to the idea and utilization of national security as an instrument of domestic government is the widening use, also since the presidency of FDR, of powerful assistants or aides in the conduct of executive power who are extra-constitutional in large part and, most important, whose loyalty is expressly personal to the President rather than rooted, as is that of Cabinet officers, say, in Constitution or statute and hence responsible to legislature. For the first time America became aware of this kind of power when FDR took with him to Washington assistants of a special kind, ostensibly to advise him but, as events proved, to wield elements of the presidential power directly. Names like Moley, Rosenman, Corcoran, Cohen, and Hopkins began to rival and then exceed the names of official Cabinet officers. True, some or all of them may have held some official post, some assistant secretaryship, but their true significance had nothing to do with that fact and everything to do with close personal responsibility to the President. Nothing like this had ever existed before—with the single exception perhaps of the role of Colonel House, also, it should be added, of George Creel—in the history of the American presidency. All preceding Presidents with rarest and most unimportant of exceptions gave to official Cabinet officers and their staffs the regard and attention the Constitution called for.

Here too what began under FDR increased steadily under succeeding Presidents. In the Kennedy and Johnson administrations the psychology of the courtier became overpowering in the White House. Roles bred originally in Renaissance political courts in Europe began to proliferate in Washington: court jester, court scholar, court chamberlain, and the like. Under Kennedy those such as the Bundys, Rostows, and Schlesingers began to exert more power over actual foreign and domestic policy than did, with one or two exceptions, those who served in official Cabinet posts. Their fundamental loyalty was of course, like the loyalty of any courtier or aide in the sixteenth century, not to office as such, much less to government in the large, but to the individual occupant of the presidency.

However unimportant the vice-presidency had been historically, it was now worse than unimportant; it was something on the order of a joke, with the flavor of the joke carefully communicated to press and public by one or other of the Kennedy and Johnson courtiers. Much the same attitude existed toward any given bureau head, unless as occasionally happened, he held additionally the position of courtier in the White House. The great power of a McNamara came less from his being Secretary of Defense than from the exalted courtier-role he enjoyed along with someone like Bundy in the White House.

Finally, it is not extreme, it seems to me, to suggest still another cherished royalist concept that has recently flowered in Washington, one that is also of Renaissance origin: *lèse majesté*. I do not mean of course that one will necessarily go to jail for a harsh word about the President. That is not the essence of the matter. The essence lies in a regard for the monarch that makes him virtually sacred in presence, that thereby gives his person a privileged status in all communications and that creates inevitably the psychology of constant, unremitting protection of the President not merely from physical harm but from unwelcome news, advice, counsel, and even contact with officers of government. Over and over during the Ervin hearings one kept hearing one or other expression of this psychology, but it did not begin with Nixon's administration; its roots also lie in the White House of FDR and those roots grew constantly during succeeding presidencies, nowhere more evident than in the Washington of John F. Kennedy.

Royalism under Johnson and Nixon lost the iridescence—and also the eager support of press and academy—it had had under Kennedy. But the substance remained, even grew, reaching its climax no doubt under President Nixon. Today, as the result largely of Watergate, there is a good deal of resentment against royalism in the White House. I think this resentment will shortly pass. There are too many powerful voices among intellectuals—in press, foundation, and elsewhere—that want a royal President provided only that he is the right kind of individual. There are those, such as Arthur Schlesinger, who argue indeed that only a strong and richly visible President can hold the fabric of democracy intact, that the President is the only vital symbol of unity and consensus. Such an argument is of course the best recipe for royalism. That it is almost totally false, without the slightest possibility of being substantiated in the comparative history of politics, will not, however, affect the tenacity with which it will continue to be urged by our political intellectuals whose fascination with centralized power is such that they do not even see the real threads of the constitutional fabric.

It is not likely that royalism in the American presidency will disappear. The moribund condition of the political community suggests that, allowing for possible lulls occasionally, the trappings of royalism will increase and spread. Precisely as papal Rome was never so imperial in style as just before the Reformation that broke the Papal See, and just as monarchical courts in Europe on the very eve of the Age of Revolutions revealed a degree of luxury and pomp that would have astounded earlier occupants, so I think it can be said today that the eruption of royalism that is to be seen in constantly quickening intensity since Roosevelt is as sure a sign as any of the diminished significance in American life of the political community.

It has been left to that very wise observer of the human and political scene in America, Russell Baker of the *New York Times*, to supply us with the ultimate demonstration of the particular kind of royalism we are afflicted by. That is the public architecture that has been filling the open spaces of Washington these past two decades. Such architecture in any society and age is a faithful reflection of what characterizes government in substantive terms. What Russell Baker is saying, in effect, in a striking article, "Moods of Washington," is that Washington royalty of the late twentieth century, like its public buildings, is always inflated and aggressive.

To Mr. Baker's anguished eye Washington is what it builds, and he does not err in seeing such architectural horrors as the Rayburn Office Building and the Kennedy Center for the Performing Arts as faithful monuments to the spirit of Washington and of the White House in our time. He writes of the Rayburn Building, "It dwarfs the forum of the Caesars. Mussolini would have sobbed in envy. . . . [But] the Kennedy Center nearly succeeds for barefaced oppression of the individual spirit. Poor Lincoln, down the road a piece in his serene little Greek temple, would be crumpled like a candy wrapper if the Kennedy Center could flex an elbow. The Pentagon of the warlike forties is matched by a monstrous new Copagon, home of the FBI, astride Pennsylvania Avenue. The vast labyrinths bordering the mall would make a minotaur beg for mercy."

It is simply not possible, as Russell Baker understands very well indeed, to work and live in such architectural monstrosities without one's mind and sensibilities being affected.

> My misgivings are not about the wretched architects, who must give Washington what it pays for, but about their masters who have chosen to abandon the human scale for the Stalinesque. Man is out of

place in these ponderosities. They are designed to make man feel negligible, to intimidate him, to overwhelm him with evidence that he is a cipher, a trivial nuisance in the great institutional scheme of things.

Those most likely to be affected are men who work in such arrogant surroundings. And so, it is not surprising that of late we have seen a curious tendency for Government people to differentiate between duty to Government and duty to country in a most ominous way.

It has always been thus. Merely compare the public architecture of Greece before and after the rise of Alexander; of Rome, before and after Augustus, and before and after the eruption of, first, Renaissance despots in Italy and then divine right monarchs. The change in American government that has taken place during the past several decades is almost perfectly evidenced by the change in the style and character of its buildings in Washington.

THE NEW CORRUPTION

"Men living in democratic ages," wrote Tocqueville, "do not readily comprehend the utility of forms: they feel an instinctive contempt for them. . . . Forms excite their contempt and often their hatred; as they commonly aspire to none but easy and present gratifications, they rush onward to the object of their desires, and the slightest delay exasperates them. This same temper carried with them into political life renders them hostile to forms, which perpetually retard or arrest them in some of their projects."

Yet, as a line of thinkers going back to Aristotle in the West has emphasized, in no form of government are forms—conventions, codes, rituals, established procedures—more vital than in democracy and popular government generally. In substantial degree the rise of democracy in the eighteenth century carried with it revolt against monarchical and aristocratic forms; but we cannot fail to note, especially in the American Constitutional Convention, a very real respect nevertheless for forms, and it is safe to say that a great deal of the stability of American democracy has sprung from dependence upon both political and social conventions which precede the rise of formal democracy. Respect for law, for office, for branches of government, protocol, and the innumerable lines of communication which become in time conventionalized, all of this bears upon what Tocqueville had in mind when he spoke of forms. Forms are, above all else, powerful restraints upon the kinds of passion which are generated so easily in religion and in politics.

Few things are more obvious in the recent history of the United States than the quickened decline of forms in all spheres of social life, but particularly, and most decisively, in the political. I believe that Watergate, whatever other sins and corruptions it may be associated with, is the crowning example of this decline. So much of what has been revealed in Senate inquiry and documents reflects, sometimes in the crudest possible way, impatience with, hostility to, all the agencies of government, all the established communications, all the *forms*, which in any way seemed to arrest political aspirations and designs in the White House.

Yet, distinct as Watergate is in its intensity and scope of violations of political and legal forms, it can be seen in a context that began a number of years earlier: a context in which contempt for and hostility to forms in government were widespread. At some point in the recent past the pattern of corruption took a significant turn. From being one rooted overwhelmingly in *economic* motivations—with Teapot Dome perhaps the classic instance—the pattern became one in which the seeking of *power for its own sake* took command. And while Watergate will remain for a long time the classic illustration of this kind of corruption, we are nevertheless obliged to see this event in an historical perspective that goes back at least as far as FDR's court-packing attempt and the general spirit of disdain for congressional and judicial branches of government, the fascination with projects and powers as ends in themselves, and the spreading desire throughout the Roosevelt administration to do things directly, with instant publicity, rather than through the accustomed offices and procedures.

Looking back on the thrust of the power that commenced in the New Deal, attained military intensity in World War II and then in the Cold War, and extended deeply into the Kennedy and Johnson administrations, we find ourselves almost feeling a sense of inevitability about Watergate and the extreme flouting of forms in the Nixon administration. One has the feeling that had even a Coolidge been elected to office in 1968 he would shortly have succumbed to the same pressures and temptations, all of which existed in abundance, the heritage of more than three decades.

The justification for the floutings of form is always either moral or drawn from expediency. In the first, some end is held so important to government, to one of its agencies or individual members, or for that matter to any individual or group in society, that a flouting of recognized procedure is permissible or even mandatory. In the second, desire to escape from the time limits which necessarily go with all forms is the justification proffered. Something, it is thought, badly needs to be done, and done immediately. Ordinary consultation, routing of the matter through conventional councils and offices, depending upon delegation and regularized communication—all of this looms as a set of traps, a thicket through which originality and dispatch cannot penetrate.

It is hard to think of a better illustration of violation of forms in recent times than the changed relation of the Secretary of State to American foreign policy; and along with this the immensely diminished place of the State Department. The Bundys, Rostows, and Kissingers, working directly under presidents, free to bypass established departments as they saw fit and to make public their disdain and contempt for such departments—these are the recent successors to a once-great line of secretaries of state. And when a Kissinger is installed in the office his manner of running it, or disregarding it and its routines, remains very much the same. That occasional benefits may seem to proceed from such direct uses of power, personal power, is in the long run of much less consequence than the opportunities which are opened for mischief, bungling, and outright disaster. Once forms are violated with impunity by the truly able among political leaders, they can and almost certainly will be violated by those a good deal less—or more!—than able. The true value of forms, as Aristotle, Burke, the authors of the Federalist papers, and Tocqueville all realized, is that they never can restrain or hinder authentic genius nearly as much as they can protect against the despotic, the covetous, and the corrupt.

THE TRANSPOLITICAL

The great military philosopher and strategist Clausewitz once wrote: "We see that war is not merely a political act, but also a real political instrument, a continuation of political commerce, a carrying out of the same by other means." So is what I call the transpolitical a political instrument, one that goes beyond what law or morality authorizes but that is nevertheless "a continuation of political commerce, a carrying out of the same by other means." The transpolitical, as presidential and executive practice, began, as did democratic royalism with its flouting of constitutional forms, essentially in the Roosevelt administration during the New Deal and especially during the years immediately prior to American entry into World War II.

The essence of the transpolitical is the use of means which are in themselves illegal, or at very least unethical, and in any event extreme violations of convention, in order to accomplish some end that is deemed of surpassing importance—an end in either foreign or domestic policy. Understandably, we think, and should think, of Watergate in the first instance when there is reference to violation of the political and to recourse to measures beyond politics. But as Vermont Royster, distinguished journalist, has recently written, we are obliged as historians to go back to FDR for earliest ventures in the realm I am writing of. It is with FDR's White House in mind that Royster writes: "With power came pomp, and with them there came, slowly at first, then increasingly, the feeling that an office with so much responsibility could not always put fine points of nicety upon what it did with its power. . . . The harsh fact is that almost every single action of the Watergate perpetrators—wire tapping, spying on political enemies, covering up political malfeasance—has its antecedent example somewhere in history." By which, of course, Royster means very recent, and American, history. He quotes George Reedy, himself a former White House aide under Lyndon Johnson and author of an excellent book on the contemporary presidency: "If it hadn't been Watergate, it would have been something else. If it hadn't been the Nixon administration, it would have been the next. . . . It's not just Watergate. A feeling has been growing for a long time—even before Viet Nam—that the presidency was somehow out of hand. The White House has been building up to some kind of smash."

Here also we are witnessing, in addition to another mark of the decay of the political community, of the consensus among contending parties that has been so vital to the whole republican system, a recrudescence of something from the era of the absolute monarchs. Then, however, the line between the political and military was regarded by almost everyone as an unimportant, even absent one. What kings were privileged to do to enemies or opponents abroad, they were just as entitled to do to enemies at home. And, as we know, many a beheading took place at the Tower in London for precisely this reason. If the state, the by-now-sacred state was to be maintained, no limit of either morality or law must be set upon actions of the king and his lieutenants. Politics and the military, politics and transpolitics, such distinctions were hardly worth the making in Renaissance Europe.

They have been worth making, however, for close to two centuries in the West. Indeed apart from distinction between politics and the transpolitical, between politics and war, there could not possibly have been a set of republican and representative institutions in the first place. However fierce the battles between two parties could be in this country, as between the historic Democratic and Republican parties, the whole possibility of the political community lay in recognition of limits, of boundaries, and of an underlying consensus that no difference on any political, social, or economic matter could legitimately violate.

I would argue that the initial impetus for scrapping this idea of consensus, for calculated turning to the uses of the transpolitical, came from the political left. Deeply rooted in the philosophy of revolution that had taken form in the nineteenth century, a philosophy that of course repudiated any thought of republican or electoral procedures, the intellectual left in this country as well as Europe began—roughly in the 1930s—to flirt with the thought of trans- or parapolitical procedures, if not actually revolution. Given a conviction that capitalism, or democracy, or the establishment, as the case might be, was overwhelmingly corrupt and dedicated to repression, it was understandable, at least from an intellectual point of view, that the minds of actors in the political drama would increasingly become riveted on ways by which the ordinary procedures of politics could be bypassed.

But irrespective of origin, the idea of the transpolitical was, as I have noted, a not unfamiliar one in the New Deal, in the Cold War, and then thereafter in steadily mounting degree in many political quarters. FDR's clandestine investigation through the FBI of political opponents on the matter of America's entry into the war after 1939 was only one of several distinctly transpolitical acts. So was Kennedy's bugging of the private life of Martin Luther King. So was his use of the FBI against the press in the steel-price incident. What was the Bay of Pigs but the transpolitical or, if we like, the transdiplomatic, given the absence of a declared war on Cuba? There was the calculated bringing-down of Diem in Saigon by White House action under Kennedy and, perhaps above all other ventures into the transpolitical by the Kennedy government, the sending, without authorization by or even significant consultation with Congress, 16,000 uniformed American troops under a four-star general in 1963. The sphere of the transpolitical widened under Johnson, reaching the use of the American Army for purposes of domestic surveillance and above all his management of the now-notorious Tonkin Gulf resolution by Congress.

Nor can we overlook here the identical psychology of the left during the 1960s—psychology and also strategy and tactics. That willingness on the part of the left to turn to the transpolitical I mentioned above, a phenomenon of the 1930s, had by the 1960s become a major element of American life. Whether it was in the name of civil rights, poverty, or opposition to the draft and to the war in Viet Nam, more and more groups on the left turned to violence, to revolt, to destruction, to, in fine, the transpolitical. In the extermination of injustice, all is legitimate. So might the leaders of the revolts in the 1960s have declared.

Precisely as the thought of one kind of injustice in American society led sizable groups to take the route of the transpolitical in the early 1960s, so did the thought of a different kind of injustice—the flouting of all ordinary proprieties, even of laws, by the militant left—lead another group, the one closely associated with Nixon, itself to take the route of the transpolitical. Putting the matter succinctly, if the transpolitical act of a Daniel Ellsberg (who had begun, as we know, as a Pentagon intellectual under Kennedy, committed to American military intervention in Viet Nam) in stealing and then broadcasting the Pentagon Papers was allowable within one moral framework, then the act, or acts, which were equally transpolitical and deemed necessary to offset and to prevent the Ellsberg type of transpolitical act were also allowable within a different and, as it was thought, even better moral framework.

So ran the thinking of central figures in the White House, starting undoubtedly with President Nixon himself, from about 1970 on. Working from a zeal that was within a short time almost uncontrollable, taking refuge in moral righteousness, it was not difficult to find rationalization for illegal use of the great amount of wealth and power at the disposition of the White House. If the political and legal approach could not be counted on to achieve certain ends quickly—ends which were in themselves moral and predictably in accord with the views of the vast majority of the American people—then, why not follow the timeworn principle of direct moral action and in the process give new meaning to the idea of civil disobedience? For a decade or more the political and legal order had been challenged in the name of conscience and of what was so often termed the real will of the people. Laws and ordinances and judicial norms of due process were toppled time and again in the name of a morality declared to be higher than anything found in ordinary politics and the law of procedure. Why not now challenge politics and law in the name of a still higher morality: the morality of peace, tranquility, and freedom from chronic violence? This was surely the rationale of Watergate.

Had the principals in Watergate been men of low character from the outset, had they sought for themselves individual financial gain or unusual preferment of status and power in the conventional sense, we might be able to draw a certain comfort from what happened. After all, the politics of corruption, whether with respect to money or to power, is an old story in the history of democracy as well as of other types of government. But it is as though the principals of Watergate were a new breed, for almost without exception their lives had been singularly free of either legal or ethical blemish, and, allowing only for their nearly limitless dedication to one man, President Nixon, they would appear to have been men of almost striking temperamental balance, rectitude, and probity. They believed, it would seem, that others before them and around them were committing crimes or gross breaches of public morality which the ordinary processes of law and order were not equal to, and, so believing, entered into the realm of the transpolitical themselves.

The fact is, quite apart from all justification that might be ad-

vanced, the White House became, beginning about 1970, a veritable command post of the paramilitary, transpolitical, call it what we
will. And the gnawing, nagging, torment in the minds of a great
many individuals in politics today, whether on the left or the right,
could well be epitomized in the celebrated words: There but for
the grace of God go I!

Will Watergate become an American Dreyfus case? There are
those to declare it such, and a certain amount of plausibility goes
with their declaration. Never mind that at present writing a large
majority of Americans willingly express their relief that President
Nixon resigned and that, on the evidence of poll after poll, a substantial majority existed for nearly a year before resignation which
believed in his guilt. Watergate even so has all the potential of a
Dreyfus case: the bitter intensity of hatred in a minority on each
side, the unprecedented toppling of an American presidency, the
ease with which innocence and villainy alike can become embroi-
dered during the months and years which follow a crisis such as
that of Dreyfus or Nixon.

The historical sociology of "followings" should teach us never to
underestimate the capacity of even the guiltiest—by all conventional criteria—for attracting to themselves fanatical loyalties which
grow, seemingly, on every fresh revelation of guilt of the principal.
Credo quia absurdum has its companion in the history of government
in *Credo quia sceleris*. Once the seamier details have been forgotten,
which will not take very long, the number of those in this country
for whom Watergate can become a veritable Golgotha will surely
grow. Whether we like it or not, the potentiality of martyrdom in
Watergate is a significant one. And, as is always the case in martyrdom in history, ordinary, conventional criteria of wickedness and
guilt do not apply.

There is another aspect that makes for analogy of Watergate to
the Dreyfus case. It is well to remember that on the side of
Dreyfus there were those who seem to have believed in his technical guilt but who felt that there were overriding social and moral

considerations which made his defense necessary and just. And conversely there were certainly those in the opposition to Dreyfus in French opinion who were obliged by strict evidence to believe him innocent of the crime he was charged with but who also believed that overriding social and moral considerations made the judgment of guilt and his imprisonment necessary.

I am inclined to think that some of this has already operated with respect to Nixon and Watergate, and that a great deal more of it will operate during the years ahead. It is too early to be certain, but on balance I think Watergate will prove to be the American Dreyfus case. If so, there are dangerous implications to the political process.

One final point should be made about Watergate and its uses of the paramilitary and transpolitical. The air is filled, as I write this, with a great deal of complacent self-congratulation on how our "constitutional" or "political" system saved us from the diseases of royalism and the calculated effort by the President and his staff to subvert constitutional processes. Repeatedly we hear the litany: Thank God for our system; it saved us!

That is nonsense. In the first place, the "system" has not prevented a transition of power that is more in line with what has existed in certain Latin American and Middle Eastern countries for centuries than with anything to be found in American history. After all, we have at this writing a new President and a new Vice-President, neither of whom has been elected to the White House or Executive Office by the people. And we witnessed the phenomenon of a four-star general assigned to political duty in the White House, General Haig, in effect superintending much of the transition from Nixon's to Ford's government.

More important perhaps is the role of sheer *accident* in the uncovering of Watergate and prosecution of its principals. Here again we are indebted to the perceptive Russell Baker. For, as he noted, it was not any "system" but accident alone that saved the country. Not the genius of political institutions but the accident of the bungled break-in—the guard's discovery, then rediscovery, of that almost incredible piece of political cretinism. There was too the accident of the presidential tapes, their mere existence a heavy strain on the imagination, their public disclosure happenstance of the highest order. What we now know to be the very worst features of the Nixon administration do not even include the attempted break-in of Democratic headquarters, which by itself was indeed a "third-rate burglary," and which had no real strategic design that has yet been uncovered. But if it had not been for the accident of this bungled affair, the whole drama would surely never have commenced to unfold.

In other words, it was not an ever-vigilant Congress that brought Watergate to its culmination. In that body there was a great deal of initial foot-dragging. Nor was there an ever-vigilant public. For many months the public seemed to want to hear little or nothing about Watergate. Nor can the press be said to have been the prime mover, though this is to take nothing away from the *Washington Post* and its two reporters who have recorded in detail the larger number of accidents involved in their investigation. As for the judiciary, this branch of government would not even have come into the matter had it not been for the accident of the bungled break-in.

The revelations of Watergate and the downfall of Nixon are almost entirely, as Russell Baker has stressed, products of—accident!

Will we be that lucky the next time? To say that the uncovering of Watergate and the resignation of Nixon make a next time impossible or unlikely is, I fear, more nonsense. If the uses of the trans-political and the paramilitary were solely confined to the Nixon administration, with preceding administrations from that of FDR on spotless in all such respects, if there were not clearly to be seen a constantly rising royalism in the White House over the past couple of decades, if there were not, especially among political intellectuals and nationalist-liberals of all stripes, a notable fondness for a powerful Gaullist type of president, we could be more optimistic.

I am afraid that the only lessons that have been truly learned in the whole Watergate business are to avoid such idiocies as tapes and illegal, unwarranted break-ins, and to restrict the operation of the fortuitous and the random to the smallest possible area. I would be astonished if the real lesson of Watergate—the Actonian principle that all power tends to corrupt, absolute power absolutely—were other than forgotten utterly once a crowd-pleasing President with the kind of luster a John F. Kennedy had for academy, press, and the world of intellectuals generally comes back into the White House.

THE OBSOLESCENCE OF IDEOLOGY

Politics in our era has become as nearly devoid of genuinely ideological divisions as is possible to conceive. We are in a condition astonishingly like that which beset Rome during the last century or so of the Republic, when all traditional intellectual and political issues disappeared, and with them parties in the true sense, to be replaced by mere power-blocs, each with nothing more than lust for office to guide it. The growth of the modern political community, ever since the late eighteenth century, has depended in large part, just as did that of the ancient Roman Republic, on ideologies which have been engines of its progress. Today the political scene is occupied by strategies and tactics, no longer by principles emerging from the three great ideologies which for so long were the stuff of politics in the West.

The first of these was liberalism, which put its full emphasis on the free individual, finding in man's liberation from political and military bonds, even those of religion and local community when these were oppressive, the essence of progress. We find this liberalism prominent in the West from about the time of John Locke, coming down through Adam Smith and John Stuart Mill to the present century. Individual autonomy is the transcending goal of historic liberalism.

Radicalism, no less important historically, originates in Rousseau and his worship of equality. Its enemy was privilege and other elements of inequality. If there is any single value that modern radicalism, in contrast to liberalism and conservatism, has made central it is equality, manifest in the ideal of a classless society and the creation of a social order in which even natural inequalities among individuals would be subordinated to the kind of equality that the collective will of the people could institute. The socialist tradition has been on the whole the main avatar of radicalism in modern history, though one would not wish to neglect anarchism and forms of social utopianism which fit almost no recognized category.

Conservatism, originating in Edmund Burke's great defense of traditional society against the depredations of wielders of what Burke called "arbitrary power," whether these were cabinet ministers in the British government, the rulers of the East India Company, or, most spectacularly in all of Burke's writings, the French Revolutionists, founded itself upon the unities of property, family, local community, and social class. Conservatism shares with liberalism a primary concern with the individual and with freedom of individual thought and action as against the claims of the total social order, but the conservative ideologists have for the most part seen this individual freedom as an inextricable aspect of a kind of social pluralism, one rich in autonomous or semi-autonomous groups, communities, and institutions.

There are innumerable variations on these three great bodies of belief and doctrine as I have briefly described them; and it is probably true that a substantial difference has long existed between America and Europe in sheer impact of ideology upon political habits of mind, with Europeans generally taking articulated bodies of political ideas more seriously than have Americans. Yet it would be highly misleading to omit ideology from consideration of some of the greatest political events and personages in American life. For a long time following the Civil War, differences between the Republican and the Democratic parties were significantly ideological, having to do with such matters of moment as role of wealth and property in the social order, taxation policy, tariffs, labor, and a score of other important topics. And it would be impossible to account for the special shapes politics has assumed throughout the West during the last couple of centuries except by recourse to ideologies.

How very different all of this is today! Principles and convictions have ceased to matter greatly in the political process—at least by comparison with individuals and issues. Apart from these latter, one is hard put to distinguish seriously today between the Republican and Democratic parties. The once-proud ideologies of liberalism, radicalism, and conservatism have dissipated themselves into often mindless devotions to this or that individual, this or that issue, irrespective of the relation of either to any seriously held body of belief.

Liberalism has for the most part lost historic objective in its growing fascination with the uses of centralized power. Where freedom from power was for a long time the chief end of liberal thought, participation in and control of power have become the chief idols of the liberal mind in our time. This and, not to be omitted, a gathering relativism, indeed indifference on matters of morality. In her profound, recently published *On Liberty and Liberalism: The Case of John Stuart Mill*, the historian Gertrude Himmelfarb has effectively shown and with an abundance of documentation the sorry decline of the liberal ideal in the West from one originally rooted in desire to be free to follow the precepts of morality to the kind of escape from morality in any form that highlights contemporary liberalism. No doubt there should be a clear contradiction between the liberal's worship of power and his indifference to moral restraints upon liberty, his all-out celebration of what he calls "civil liberties," but for reasons I shall describe later in this book there is no such contradiction. The two impulses have often gone together in Western history.

Conservatism is hardly better off. The resurgence we were treated to for a few years just after World War II and that promised so well has declined into mere rightism, into mere aggression and defense, with positions set oftener by what adversaries do and say than by anything that comes from philosophy or principle. The reaction to Watergate from the American right is an unhappy illustration of this. If there is one identifying element of the conservatism that began with Burke in the late eighteenth century, it is opposition to the extension of political power into the social order. The great value of the conservative right has consisted precisely in its challenges to and criticisms of such power, in a line of thinkers beginning with Burke and including Coleridge, Tocqueville, Burckhardt, Acton, Albert Jay Nock, and others. Such opposition to power was rooted from the beginning in the conviction that all power must be anchored in and limited by moral principles, basically those of the Hellenic-Hebraic tradition. Can one imagine either a Burke or a Nock being other than revolted by every aspect of Watergate, its flouting of morality and its consecration of arbitrary power?

But the whole strategy of the present American right, with a tiny few distinguished exceptions, seemed from the beginning to be little more than a search for, or manufacture of, extenuating circumstances—at best; at worst there was a seeming willingness to call for, if not aid in, continued concealment and cover-up. It is entirely possible that American conservatism has been grievously, perhaps fatally, wounded by Watergate, and if this proves to be the case, the reason lies squarely in the passivity with which the Nixon administration's moral delinquencies were greeted from the start. Only when Watergate became overwhelmingly and crushingly a legal matter, impossible to ignore, can it be said that much in the way of a conservative opposition to Nixon was mounted. In Burke's day, indeed in the day of each of the great conservatives I mentioned above, the idea of a dishonor too great to be borne was a familiar one; resignation was what was expected from any public servant whose honor had been tarnished, in whatever degree, by his own acts or by those of his trusted aides. Not least among the tests of a truly great ideology or party is that of the limits it places upon its willingness to support its own in public life. It would be hard to think of anything more fundamentally vandalistic in respect of traditional conservatism than the acts of the Nixon administration toward the opposition party, toward the public, and toward the whole fabric of political morality that was given representation by the Constitution's makers at the end of the eighteenth century.

The prospects for conservatism are hardly bright. It became great by virtue of its fight against power, which now is being converted into a fight for capture of power, central power.

Nor can we overlook the deeply changed character of radicalism. From the time of the American and the French revolutions in the eighteenth century until very recently, radicalism in the West has been overwhelmingly objective and political in its character. I mean by objective in this context radicalism's preoccupation, with rarest exceptions, with external social institutions and structures and their place in historical time. Through drastic reforms and reconstructions in this external sphere, it was thought by radicals from the Jacobins down to the Bolsheviks, lay the best hope for rehabilitation of morality and of man's inherited nature. The political character of Western radicalism flowed directly from its objective concern. The state was the seat of power in society—the society, at least, that had been brought into existence by the Age of Revolution—and capture of this power was therefore the sovereign objective of radical movements throughout the nineteenth and early twentieth centuries.

Very different is the radicalism of our day. That a considerable residue of the Old Left continues to exist is not to be doubted. But far outweighing it in significance is a New Left of which flight from both objectivity and politics is apparently the very essence. This flight from or repudiation of politics—that is, of the political community and the political habit of mind—is revealed at one extreme in consecration to senseless, meaningless violence for its own sake and, at the other, in individual retreat to innermost areas of consciousness and in a kind of consecration to self, self-awareness, and the undilutedly subjective.

I shall have more to say about this subjectivism in the next chapter, where its implication not only for politics but for culture will be considered. Let us note here only that few states of mind have greater and more destructive impact upon the political community than this particular form of failure of collective nerve. Such failure of nerve, as historians of post-Alexandrian Greece—foremost among them Sir Gilbert Murray—of imperial Rome and, far from least, of Renaissance Europe, when fascination with the subjective, the irrational, and the occult accompanied widespread intellectual assault upon every form of objective reality, tends almost uniformly to go with the decline of philosophy of government and with the sharp upthrust of personal despotism punctuated by internecine strife that has become devoid of any kind of genuine ideological content.

Such conditions are evident in our time. With the abdication of true philosophy and of rooted ideology in the present age, we are bound to see an intensification of emphasis on personal power on the one hand, with the assertedly charismatic qualities of the political leader foremost, and, on the other, an increasingly savage struggle between factions variously termed "Left" and "Right" but which, like those of late Republican Rome, reflect little more than the lust for power and its capture through whatever means.

THE TOILS OF BUREAUCRACY

We are indebted to Karl Marx for words on the executive power and its bureaucratic apparatus which most persons in our day would find wonderfully apposite to the present even though they were written to describe the European governments of his own time:

This executive power with its monstrous bureaucratic and military organization, with its artificial state machinery embracing wide strata, with a host of officials numbering half a million, besides an army of another half million, this appalling parasitic growth, which enmeshes the body of French society like a net and closes all its pores, sprang up in the days of the absolute monarchy, with the decay of the feudal system, which it helped to hasten. . . .

Of all aspects of the contemporary state none has proved to be so repugnant to populations as has the structure of bureaucracy through which, today as in earlier centuries, government discharges its obligations to citizens. However widespread and oppressive political bureaucracy may have seemed to Marx and other nineteenth-century minds, it was as nothing in comparison with what is to be found in every Western—and many a non-Western—nation today. One need but think of the immense burst of social legislation in each of the Western democracies that has taken place since Marx's time. In the beginning there was a strong effort made in some parts of Europe to counteract the heritage of centralization from Renaissance monarchy and also from the French Revolution through revival of local and regional organizations. The wave of voluntary association to be seen in the nineteenth century—reflected in trade unions, cooperatives, and mutual aid associations of one kind or other—was also, in effect at least, a strategy of meeting, or seeking to meet, social needs through instrumentalities other than the national state. A great deal of the guild socialist and syndicalist writing of the time was oriented in this direction, and it is larded with frequent criticisms of the tendency of modern democracy toward collectivism and centralization.

Most of that is gone, however, from the contemporary scene. Few things so clearly separate the liberalism of the nineteenth century from twentieth-century liberalism and progressivism as the nearly complete acceptance by the latter of bureaucracy. It is one of the tragedies of our age that the pluralism to be seen in so much

of the social thought of the late nineteenth century and the concomitant inclination toward the local and the voluntary have virtually disappeared in our time, commonly referred to, if referred to
at all, as archaisms and atavisms. That a very substantial majority
of Western peoples, including American, favor the principle of national aid where necessary to the indigent and infirm and unfortunate is not to be doubted. Nor can we reasonably doubt that in
some instances at least, the nation is the only setting for such aid,
national government its source, and Federal bureaucracy the instrument.

Unhappily, as is now a matter of full record, the bureaucratic instrument has taken command. It is impossible to so much as glance
at the thousands of miles of bureaucratic corridors, the millions of
file cases, the millions of bureaucratic employees organized in a
complexity that gives fresh meaning to Laocoön, as all these become revealed in ordinary human experience, without realizing
that once again in history means have conquered end. What Marx
and others of his day saw and recoiled from in the way of bureaucracy, what Tocqueville foresaw as the melancholy future of mass
democracy, is, in the judgment of a large number of people today,
present reality.

It is not as though we had not been warned—by Max Weber and
Robert Michels perhaps foremost at the beginning of the century.
As Michels wrote: "Bureaucracy is the sworn enemy of individual
liberty and of all bold initiative in matters of internal policy. . . .
We may say that the more conspicuously a bureaucracy is distinguished by its zeal, by its sense of duty, and by its devotion, the
more also will it show itself to be petty, narrow, rigid, and illib-
eral."

One thing has to be said in behalf of those in the White House
who, beginning with FDR and culminating with Kennedy, Johnson, and Nixon, brought presidential power to the point of both
royalism and the transpolitical. Each of these presidents could see
himself as in some sense the tribune of the majority that elected

him, responsible for the expeditious carrying out of policies, domestic and foreign, in his campaign platform. Each, however, found himself in the presence of bureaucratic offices and agencies, some very powerful indeed, whose internal policies and structures made presidential action in any normal, constitutional way often difficult if not impossible. Hence the strong appeal of direct action, the violation of forms, and the massing in the White House of aides whose sole loyalty was to the President himself. Such aides could hardly avoid becoming first task forces seeking every means to overcome established bureaucratic power, and then, in a short time, bureaucracies themselves, however small. Even these, appointed directly by the President, responsible basically to him alone, could become, as Watergate demonstrated, increasingly autonomous entities, more and more impervious to the command of the President himself, much less the Vice-President and other constitutional officers. George Reedy is only one informed mind that has told us of the number of hours spent by the President simply to find out whether an order given by him had managed to get through first the White House bureaucracy and then the larger bureaucracy surrounding it.

This is, of course, precisely the situation that Weber had in mind when he wrote early in the century about the conflict between bureaucracy and democracy, with the latter tending toward ever greater excesses of demagoguery. The paradox presented is tragic indeed. Through democracy, historically, bureaucracy has constantly expanded, the result of the rising number of social and economic functions taken on by the democratic state. But when bureaucracy reaches a certain degree of mass and power, it becomes almost automatically resistant to any will, including the elected will of the people, that is not of its own making. Hence, at best, the frustration not merely of Presidents but of all other elected officials; and, at worst, the transpolitical, paramilitary stratagems devised by the more powerful of the latter.

It is no wonder that bureaucracy has so visibly entered the mind of the contemporary left. One of the most striking differences between the Old Left and the New Left, as these differences first became dramatic in the 1960s, was the attitude of the New Left toward bureaucracy, the effort it made, at least in the beginning before a mindless spirit of vandalism took over, to include centralized political bureaucracy with the older economic enemies that the older protest movements had fixed attention on. But that brief—as it turned out—intellectual revolt against bureaucracy aside, the record of the political left is, as it has been generally ever since World War I, almost solidly on the side of administrative centralization. Only the West's experience with mass warfare during the past century and a half has done more to accelerate the growth of bureaucracy, through the enormous pressure that modern war by its nature places upon central governments; and, as I shall develop in some detail later on, it is this fact undoubtedly that accounts for the otherwise curious affinity between the Western intellectual and the military state, or at very least the military departments of the political state. It is difficult to distinguish at times between the political and the military intellectual.

John Stuart Mill thought it better to allow people to do for themselves, through individual and associative activity, everything they possibly could in the social and economic realms, even when the evidence might show that bureaucrats could do these things more efficiently on a rationalized basis, simply because—quite apart from any issue of freedom—of the development such self-help gives to the individual faculties. Thus, as Mill, following Tocqueville, notes, the greatest value of the jury system is what it does, not for the accused—who might indeed be better and more fairly dealt with by a professional magistrate—but for the jurors themselves: that is, bring them into direct experience of the exercise of political and legal judgment.

The word *bureaucracy* has come to symbolize, above all others in our time, the transfer of government from the people, as organized in their natural communities in the social order, as equipped with the tastes, desires, and aspirations which are the natural elements of their nurture, to a class of professional technicians whose principal job is that of substituting *their* organizations *their* tastes, desires, and aspirations, for those of the people. It is this seemingly ineradicable aspect of bureaucracy that makes for the relentless, unending conflict between bureaucracy and freedom that more and more people in the present age have come to regard as very nearly central. And it is this same aspect that has led so many persons in the present age to despair of restoring to political government those foundations in popular will which are utterly vital to the political community.

As I write this, the newspapers are filled, day after day, with accounts of one or other effort by individuals, by Congress and by state governments, to liberate themselves from some toil or torment imposed by a Federal bureaucracy that chooses to be the arbiter of the people's happiness and safety, that does everything it can to spare people the demands of self-help and individual thought, even the business of living their lives. It may be something as trivial and banal as the elaborate mechanism perfected to compel people to strap themselves against their will into seat-harnesses in automobiles. Or it may be elaborate and labyrinthine programs of busing school children tens and tens of miles for no purpose other than that of meeting some bureaucratically arrived at quota. Or it may be some fresh violation of neighborhood and community in the name of urban renewal or control of poverty. Poll after poll among all elements of the population will reveal widespread hostility, but for the bureaucracy such evidence bespeaks only ignorance and the need of still greater bureaucracy for the purpose of liberating the people from their prejudices.

It was the inherent despotism of such bureaucratic regulation of life that Tocqueville referred to as "absolute, minute, regular, provident and mild." Such power, Tocqueville continues, "would be like the authority of a parent if, like that authority, its object was to prepare men for manhood; but it seeks, on the contrary, to keep them in perpetual childhood. . . ."

In childhood and in a state of permanent invasion of privacy! Already it has become difficult for us to remember that as recently as half a century ago, most Americans were so free, relatively, of the bureaucratic invasions of privacy which are now commonplace that the word "bureaucracy" was scarcely to be found in either scholarly or lay writing in this country. What a minimum of information about one's self was then required when applying for a government job! Or in completing one's tax return! Or in making any application to a government office! It is depressing to think of the number of first-rate, trustworthy, loyal, and otherwise motivated individuals today who are self-barred from a responsible government career by the thought of the intolerable assaults upon their privacy and personal freedom which are the price of any office, appointive or elective.

Max Weber, looking around him in the Germany of already advanced social democracy, contemplating the constantly rising number of those in bureaucratic office, wrote:

> It is horrible to think that the world could one day be filled with nothing but those little cogs, little men clinging to little jobs, and striving toward bigger ones. . . . This passion for bureaucracy is enough to drive one to despair. It is as if in politics . . . we were deliberately to become men who need "order" and nothing but order, become nervous and cowardly if for one moment this order wavers, and helpless if they are torn away from their total incorporation in it. That the world should know no men but these: it is in such an evolution that we are already caught up, and the great question is, therefore, not how we can promote and hasten it, but what can we oppose to this machinery in order to keep a portion of mankind free from this parceling-out of the soul, from this supreme mastery of the bureaucratic way of life.

Albert Speer tells us in his memoirs that Hitler—*Reichsführer* though he was, possessor of supreme political power in the Third Reich, architect, as he saw it, of a new political order that would last a thousand years—during the greater part of his career made a vain effort to persuade, through applications and letters unending, the pension-bureaucracy in Germany that he was entitled to a certain increment, based on World War I service, that this agency was unwilling to grant. It is impossible not to find this amusing: the master of all Europe held at bay, so to speak, by a single department of his own government. No doubt the humor could be extended if we made analogous inquiry into the careers of Caesar, Cromwell, and Napoleon at their zeniths.

There is no humor, however, in the minds of the countless millions of citizens in our time for whom modern government—indeed modern society as a whole, its economy, educational system, health institutions included—has become indistinguishable from what Marx called "the monstrous bureaucratic and military organization" of his own age, an organization very small indeed by present standards.

More and more, I suspect, revolt in the West in whatever form it takes—peaceful and political, violent and terroristic, or military—will consist of hatred of bureaucracy and passionate desire to destroy it. It is the immensity of bureaucracy at the present time, and the growing immensity of opposition to it, that promises a drive toward total reconstruction that must itself be laden with implications of despotism. For what we have learned in other ages is that oftentimes it is bureaucracy that the aspiring despot castigates most bitterly in his efforts to create a base for his power in the popular will. That the history of despotism, even of ordinarily "strong" executive government, has contained invariably fresh additions of bureaucracy once the ruler or executive was in office is seemingly forgotten quickly.

Bureaucracy in Western governments has come, overwhelmingly, from two sources: mass war and mass social reform of socialist or quasi-socialist character. I nevertheless predict that in the years just ahead the most constant criticisms of bureaucracy will come from the military and from the left. Bureaucracy has long since replaced capitalism and its factory system as the object most hated by the popular will.

THE SPECTER OF VIOLENCE

Of all the really fundamental desires in human life, protection is surely first: protection from the kind of violence or threat of violence that Hobbes made the very essence of the state of nature. Never mind that the fear and torment Hobbes ascribed to the prepolitical condition of mankind might on better ground in many parts of the world be ascribed to the political condition; never mind either that Hobbes' ascription was a piece of selective and tendentious argument in behalf of absolute power, buttressed in part by some rather bad ethnology. No one has ever described more pungently the nightmare of disorder and endemic violence than did Hobbes in his imagining of the aboriginal state of nature—a state of nature, be it remembered, that Hobbes specifically declared to be present always, *in potentia* at least, just under the skin of political law.

There is irony as well as tragedy in the present relation of the political state to the maintenance of order in the hundreds, even thousands, of towns and cities in the West where today disorder has become the rule, where human beings quite literally live, in large sections, in "continual fear and danger of violent death," to use Hobbes' famous words on the state of nature. I say irony, for the selling point of the modern national state in the political theory that begins with Machiavelli and his contemporaries, that continues through Bodin and Hobbes and reaches its high level in the works of writers such as Rousseau, Bentham, and Austin, has always chiefly been the claimed capacity of the political state, of the heralded doctrine of sovereignty, to create solid and predictable public order. In many respects this is the single greatest failing of the political community in the West at the present time: a failing, as I shall stress, that will certainly, if it becomes magnified, lead to ever more extreme uses of police, eventually military, power.

A genuine, politically based, public order did not, assuredly, come into being with the political theory that first hailed it. The concept of a public order, like the concept of a public law, was almost completely foreign to the medieval legal mind. Order, like liberty, rights, and membership in society generally, was conceived of as a tissue or network of "private" relationships in the Middle Ages. Law, to be sure, was held to transcend everything, including the king and his claimed powers; in medieval political theory everyone, the prince included, was "under the law," in the common phrasing at that time. So far as security and protection were involved in individual lives, associations like the kindred, guild, church, and monastery accounted for more than did anything properly called the political state. Even so, from earliest times in medieval Europe there seems to have been the germ of a conception that eventually became known as the King's Peace—a mandate, small and no doubt precarious in the beginning, that sought to rival and even exceed the "religious peace" that had been the Church's answer to the occasional excesses of war among feudal nobility.

In a very real sense the modern notion of public order is an evolution of the medieval idea of the King's Peace: a claim that the normal state of things shall be peaceful, with the military power of the king available if need be in enforcement of this peace. Not until the nineteenth century would the idea of a standing, visible police force with the primary function of protection rather than harassment of individuals become an increasingly common one in the West. And it is in that century too, on both sides of the Atlantic, that the idea of a public order began to be taken for granted, at least in the settled and civilized areas—in contrast, say, to those areas such as the Far West during the Gold Rush where vigilante justice sometimes flourished and where at the worst it was every man for himself on the frontier. It can be safely said that by the beginning of this century the concept of public order was understood—and indeed taken for granted—throughout Western European civilization.

What we are witnessing today, foremost perhaps in the United States but increasingly in other parts of the West, is the breakdown of that concept and with it of confidence in political government and its ordinary police and judicial powers of protection. Not very old, the idea of public order has already become the object of derision. We observe on a constantly rising scale the use of techniques of "private order" which range from bodyguards and complex electronic systems down to twenty-four-hour security personnel and triple locks in apartment houses that as recently as a quarter of a century ago were immune to such necessity. One reads too of increasing recourse to neighborhood associations, operating voluntarily with inevitable unevenness of results.

What has happened is that political government, in taking on itself a great variety of social, cultural, and economic responsibilities, for many of which it is ill-fitted, has ended up derelict in performance of its timeworn function of preserving public order. Police forces rise incessantly in size, but crime rates rise faster, with the number of persons annually reported in commission of felonies, especially those involving violence, at times doubling from year to year. For a while it was fashionable in some circles to dismiss reported increases in crime as merely statistical in nature, the product of reporting where once reporting of crimes was absent or else of refinements in classification. It is no longer fashionable. The inescapable fact is that crimes of violence and of robbery and theft increase significantly every year in Western countries, and nowhere as steeply as in the United States.

One of the byproducts of this increase is diminished loss of confidence in humanitarian works. For decades it was conventional wisdom in the social sciences that crime is the product of poverty, unemployment, and poor housing. We might have looked to large cities in the world where these blights were commonplace but without appreciable incidence of crime. Any such comparative analysis would have quickly disabused us of the idea of a one-to-one relation between social and economic deprivation and criminal behavior. In point of fact, as such perceptive students of poverty as Robert Coles and the late Oscar Lewis have pointed out, hard-core poverty is if anything a preventive of crime. Precisely as the impulse to rebellion is muted in such conditions, so is the desire for crime. As Eric Hoffer has written, if poverty were indeed the fundamental cause of crime, history would be about almost nothing else, for the vast majority of people in world history have lived in poverty.

Poverty is its own evil, a unique form of human degradation. It deserves obliteration on its own ground, not on the imagined ground that it generates crime. The sad fact is, though, that because of the long insistence to the public by social scientists and government officials that huge sums spent to eradicate slum and ghetto conditions would also work to reduce crime, there is a greatly diminished public interest in public humanitarianism. The effort to prove too much—falsely, as it turned out—has resulted in spreading disenchantment with good works.

Crime in rising volume is one aspect of the specter of insecurity that hovers over Western society; another is the increasing threat of terror. If it is true, as seems to be the case, that revolution in the old sense is now virtually impossible in Western countries, and of course many others also, it does not follow that terror has become obsolete. On the contrary, it is probable that the vacuum left by receding revolutionary hope is being filled by mindless, purposeless terror as an end in itself. Thus far, terror, formidable as it is in a few locations, is restricted. There is the IRA operating in Ireland and England; the PLO in a few capitals and major airports; in this country the relatively insignificant SLA and, earlier, the Weathermen. But there is, on the sober judgment of scientists and officials alike, every reason to expect constant rises in the rate and incidence of terror in the modern world—with the exception of the military totalitarianisms where, in effect, terror is monopolized by the government. Terror is now a way of life for certain groups in the world, and we may be certain their number will go up constantly.

If ordinary judicial and police measures are merely inadequate against crime rates, they are clearly ludicrous against systematic outbursts of terror: the kind generated, say, by the IRA, which has led in Northern Ireland and parts of England to what is nothing less than martial law. Only the military—in full, uninhibited operation, unrestrained by ordinary due process and respect for normal immunities—would appear to be effective. But what this means basically is the institutionalization and the legitimization of terror as a weapon against terror.

I shall deal later with what I call the lure of the military and of the war state. It suffices here to say that high among the attractions of that kind of state is belief in the military's unique power to put an end to terror and to crimes of violence.

THE EROSION OF PATRIOTISM

No one would declare patriotism as strong a sentiment in any Western country today as it was at the beginning of the century, even down through World War II. There are no doubt many, with memory fresh of some of the excesses and stupidities of legislative committees and other agencies committed to an all-out Americanism, however defined, to take pleasure in the reality of this erosion. Although, as I shall indicate in a moment, the modern character of national patriotism was largely given by the intellectual class in Europe and America in the nineteenth century, the fact remains that patriotism has hardly been one of the cherished values of recent generations of intellectuals.

Whatever we may think of it, patriotism is a form of spiritual cement in the political community, as necessary to it as piety is to church or the sense of kindred is to family. The ascendancy of the political state in popular opinion, the lengths to which political government has been taken in social and economic affairs, and the overall acceptance of the state as a form of community would never have been possible apart from the tie of patriotism, now a severely weakened tie.

Patriotism and piety have much in common. Each has its sacred dogmas, its festivals, saints, hymns, art, and ritual. And historically each is in the beginning basically a tie relating to people rather than to a given piece of territory or an institutional structure. In the Greek the word *patriotism* goes back to love of one's fathers, and to this day it is quite evidently strongest where a political nation is overwhelmingly composed of citizens who can be thought to be of common ethnic descent. The territorialization of the patriotic sentiment has its modern roots in the political state that emerged in the Renaissance, but it was not brought to high intensity until the French Revolution. Then it was that the idea of France, "one and indivisible," became the mainspring, working through Jacobin decree and military successes in the field, of what we think of as modern nationalism and also patriotism.

Patriotism in the form we have known it for nearly two centuries has been inseparable from war and revolution. Each of these forces, destroying or diminishing as they have the more ancient ties of race, locality, religion, and kinship as effective allegiances, has been closely involved in the creation of the sense of *La Belle France*, *Deutschland über Alles*, John Bull, Uncle Sam, and the like. Undoubtedly the high point of modern national patriotism was reached throughout the West in World War I. There had been pacifists and idealists in the decades leading up to that war who had thought the bond of national patriotism so weak in substance, as the result of new economic and social ideals, that national war had virtually become obsolete. The dispatch and unanimity with which the political lefts in Germany and France alike voted war credits to their respective governments took care of that illusion. It is doubtful that anything in history matches the readiness of literally millions of Europeans to give their lives to a war that almost from the beginning guaranteed highest probability of death or mutilation in the trenches. Belief in the sacred mission of one's nation was as powerful and governing in Russia among the peasants as it was among German or French industrial workers. There was, on the evidence, nothing that would not be quickly and even cheerfully given to one's nation in World War I. A whole upsurge of song and poetry testified to the buoyancy of patriotism in Western nations. The First World War has been accurately termed "the singing war," and strange though it may seem today the singing was as much to be heard on the Western Front as back at home. That war was also, in a genuine sense, the poet's war. We know how very bad most of that poetry was, but the important fact is that it was poetry inspired by patriotism. There were many millions to read and be deeply moved by the lines of a Rupert Brooke.

In a way this ascendancy of song and verse in the patriotism of World War I was symbolic, for it would be impossible to account for the peculiar form modern nationalism has taken since the French Revolution apart from the services of the intellectual class in each Western country. There is nothing spontaneous or natural in the intense devotion we find given to a Germany or France or a United States in the nineteenth and early twentieth centuries. To a given locality, region, or ethnic body, yes, but not to a vast expanse of territory that had had its boundaries and its actual component subjects or citizens so often altered by the exigencies of war, diplomacy, and sheer historical accident. It was easy to find Burgundians and Britons in the France of the eighteenth century, but not Frenchmen. Precisely the same was true of Germany, Russia, and other modern states. Even England, as many an intellectual lamented in the nineteenth century, lacked, despite its relative smallness and homogeneity of population, the "true" sense of nation with its attendant patriotism.

The fact is that the territorial state could never have aroused the fierce flare of patriotism it did from the French Revolution on had it not been for the histories that were written, the songs that were composed, the speeches and orations so carefully contrived and so powerfully delivered, the rituals and feast days given credibility by writers, and the whole gamut of intellectual contribution that ranged from tract to solemn historical or philosophical tome. The role of the school and the college, and thereby of the teacher and the textbook writer, was, as countless studies of the formation of national patriotism have shown, utterly vital. To make Frenchmen out of Burgundians, Germans out of Bavarians, and Americans out of Virginians or Californians was no easy matter in the nineteenth century, and it is inconceivable that ordinary, unspoken, unwritten economic or political forces could have accomplished this. Precisely as a very different set of intellectuals had helped bring Christianity into great power and endow it with intellectual substance and popular allegiance in the late Roman Empire, so in the nineteenth century it was a body of diverse intellectuals in each of the Western nations that gave comparable substance and possibility of attraction to the great successor of the church, the modern nation.

I do not say that institutional contexts were lacking: those provided by the military, by political aggrandizement, and by a new form of business enterprise that increasingly sought large markets. Nor can the mere existence of national governments and their nationally oriented laws be omitted. But if words and songs and rituals must have their institutional settings, these latter must be made to seem real in the popular mind, must be made evocative and allegiance-commanding, and that can only be done by symbols, the kinds of symbols the intellectual class, taking this in the large sense, alone works with skillfully and professionally.

Nor was it difficult to enlist, and widely, the intellectuals of the nineteenth and early twentieth centuries. So many of these were drawn to the new territorial nation and its sovereign government for the very reason a Fichte in Prussia or a Michelet in France was: the accomplishment, at one and the same time, of destruction of the hated (chiefly religious and feudal) past and the creation of a setting in which rationalism could take command. Suspicion of government, especially distant government, has always been large in the history of populations on earth. Such suspicion is still a vivid reality in Asia and Africa, and in the nations of those continents just now coming into full existence the function of the intellectual class, through press, radio, and television, working for the central government, is not very different from what it was in the West in the nineteenth century.

But what the intellectual class gives, it can take away! After about 1920 in Western nations the same adversary mentality that had been for a century or two directed against church, local community, and family began, on a steadily widening front, to be directed against the patriotic sentiment. The memory of World War I and its terrible toll of human life, a toll that was often senseless and purposeless beyond ordinary belief in retrospect, helped here. So did the spread throughout the West and other parts of the world of Marxism with its denigration of national consciousness, its repudiation of patriotism. Depression, Fascism, and largely impotent efforts of governments in the West to counteract unemployment provided additional ground on which to mount intellectual assault upon patriotism as a sentiment. There was a quickening of the patriotic impulse with World War II, but it was nothing by way of comparison with what the earlier world war had brought. Where was the poetry, the song, the patriotic speech in every town hall, the rich symbolism of every kind that had highlighted World War I? The roots of these had all become weakened by a mentality that had become increasingly hostile, or at very best indifferent, to the idea of national patriotism.

There is another aspect to this that deserves comment. Burke, in his *Reflections on the Revolution in France*, had warned that in the long run a nationalism or patriotism that sought foundation in the ruins of what he called the "smaller patriotisms," that is, family, neighborhood, locality, and region, was destined to fail. Large, impersonal, absolute government at a distance would never, Burke thought, generate for more than a short time the kind of human loyalty that is given naturally to family or neighborhood. Thus as the forces of centralized nationalism, which, as I say, included so much of the intellectual class, did indeed create for more than a century a truly imposing patriotism resting upon national rather than local or regional ground, the long-run effect of their work was the kind of erosion of national patriotism that we have been aware of for several decades now.

It is, or has been, often said that it was Viet Nam and its unpopularity in the American mind that killed patriotism, that has brought flag, anthem, ritual of every kind to their present low estate in national consciousness. But this is absurd. The erosion of patriotism in America was well under way before Viet Nam, as it was in each other country of the West. The same forces which were eating away at the fabric of the political community were bound to reach the sentiments and rites of patriotism. If the national state can no longer be believed in, be the object of belief and trust, how can patriotism be other than a hollow word?

For a long time now it has not been popular among the educated classes to be or seem patriotic in the sense this word had even half a century ago. Patriotism is without question one of the values we have jettisoned this century in the West. In some ways one can be grateful. The spirit of nationalism and of the patriotism that went with it has never seemed to me as fertile in the creation of the greater values and ideas of Western civilization as other spirits and other loyalties. And from the beginning it has been almost impossible to separate the spirit of patriotism from war and its symbols.

So much is true, but what is equally true is that no government can hope to achieve anything of a political, social, and economic character that rises much above the level of a written statute unless there is present a sense of veneration for that government that is but another way of expressing patriotism. Those who take delight in the fact that a recent poll shows only a minority of Americans now willing to see "Americanism" spread to other parts of the earth might with good reason reflect on the fact that apart from some manifestation of this special devotion the cause of the national planning and social and economic regulation so many of these selfsame critics of "Americanism" cherish is made hopeless in the long run. As Cardinal Newman wrote, men will die for a dogma who will not even stir for a conclusion.

THE NEMESIS OF POLITICS

What grim irony there is in our present political condition. Almost everything that has ever been dreamed of for the political sphere by its major prophets from Hobbes through Locke, Rousseau, and Bentham down to the Galbraiths, Schlesingers, and Goodwins of the contemporary age has either been accomplished or is well on the way to being done.

The kind of absoluteness in the state that Hobbes demanded as the sole alternative to the state of nature is, and has been since at least the French Revolution, a fact; as much so in the democracies as in the total states. In Hobbes' day the power of the political order was still being effectively challenged by social class, church, town, and family. It no longer is so challenged. For at least the past century and a half, perhaps longer, the state has elicited from its citizens in the West the kind of loyalty that prior to the eighteenth century was much more likely to go to other institutions in society. Say what we will about abridgments of individual freedoms, civil rights have nevertheless reached a status in the Western state that a John Locke or John Milton would have scarcely dared to hope for. And whatever substantial inequalities may still remain in the state and in participation in the political process, the long-run pattern is as clear as any to be found in modern European history; it is a pattern of almost constantly increasing equality. And finally, on the evidence of each of the Western states in our day, the use of the state's power to effect social reforms is and for some time has been monumental.

Not Jeremy Bentham with his numberless projects for directly adding to human welfare and happiness, not the most ardent and optimistic of early nineteenth-century socialists, egalitarians, and social progressivists, could have conjured up visions of direct political action in service to mass needs equal to what has actually come about in all countries in the West. The steps which Marx and Engels listed in their *Communist Manifesto* as being necessary to the establishment of socialism look almost comical today in their paucity and meagerness—compared, that is, to reigning reality in our time.

George Bernard Shaw once said that the only thing worse than not getting what you have striven for is getting it. Whether in that Shavian cynicism there is an iron law of human nature, I cannot be sure. But I do know that the present political scene suggests its appositeness so far as nineteenth-century political and social ideals are concerned.

For where the centralized, bureaucratized, collectivist state was, only a century ago, scarcely more than utopian dream for progressivists of all stripes and colors, such a state is omnipresent reality in our society. And, on the evidence of polls and surveys, it is not much liked. It is not even much liked by intellectuals of a type that helped make such a state reality, though their only prescription is more of the same thing.

We have brought state and individual very close, largely through destruction or weakening of ties which once lay intermediate, providing the state with institutional checks upon its expansion and the individual with sources of security. Clearly, neither state nor individual has profited from this pincers process. The political order, swollen by economic and social responsibilities, so many of which it performs ineffectually and at awesome cost, has manifestly lost the capacity to do at least one of the things for which it is uniquely fitted: maintain internal order. Whether the Western state has also lost, or had severely diminished, its other great historic function, that of making war against foreign enemies, we cannot yet be certain, though it would be remarkable if the internal rot that rendered both Italy and France ineffectual in military terms by the beginning of World War II has not spread to other Western countries.

As for the individual, I have adduced enough evidence in this chapter, I believe, to suggest his impotence in political affairs in the contemporary state; his impotence and also his loss of sheer political will. The individual's political identity, far from waxing with the enlargement of popular and public opinion as a force in democracy, has decayed. So, as I wish to stress in the next chapter, has the individual's identity in the social order and in culture.

The proliferation of civil rights in the areas of speech, press, theatre, and the arts generally is attended by license and anarchy, in the judgment of many, rather than the hoped-for liberation of the creative mind and the sense of intellectual buoyancy that liberty carries with it. "Men are qualified for civil liberty," wrote Edmund Burke, "in exact proportion to their disposition to put moral chains upon their own appetites." Few such moral chains are to be seen at the present time. We have more than a few evidences in history that civil freedom comes to be detested by widening numbers of people when its fruits are more likely to be the decayed ones of freely exhibited obscenity and morally irresponsible demands and threats in the marketplace than those which the greater philosophers of individual freedom intended. We might take note from the very recent writings of the now-exiled Solzhenitsyn that not even this remarkable mind, dedicated to freedom for the creative mind, willing indeed to spend years in first prison, then exile, believes for a moment in unrestricted, untrammeled rights for individuals. So clear indeed in his own mind is this extraordinary Russian on such matters that he has been quite willing on several occasions to intersperse his criticisms of Russian bureaucracy and ideological rigidity with some stinging reproofs to Western, particularly American, intellectuals for what seemed to him unconscionable betrayal in their writings of their national community.

And as for spreading equality and social justice in modern democracy, there is, as we know, a constantly enlarging number of people whose disillusionment with these ends is in exact proportion to their hatred of the means through which the ends have been sought. Nothing so leads to popular resentment as does the combination of welfare taken for granted—exhortations indeed to take welfare for granted—and means which are acutely distrusted or despised. It is not a greater sharing in affluence that results from the political mentality we have known only too well since the New Deal but, rather, a greater sharing in blunted, defeated expectations. There is not the slightest evidence that any of the real increase in standard of living we have seen take place in the West for a long time now, most especially in the period since World War II, owes anything in any degree to political planning or control. It is entirely the result of economic growth. But the by now habitual association of such growth and political action—and promises—is bound to direct to the state and its governing agencies and officials all the resentments and hostilities which are generated by the feeling of deprivation or loss in economic matters. It is no wonder that the political order bears today a load of recrimination and resentment it never had to bear in earlier periods when standard of living was a great deal lower. Then the state, not demanding credit for what it had done *for* people through its servants, was less likely to win hostility for what it had succeeded in doing *to* them.

There are a great many intellectuals at the present time who clearly believe correction of all these reversals and pathologies lies within the power of the state—the state, that is, properly governed. Reform of political institutions, it is said, is all that is needed to end the current malaise, dissolve present accumulating hostilities and distrusts, re-achieve the bond of genuine political community. A strong presidency—in proper hands, of course—and an active, responsive Congress coupled with a national grass-roots type of common cause or populism: this, many continue to believe, will restore faith in politics and its distinctive kind of power.

I cannot agree. Such means seem to me, even in the best light, hardly more than a use of combustible materials in putting out a fire. The heart of our problem with the state and its governing agencies does not lie in the state, much less in the type of individuals who make their way to the top in politics, but instead in *the relation of the state to other, nonpolitical institutions.* These latter have been the essential walls of the political community, the indispensable means by which checks and limits have been placed upon the state's power and upon the tendency, always great in democracy, for that power to seek constantly to encompass all manner of ways of life. Say all we will about the wisdom of the Constitution and the merits of the internal system of government it prescribes: the success of liberal democracy in America and elsewhere has depended overwhelmingly upon the social and cultural walls which have, as it were, protected the Constitution and liberal democracy from the demands and strains which would otherwise be placed upon them.

But it is a mark of the age we live in that these walls are crumbling before our eyes. Unless we see this fact in some detail and clarity, we shall be unable to appreciate the true crisis of the political community.

THE CRUMBLING
WALLS OF POLITICS

WHEN THE FUNDAMENTAL ideas of modern liberal, representative democracy were being set forth in the late eighteenth century on both sides of the Atlantic, certain important assumptions were present in the minds of the Founding Fathers. These assumptions had less to do with politics than with the non- or pre-political values and structures of society. The political and legal would for the most part be inscribed in constitution or organic act. What was not so inscribed, what was thought to be self-evident enough to be virtually taken for granted, was a series of propositions regarding the relation between the social order and the political state.

Except for certain of the French *philosophes,* and subsequently the more zealous leaders of the French Revolution, a substantial degree of *pluralism* is to be found in the minds of those who, like Montesquieu, Burke, Jefferson, and Madison, gave the basic intellectual temper to Western democracy. I mean by this only that it was never intended for a moment that political government would be, indeed could be, the answer to all the needs of human beings living together in a social order. Apart from a social structure rooted in kinship, locality, and voluntary association—not to emphasize here a largely Christian-Judaic morality that was assumed to be a part of every individual's very nurture—and apart from a human nature presumed to be anchored in this social structure and this morality, modern liberal democracy could not have seemed even a faint possibility to the architects of the constitutions which began to take shape in the West by the beginning of the nineteenth century.

Neither in man's innate character nor in any magical properties present in a political general will was the future of democracy thought to be rooted. We need read only the Federalist Papers in this country to be made quickly aware of the wisdom of the Founding Fathers regarding man's inherited nature. Far from its being thought necessarily good at birth, with the possibility of corruption lying only in institutions, the opposite is more nearly true. Like Montesquieu and Voltaire in France, Hume and Burke in England, the makers of American constitutional democracy thought it best to presume, if anything at all about human nature, a certain ineradicable tendency toward mischief and even evil. It is absurd to charge the philosophers of democracy with any of that romanticism regarding the child and untutored savage which we find in so much of the popular literature of the time and in the works of a few anarchists or proto-anarchists like William Godwin. There is nothing in the slightest degree naive in the ideas of human nature we find in the primary works of those responsible for the system of representative, liberal democracy that achieved its high point in the early part of the present century.

But what was present in very substantial measure in the basic works of the founders of political democracy was respect for such social institutions as property, family, local community, religion, and voluntary association, and for such cultural and social values as objective reason, the discipline of language, self-restraint, the work ethic, and, far from least, the culture that had taken root in classical civilization and grown, with rare interruptions, ever since. If we neglect the role of these institutions and these values in the minds of the Founding Fathers, we have omitted the elements on which alone, in their minds, political democracy could be made a reality. If, in their bold view of the matter, a less than arbitrary and powerful political state could be safely contemplated, this was not because man was deemed naturally good and law-abiding, but only because common sense suggested that such institutions as family, local community, and religion, having been for so many thousands of years the universal contexts of human nature, and such ideals as charity, brotherhood, reason, and justice, having been for more than twenty-five hundred years the principal threads of Western morality, would continue indefinitely into the future. Was it not reasonable to assume that human beings would go on being nurtured in these institutions by these values during the centuries ahead as they had been during the millennia past? Was it not equally reasonable, despite the worst excesses of Jacobin democracy, to assume that individual and social privacy would continue to be cherished, with cooperation and spontaneous association the primary supports, after family and church, of the individual? The architects of Western democracy were all students of history, and they had every intellectual right to suppose that moral values and social structures which had survived as many vicissitudes and environmental changes as these had over the two and a half millennia of their existence in Western society would go on for at least a few more centuries.

But in fact they have not. If there is anything distinctive about the twentieth century in the West—in addition to the most destructive wars in all human history—it is the condition of moribundity in which we find these selfsame structures and values. I do not question the fact that we can find the beginnings of this moribundity well before the present century. I shall argue indeed in a later chapter that from the time the modern national state came into being in the West during the Renaissance and Reformation, there came into being also a kind of built-in, endemic process of annihilation of traditional social and moral institutions. The centralized, potentially collectivist nature of the sovereign power claimed by its philosophers and protagonists for the modern state made such annihilation inevitable in the long run. But such was the accumulated authority to be found in traditional society and culture, such were the accumulated allegiances to this traditional authority, such was the autonomy that for a long time continued to characterize the whole social and culture sphere in its relation to the political state, that thinkers in the eighteenth century can be forgiven for having supposed that this authority, this allegiance, and this autonomy would endure for a long time, thus making possible political freedom and a vigorously representative democracy.

It is the failure of traditional social authorities, allegiances, and their embedded autonomies to endure to our century that, above anything else, is responsible for the intolerable strains which have been placed upon the traditional political community and for its present malaise.

THE LOSS OF SOCIAL ROOTS

During the past two centuries mankind has undergone the most traumatic social change it has experienced since the beginnings of settled culture in the Neolithic age. I refer to the decline—even disappearance in spreading sections—of the local community, the dislocation of kinship, and the erosion of the sacred in human affairs.

It would be difficult to exaggerate the significance of this change, which began in the West in the late eighteenth century and has by now spread to most parts of the world. The historical roots of culture and personality alike lie deep in neighborhood, family, and religion. The symbols of the distinctive form of community each represents remain with us in countless manifestations, but their power to awaken response is bound to diminish constantly, given the profoundly altered position of these types of community in modern industrial and political society.

It is a striking fact that through approximately ten thousand years, the period since the appearance of agricultural arts made settled community possible, the basic strength of these social ties remained intact: this despite the innumerable wars, migrations, famines, plagues, and other kinds of catastrophes to which mankind was subjected.

Very different, however, has been the case since the onset of the two great revolutions of modern times: the democratic and the industrial at the end of the eighteenth century. Unlike all preceding major changes in human history, these revolutions went below the superstructure of society, went right to man's most ancient and cherished sources of identity. With the rise of the factory system and the mass electorate, there was inevitably a wrenching of the individual from his accustomed family, local, and religious contexts. As Ostrogorski wrote in this classic study of democracy and political party, the advent of the new forces "shattered the old framework of political society. The hierarchy of classes and their internal cohesion were destroyed, and the time-honored social ties which bound the individual to the community were severed."

New organizations rose, to be sure, and sought in one fashion or other to capture the allegiances of individuals: factories, offices, labor unions, cooperatives, and the whole host of associations which began proliferating in the nineteenth century. Without question many of these have proved effective in the larger realms of function. But so far as the individual and his loyalties are concerned, the ties contained in these new organizations have too often seemed mechanical, without power to create the sense of membership in society that had lain in the bonds of kinship, locality, and religions.

The increasing isolation of the individual in electorate and marketplace carried with it a large literature in the eighteenth and nineteenth centuries that, in effect, justified it. An individualistic psychology found the basic springs of human stability, of motivation, and of freedom in the biologically inherited nature of man. Economics, with its celebration of enlightened self-interest and what Adam Smith called "the instinct to truck and barter," its envisagement of society as little more than a scene of conflicting individual forces, and its general neglect of the moral and the social, was a perfect intellectual analogue to what was going on in the institutional sphere. Moral philosophy took refuge in a highly individualistic utilitarianism. Just as early Puritans had seen external structures of religion as fetters upon individual faith, so, now, did many philosophers see nearly all social institutions as limits upon the individual's freedom and self-reliance. There were exceptions, among them Burke, Coleridge, Hegel, and Tocqueville, but they were few.

It is against this background of change that present assaults must be seen. It is always this way, as we know from the comparative study of revolution. There is seldom a major attack on institutions and values until well after processes of decline and erosion have begun. By a strange law of social behavior, decline actually causes attack. Let a government, economic enterprise, or church reach a certain point of enervation, the result of random causes or tidal forces of history, and it is virtually certain that some kind of assault will be mounted on it. As Tocqueville pointed out in his classic study of the French Revolution, it was not the Revolution that brought down the monarchy; it was the steady decline of monarchy, and all that went with it, that brought on the Revolution.

It is in these terms, I believe, that we are obliged to see contemporary assaults upon the historic family and upon the ties and the roles which the family has sustained for so many thousands of years. The kinds of revolt which we see in youth's restiveness under any form of parental domination, in the constantly rising divorce rates, in the forsaking of traditional family for novel forms of communal living, and in the more radical expressions of the women's liberation movement—all of these, while strong in their own right, are manifestations, I believe, of prior decay of the family's—especially the extended family's—functional importance in the social order, as the consequence of the great political and economic changes which have swept modern society during the past two centuries.

The essential base of a strong kinship system is not affectional, nor is it primarily moral; it is economic and political. Where family has possessed economic significance either as a producing unit or as the result of its being fused into the economic system, and where it has been closely linked with property, a whole morality could be built around this economic significance. And in societies where the family tie is fundamental, the power of the government stops literally at the threshold of the house. The state is an association of families, not of discrete individuals.

But the two great Western revolutions have loosened the economic and political ties of the family and, in the process, have blurred accustomed roles, have separated the sexes and also the generations. It is not "sexual immorality" that weakens the family; it is a weakening of the family that generates what we call "sexual immorality." Similarly, it is necessary to see the radical phases of women's liberation not as cause but as reflection of the diminished significance of marriage and family in our time.

I am not trying to take anything away from the revolutionary thrust of much of the literature and action of this movement. Women's liberation, along with black civil rights, must be accounted one of the genuinely revolutionary movements of this age. It is too soon to tell how far it will go, how great will be its consequences. I am saying only that this revolution, like all others known to us in history, has to be seen against a background of prior destruction or erosion of key values, of prior dislocation of an institution from its historic contexts. Had human beings not already become separated in substantial degree from kinship, as the result of progressive loss of the relation of its dominant roles to the larger economic and social order, it is exceedingly unlikely that a conscious and systematic women's revolution would have come into being. Precisely the same is true of the relation of youth to the traditional kinship structure. The important point is that it is not either women's or youth's revolt that is the primary cause of a weakening of the authority of the family; it is, rather, the weakening of the family's authority over the past century or two that is the cause of the contemporary revolts.

This said, it is still important to give the ongoing women's liberation movement its due. Potentially, it is the most fundamental of modern revolutions, for unlike all others, which have been political or have dealt with the relationships of large groups in the economic sphere chiefly, this one is directed at the most ancient roles in human history: those of the two sexes. It would be difficult even to guess at how much of human culture, of the social bond in all its complexities, has rested, indeed still rests, upon the highly unequal role differences of women and men, of girls and boys. Such differences have for millennia furnished the themes of art, literature, religion, politics, and it can be said that an entire civilization, in the West certainly, reflects in countless ways the historic acceptance of woman's inferiority to the male.

Leaving aside those few and debatable instances in primitive society of matriarchal kinship relations, it has to be said that the family—conjugal and extended—has been a tissue of these role inequalities. It is impossible to deal with the traditional family as a center of authority and a nursery of human affection, loyalty, and the several traits by which sex is defined socially apart from its overwhelmingly masculine orientation. Clearly, one is not obliged to defend this orientation or the inequalities which are necessarily stitched into the fabric of kinship in commenting upon the radical character of any change that significantly transposes, reverses, or modifies them.

Earlier women's rights movements were essentially that: efforts to achieve for women a larger share of economic, educational, and cultural benefits—*but within the family structure;* or at least without seeking to alter that structure seriously. What gives present manifestoes, political actions, and movements toward legal reform their revolutionary character is the degree to which the substance of the family is changed. For with sure revolutionary instinct, the women's liberation movement—at least in its radical expressions—goes right to the heart of the matter, which is the historic nature of the *role* of each of the sexes.

Youth's relation to the traditional family is also worthy of stress, for just as the family has always had an overwhelmingly masculine character, so has it had a strong tilt toward parent, particularly father, rather than child. This, as we know, has been visibly changing for some time now, especially in America. As long ago as the nineteenth century it was possible for European and Asiatic visitors to this country to be impressed by the greater freedom and mobility of youth, male and female. The *marriage de convenance,* even among the wealthy and aristocratic, was scarcely known in this country. That freedom and mobility increased rather steadily during the first half of this century, and in retrospect we should probably have been able to predict the immense explosion of youth culture in the late 1950s and 1960s. It is said that this has subsided, that it will not occur again—simply by virtue of the disappearance of its demographic base through profound changes in rates of birth and longevity—but I am skeptical. I think it as likely, at least on the basis of present indicators, that the youth revolt will continue, taking diverse forms—economic, marital, political, and educational—as that the women's liberation movement will continue and grow.

It is idle to comment in moral terms here, either to lament or to rejoice. As the great Bishop Butler wrote: "Things and actions are what they are, and the consequences of them will be what they will be; why, then, should we desire to be deceived." I think something in the way of a renewal of the kinship ethic may be taking place at this moment, partly in reaction to disillusionment in state and social order, but it is impossible to be sure, and all we know is that among other great changes in our social order that in kinship is perhaps foremost.

The irony, though, is that dislocation of and revolt against family takes place at a time when we are learning, with a wealth of information through careful study, just how vital the family is in the crucial areas of individual motivation, personality structure, and creativeness. In study after study we learn how relatively weak are other influences—school, peer group, church—upon the child's mind compared with influence of family; sometimes, to be sure, for bad instead of good. There seems to be something unique in the special type of intimacy of sexes and ages the family makes possible. Whether this is irreplaceable we cannot of course know. Suffice it to say that heretofore in nearly all of the utopian or other communities founded upon rigorous subordination of family tie, not very many years passed before the tie reasserted itself. But nothing quite like our present society, with its multifold changes in morality, economic possibility, and residential patterns, has ever before existed.

Similarly there has been profound dislocation in the second oldest of man's social ties: the local community or neighborhood. Here too we are being reminded almost daily of how deep the urge to neighborhood is among human beings by the impact of something like busing to achieve ethnic quotas. But it was not busing that first reawakened the sense of neighborhood; it was, rather, the destructiveness of ill-thought-out programs of urban renewal. In the razing of the whole blocks of tenements and houses there often occurred a bulldozing of neighborhood patterns which were not recreated in new structures of human habitation, whether these were public or private in construction.

But even before urban renewal there was the suburban movement which, on the testimony of scores of studies, did not often establish the sense of rootedness in place that human beings had become accustomed to during the many thousands of years since the small local community came into existence. I am inclined to think that the city, as such, has been too often maligned in this respect. The evidence of even a New York suggests that all other things equal, people will congregate in neighborhoods which have significant meaning in their lives, which become evocative contexts of stability and relatedness to the larger society. And what is true of New York is even more true of European and Asiatic cities. There is no necessary conflict between the city, even a large one, and the sense of close, local membership.

Even so, no one will seriously question that the place of the local community, of neighborhood in any form, has been made difficult by major tendencies, political and economic, in modern Western history. Forces of economic rationalization, of patterning of industry without respect to environment and local community, and of combined centralization and individualization in the political sphere, have without question cut from neighborhood and its unique form of community a great deal of the ground that it requires. Neighborhood and locality, if they are to have psychological effect in human lives, must have a functional significance in the economic and political organizations around them. They must *seem* important, but to seem important they must *be* important. And, quite obviously, local community has been no more functionally important than kinship in the kind of society that the industrial and political revolutions brought into being. State and economy alike have, in effect, bypassed family and community to go straight to the individual, thus leaving him so often precariously exposed to the chilling currents of anonymity and isolation.

The rootlessness of our age is attested to by the ease with which human beings turn to the symbols of power and politics, to movements and crusades of one kind or other. For a long time it could be thought that the political community would be modern man's substitute for the older types of membership in society. But the political community itself now suffers. There is little to take its place. Technology's wonders do not, alas, suffice. The rate of attrition, of diminishing returns, accelerates all the time. Think only of the impact of the airplane on human consciousness and on culture by comparison with the earlier impacts of railroad train and automobile. Even the remarkable jetliner does not come close to the earlier inventions in power to enchant, to fascinate an entire people at all ages, and to become the basis of legend, song, tale, and drama. Our launch to the moon should certainly rank with the greatest exploits of man in history so far as boldness and audacity are concerned. But the difficulty we have, only a few years later, even in remembering the names of the astronauts is some indication of what I mean. It would seem that technology has limited, and presently declining, power to inspire a sense of either the communal or the sacred.

What Susanne K. Langer wrote a generation ago in her profound *Philosophy in a New Key* is pertinent here:

> In modern civilization there are two great threats to mental security: the new mode of living, which has made the old nature-symbols alien to our minds, and the new mode of working which makes personal activity meaningless, inacceptable to the hungry imagination. . . . Most people have no home that is a symbol of their childhood, not even a definite memory of one place to serve that purpose. Many no longer know the language that was once their mother-tongue. All old symbols are gone, and thousands of average lives offer no new materials to a creative imagination.

What Susanne Langer is pointing to is the striking decline of the sacred in our lives. Centuries of gradual secularization of human belief have been followed in our time by an acceleration of secular tendencies beyond anything the West has before known. Mechanization and bureaucratization crowd out those ritual commemorations of the social bond which are the central elements of sacred experience everywhere. Christmas, Easter, Halloween are today but impoverished reminders of a time when the year was rich in celebrations of the seasons—and, far more important, of human community and its relation to the forces of nature. If it were solely

a matter of loss of these ritual experiences—through commer-
cialization, rootlessness, and general disenchantment, the product
in large part of rationalization of life—the matter would not be as
grave. But even, and perhaps especially, in the smaller areas of society, in family, neighborhood, and church, a conspicuous erosion
of the sense of the sacred is to be seen, also witnessed by the loss of
ritual expressions in so many lives.

The greatest of all distinctions the human mind is capable of,
Durkheim wrote, is that between the sacred and the profane or
merely utilitarian. Even the distinction between good and evil is
small by comparison, for both good and evil are but representations
of the sacred, positive or negative. To endow anything with sacred
significance—human life, birth, marriage, death, the community or
nation—is to remove it from the sphere of things which must be
justified by expediency or pragmatic consideration. Almost anything is capable of becoming, at some time or in some place, sacred
in significance, but by the same token almost anything that is
sacred can be lowered into the purely utilitarian.

Rightly did Durkheim declare the sacred but the other side of
the coin on which community is written. Human aggregates are
possible, or at least conceivable, without a sense of the sacred, but
not, Durkheim declared, community. But it is community that
gives to the sacred its most vital expressions everywhere: birth,
marriage, death, and other moments in the human drama.

Particularly important is the sense of the sacred in death. Religion's power over us in this world is closely related to its
imagined powers over the next world, specifically to that of remov-
ing our fears in contemplation of death and what may follow.
Without question, those religions strongest in ritual, liturgy, sacrament, and other forms of external authority over faith are strongest
in their appeal to individuals over long periods of time and
strongest also in their manifest capacity to prepare us for the uncer-
tainties of life, death included and foremost.

There is another value to institutional religion, one that, as Tocqueville perceived, is never so great as in democratic political orders. Religion is a powerful means of containing millennialist energies which can only too easily be released in political contexts, revolutionary and totalitarian. "When there is no longer any principle of authority in religion any more than in politics, men are speedily frightened at the aspect of all this unbounded independence." Democracy, as Tocqueville further observed, only too easily becomes a religion itself, a form of pantheism, with a transfer to the people of what is taken from God. Not seldom in history have political despots sought to assume personal sacredness. When the emperor Augustus caused an image of himself to be placed on every Roman hearth side by side with the traditional lares and penates he was but copying what Alexander had done in effect several centuries earlier; he in turn had found inspiration in Persia and other parts of the Near East long accustomed to seamless unity of religion and political power. The Jacobin de-Christianization decrees at the height of the French Revolution, like the later Bolshevik assault on traditional Orthodoxy, sprang from a well-founded realization that power can become truly absolute only when an autonomous institutional religion has been displaced and succeeded by an increasingly sacralized government.

For a long time now we have seen the secularization and individualization of religion intensify in the West. Ritual and sacrament and liturgy have been among the chief casualties of religious modernism. The results are to be seen in progressive loss of religious belief on the one hand and on the other in the outpourings of relatively unstructured pentecostalism. There is no mystery at all in the high correlation between the millennialist spirit in religion and that same spirit in politics, for there is close affinity psychologically between religion and politics, and the millennialist spirit in the two is drawn from the same sources. The distrust of "enthusiasm" in the great institutional religions is well founded.

The greatest religious event of our age will prove to have been the signal transformation of the Roman Catholic Church by the

Vatican Council summoned by John XXIII in 1960. For the Roman Catholic Church was the last real stronghold of the kind of authority that lies in religious institutions, in ritual and in sacrament. To an astonishing degree it had resisted the acids of modernity which in the Protestant faiths had virtually destroyed the sense of visible community in religion and that had driven more and more of their members either out of religion altogether or to the work of further secularizing these faiths in the interests of either politics or Mammon. I do not think it too strong a statement to say that in large areas of Protestantism—and the same applies to Jewish areas also—the capacity of religion to inspire respect, to provide spiritual anchor, to offer community worthy of the name, had just about vanished. Only, really, in the Roman Catholic church did ritual, liturgy, and sacrament remain vivid, a fact attested to in some part by the rising number of conversions to Catholicism from Protestant and nonreligious sectors.

Vatican II changed that, though we cannot be sure at this juncture exactly how much. If the Roman church, by virtue of the acts of this momentous council, goes the way of the Protestant churches, if escalating secularism is accompanied there as it has been in the Protestant faiths by loss of visible community and authority in the vital sphere of faith, then one more wall of the political community will have been weakened. Religions like Christianity and Judaism were once both strong in the authority of the sacred, and in this fact lay their internal strength and also their extraordinary value to the whole idea of the political community, together with its liberties and rights, in Western society.

I cannot help thinking that the often mindless nostalgia that has come over American society during recent decades is related to the loss of the sacred and of the power of ritual in human affairs. The great effect of ritual is its capacity to bind past and present in a single act, with the emphasis, of course, on the present. In ritual the past, and also by implication the future, are *enacted*, but, as I say, in the present. There is nothing in ritual that leads one to look

back at all, least of all fondly, on the past, for it is the merit of
ritual that it keeps the past around us in our daily existence. But
when ritual declines and disappears the sterile spirit of archaism or
nostalgia takes command. Nostalgia is the rust of memory. Having,
as it were, lost the past from our present, we look back on it
fondly, and so often vapidly. It is a poor substitute for the sacred.

THE PAINS OF AFFLUENCE

Adding to the strains and tensions of politics in our time is the
problem of affluence: I mean the problem that has so evidently
been created in the minds of the middle class by sheer possession of
a material prosperity mostly undreamed of by their forebears in the
last century. The problem I speak of is a complex one. It is in part
the result of a relatively sudden, often traumatic, catapulting of individuals ill-prepared socially and psychologically from a lower to a
higher income level. What Durkheim called anomie, that is, being
wrenched from one set of norms but not fully established in another, has something to do with the problem of affluence as it is to
be seen in so many sectors of the middle class today.

Affluence leaves a great many of us with strong guilt feelings
which are in no way anchored in piety—that is, in the sense of
religious austerity—but, rather, in contemplation of the plight of
the poor. As Bertrand de Jouvenel wrote a quarter of a century ago
in his profound and prescient book, *The Ethics of Redistribution*, the
revelation of poverty has in all ages come as a shock to the select
and affluent few, and has commonly driven them to regard personal extravagance with a sense of guilt rooted in some kind of
religious experience. Hence the periodic feasts open to all; hence
too the sacredness of alms, and the accepted role, the legitimacy, of
the beggar on the streets. Behind all this lay, of course, a religious
ethic.

But that ethic is gone, or at least seriously atrophied, in our time, and the presence of poverty is more likely to induce *ressen-timent*, the feeling behind George Bernard Shaw's "I hate the poor," than to lead to anything remotely comparable to the kind of ethic, corrupted though it could assuredly become at times, that existed in the West prior to the Reformation and the rise of Puritanism with its profoundly changed sense of poverty in the social order. As de Jouvenel writes: "Riches had been a scandal in the face of poverty; now poverty was a scandal in the face of riches." To a society increasingly committed to the secular idea of progress, the perception of poverty was not only embarrassing but alienating. Poverty must be abolished because it is hateful. No one will quibble with this view, thus stated. The trouble is, poverty having come to seem hateful, noxious, and altogether repugnant, leads to the desire on the part of enlarging numbers to be spared the sight of it, and above all contact with it. Hence the willingness on the part of the middle classes to see large amounts of money go to the poor, or at least be raised in the name of the poor, provided only that the disbursing be done through more or less aseptic, bureaucratic agencies of the government. All one asks is that in the process of poverty's being abolished, we the middle class be spared participation.

Few things are more vivid and galling, however, than our seeming incapacity to remove poverty, at least to the taste of the politically motivated and politically powerful intellectual. As Milton Friedman has been pointing out for years, every fresh infusion of large public monies, whether in the form of urban renewal, public housing, or even more direct "wars" against poverty, has little if any tonic value to the poor—who are more often actually hurt than helped—and is chiefly useful to the middle and upper classes. But the middle class—less often the upper classes, the very rich—all the while benefiting from funds spent ostensibly for the poor, remains guilt-plagued. The torments of affluence are only intensified, it would seem.

Hence the lure of the so-called zero-growth society among

widening circles in our age. I do not think very many persons fully appreciate what the toll would be economically, and socially and psychologically, in our society were a policy of no-growth to be actually instituted and reinforced. But the attraction of such a society is there nonetheless; it is idealized and romanticized into a veritable Garden. It is interesting to realize that as far back as 1848 John Stuart Mill gave the world a kind of preview of the lure that would someday be exercised by the idea of a static society in place of one charged by the goals of mobility, achievement, and competition:

"I confess that I am not charmed with the ideal held out by those who think that the normal state of human beings is that of struggle to get on," wrote Mill. The ideal state of society, he continued, is one in which while no one is really poor, no one desires to be rich. "This condition of society, so greatly preferable to the present, is not only perfectly compatible with the stationary state, but, it would seem, more naturally allied with that state than with any other."

It is not difficult to imagine the spreading appeal of that image of society during the years ahead of us. Not only will it seem a solution to the torments of the achievement psychology, of the curse of rising expectations, it will also fit in superbly with the equalitarian ethic, of which I shall say more in a later chapter. All I want to stress here, though, is the pressure that is bound to be exerted upon the political community in the present by a set of cultural and psychological forces that, in their sheer mass, could not even have been dreamed of by the Founding Fathers.

Since at least Hesiod's *Works and Days*, there have been ruminations on the paradoxes of civilization. The Golden Age for Hesiod was the state of mankind in the beginning when the very dearth of the arts and comforts of civilization had been attended by happiness and fundamental decency. His own age, thought Hesiod, was truly the Iron Age, one in which an abundance of knowledge and of the arts of culture was set in circumstances of unhappiness, frustration, and breakdown in morality.

That theme has been a recurrent one in Western thought. Although it was by no means the entire Greek view of the matter—there being those on record for whom the growth of the arts had added to human happiness—it was a fairly common one. So was it among Romans, especially in the Age of Seneca, whose account of the Golden Age at the beginning, rich in moral virtues, lacking in the arts of civilization, is nothing if not Hesiodic. The late Arthur O. Lovejoy put together a fascinating and encyclopedic study of the concept of primitivism in Western thought, showing how common is the idea of conjoined poverty—or at least economic simplicity—and moral goodness. The idea is far from alien to modern writing. Although it is false to imply that Rousseau wished to see mankind revert to a state of nature, he made evident in his *Discourse on the Origin of Inequality* how many of the ills and torments of civilization have their roots in affluence. Freud, in his later years at least, thought there was almost necessary malaise to be expected by human beings in the more advanced states of civilization. Durkheim, in his first major work, *Division of Labor,* declared that increase in unhappiness, boredom, and alienation was a demonstrable part of the progress of civilization.

Lord Keynes, in an essay titled "Economic Possibilities for our Grandchildren," once wondered what the relaxation of economic discipline, of previously unalterable processes of economic survival, would do to the social bond and to human personality. For countless millennia man's primary problem and hence goal has been the struggle for economic existence. "If the economic problem is solved," Keynes wrote, "mankind will be deprived of its traditional purpose. Will this be a benefit? If one believes at all in the real values of life, the prospect at least opens up the possibility of benefit. Yet I think with dread of the readjustment of the habits and instincts of the ordinary man, bred into him for countless generations, which he may be asked to discard within a few decades."

Until the present no civilization has ever existed in which more than the tiniest minority could escape work's discipline. Always, everywhere, those who worked, got; those who didn't, didn't. It was just about as simple as that.

Not without good reason have the ideas of work and punishment gone hand in hand in history. The Greek word for work was the root of the word for punishment; the Hebrews saw unremitting work as the expiation mankind must do for original sin. From the idea of work as punishment and expiation to the idea of work as morally and psychologically salutary is not a difficult evolution of meaning. In each case work remains, though, an important discipline in the social order, a strong bond between individual and environment as well as between individual and individual. Variations of the fables of the Busy Bee and the Industrious Ant are to be found in most of the world's folklores. In few peoples has work occupied quite the place of ethical imperative it has in the West since the rise of Puritanism. But the constraints of labor and of economic necessity have been nonetheless vital elements of the social bond everywhere for all but a few in society.

It may be doubted that work holds this significance at the present time in our post-industrial, technological, and welfare-committed society. It is not alone a matter of the Protestant Ethic becoming ever less evocative in middle-class society, a matter of scorn among more and more of the young. It is in larger degree the fact that a combination of sheer technological productivity and of political commitment to universal welfare is bound to reduce both the actual amount of work done by individuals for the most part and the age-old compulsion to work.

As I write, a worker, Ray Evanoski of Pennsylvania, is quoted in *The Wall Street Journal* as regretting the fact that in this period of recession his employer did *not* see fit to lay him off. Had he been laid off, he told the reporter, he would have collected $100 a week in tax-free unemployment benefits, with food stamps undoubtedly thrown in. As it is, he goes on, he is stuck with working and taking home $130 each week. The difference, he says, "pays for your gas to work and your lunch. So you don't make out."

Too much should not be made of that. In most of us there is an urge to keep busy irrespective of reward. But there is something paradigmatic nevertheless in that worker's experience, and his reflections. Allow all we will to the human instinct to work, an environment in which work is *not* vitally necessary to survival is assuredly a different one from anything our forebears ever knew, and it is impossible not to see what Lord Keynes had in mind so far as the constraining influence of work upon the social bond is concerned. The inescapable fact is that the ethic of work cannot for very long have the compulsion it has immemorially had in a society now politically committed to unemployment compensation, food stamps, Social Security, and Medicare. Few in our day will be so callous as to say: away with all such benefits! Some degree of security for the individual would seem a minimum essential for any form of human community. The problem, clearly, is the finding of that exact balance between an order in which the Industrious Apprentice flourishes and one in which he finds excellent economic reason for abandoning industry of any kind. It is elementary in psychology that human behavior is goal-oriented, which means in fact *norm-* or *incentive*-oriented. The consequences to both economic and social motivations of a society in which incentive to work has been extinguished or diluted are necessarily very great. We know too little about them.

Perhaps I exaggerate the unique modernity of liberation from work. Sir Denis Gabor in *The Mature Society* describes what he calls "undeserving elites" of past ages: aristocracies no longer rooted in actual service, as in imperial Rome, the French *ancien régime*, and modern Britain. He also reminds us of the large body of the idle in ancient Rome when more than a fourth of the city's nearly two million inhabitants were chronically jobless. The heavy strain imposed upon Roman policy, foreign as well as domestic, can be surmised well enough from the very existence of the public theaters, the constantly rising number of games and spectacles for the class of idlers, among others, and the fact that from the time of the Civil

Wars of the first century B.C. Rome rested on whatever stability could be given society by the army.

But we have abundant ways of assessing the impact of worklessness upon human character and upon the social order in our own time. One need but examine the consequences, in the forms of deterioration of mind and personality, of morality, and of the social bond, in areas, such as some of the coal-mining regions, where by reason of loss of market or technological displacement large numbers of men have not worked for a long time. There is also the grim phenomenon of rising numbers of young persons confronted by the choice between school they do not want, that they come to hate in fact, and joblessness by reason of Federal minimum wage laws which have in effect priced unskilled youth out of the job market. A great deal of the urban problem of crime, violence, and drug use springs directly from this group.

Nor can we overlook the social effects of spreading affluence in our middle class. What Durkheim pointed out many years ago is relevant here. Whereas poverty exerts its own disciplines and limits, affluence, by its nature, usually does not. Affluence breaks down these limits, and it substitutes for them only a set of expectations which rise almost constantly.

Affluence may also, and on the record surely does, produce boredom. A few years ago the Harvard scientist Harlow Shapley ranked boredom third among some five principal possibilities of world destruction. Tocqueville thought that one of the dangers which lay ahead for middle-class democracy was the oppressive sense of monotony, punctuated occasionally by seizures of religious fanaticism or political crusades—a monotony brought on by the combination of a quest for material possession and an abiding sense of monolithic public opinion. Much of the contemporary disdain for the marks of affluence that one sees among the young springs in some degree from sheer boredom with affluence. It is said that in the organic world apathy is induced when an organism's environment becomes too conflicting, too stimulating. Perhaps there is something analogous in man's relation to the special kind of society the two revolutions have brought into existence in the West.

Whether, however, from boredom or from passionate spiritual conviction, a substantial revulsion for affluence is present in our society today, and I think it will only increase. Without exception the major world religions—Buddhism, Christianity, Islam, and others—consecrate the ethic of poverty, recognizing full well the dangers to piety which lie in wealth and luxury. If I am correct in believing that another great, rhythmic religious seizure is in store for us, it is almost certain that poverty will once again be extolled. One thing is clear: it is a great mistake to suppose that bourgeois ideals of culture are forever rooted in man's nature.

THE RAGE TO INFLATION

"There is no subtler, no surer means of overturning the existing basis of society than to debauch the currency. The process engages all the hidden forces of economic law on the side of destruction." So wrote Lord Keynes. From the point of view of the social bond, of the sense of community, I believe inflation to be more devastating than depression. This is in no way to underestimate the degradation of individual life involved in depression or the toll that it can exact from family stability and community life at every level. Still it is a matter of historical record that uncountable numbers of people have combined poverty with social structure. Moreover we have learned more or less in the West how to cope with depression, to avert it in its worst forms; but the same cannot be said of inflation.

The answer to depression is affluence. But what is the answer to affluence when it becomes widespread in a population, with expectations of further affluence generated almost geometrically? That question will surely be the dominant one economically during the rest of this century in the West, assuming war economy has not taken command. A generation ago Charles Beard and other historians could cast doubts on the motives of the Founding Fathers, seemingly manifest in their fixed concern with financial structure, with money, credit, and allied matters. We know better today. There are excellent economists who doubt that democracy can very long survive an inflation rate of much more than 20 percent.

As is only too well known, the major current economic problem of the democracies is to harmonize reasonably stable employment with stable prices. Once, so relatively low was the scale of human desires, inflation presented no real difficulty to society except during exceedingly short periods as the result of some adventitious form of speculation in critical areas. That time is long since past. The period of affluence we entered into after World War II was in substantial part made possible by the virtual guarantee of full employment by government. No one who remembers the Depression will pretend that unemployment is other than a degrading form of torture for human beings, but the fact remains that the greatest single cause of the inflation that now threatens the economic foundations of the social order is something very closely associated with full employment: the unleashing of buying-demands which are themselves the consequences of rising expectations. Who is to say that one is not entitled to whatever expectations and demands he chooses, that a small part of society should be affluent, but the larger part not? Plainly, no one is likely to say that; certainly no one in government at the present time. But the harsh, uncompromising fact remains that no one knows or is likely soon to know how individual demands can increase constantly on a mass scale without debasement of currency, without incessant increases in prices, increases which quickly turn the foundations of social stability and morality to sand.

That there are strictly economic causes of inflation I do not doubt. But these, I believe, are outweighed by other forces which greatly exceed economic ones in number and intensity. Such forces are generated by two basic factors, which Tocqueville was the first to identify: priority of economic or material values on the one hand and social equalitarianism on the other. If through some kind of spiritual miracle the peoples of the democracies were to renounce, in timeworn monastic fashion, such material values and consecrate themselves to austerity, if not poverty, equalitarianism would present no problem. Similarly, if by some social miracle the desire for equality in the democratic population were to wane, it is unlikely that a great many people now engaged in increasing their incomes would continue to do so, or would continue at such a frenetic pace. The combination of equalitarianism and material values is a deadly one for the social structure, however normal each may seem to be in light of the whole democratic ethos. For, to repeat, who is to declare either material comfort or equality an improper goal? But an answer has not been found to the problem created for an entire social order by the fusion of these two goals in the minds of vast numbers of persons. It is the sober guess of some very responsible economists that no answer can be found.

Not, that is, within the confines of liberal democracy, of the historic political community. The only economies which have escaped the worst ravages of inflation are the so-called "command" economies of the military-revolutionary societies of Albania, China, and, to a lesser degree apparently, Soviet Russia. We call for democratic controls of prices and refer wistfully to the controls which were set during the two World Wars of this century. But there is the rub. Both the economic and the psychological elements of major warfare were required for price controls to work with some degree of success. There is little reason to believe that the massive inflation that now torments democracies can be affected significantly by ordinary, democratic price and wage controls.

The revolution in aspirations and expectations is the greatest single revolution in our time, both at home and, on an ever-widening scale, in the world at large. For a long time inherited class attitudes restrained large numbers of persons from indulging material aspirations, from seeking more money for the express purpose of raising their social status. Still-ascendant religious attitudes also tended to restrain such aspirations—and still do among those sections of the population where deeply fundamentalist religious values exist. The strength of the family tie, of neighborhood, the whole feeling of roots, also discouraged in some degree the kind of individual quest for economic and social status that has been a dominating feature of the democracies for a long time now.

But such checks and discouragements have, as we know, been high among the costs of modern affluent society. The erosion of social inequalities which began with the grossest forms continues without let, and all the while the philosophy of materialism spreads among us. "Materialism," Tocqueville wrote in *Democracy in America*, "is amongst all nations, a dangerous disease of the human mind; but it is more especially to be dreaded among a democratic people. . . . Democracy encourages a taste for physical gratification; this taste, if it becomes excessive, soon disposes men to believe that all is matter only; and materialism, in its turn, hurries them on with mad impatience to these same delights: such is the fatal circle within which democratic nations are driven round."

As Tocqueville saw so plainly in his own France, the France that Balzac portrayed in such rich detail, the disappearance of the older ties of class and community, the erosion or corruption of religious values, and the ever-increasing use of money as the dominant symbol of status and power combined to create a kind of mental feverishness that could assuage itself only through incessant expansion of desires and, in prospect at least, of gratifications. "Since money has not only become the sole criterion of a man's social status," Tocqueville wrote in the Foreword to his study of the old regime and the French Revolution, "but has also acquired an extreme mobility—that is to say, it changes hands incessantly, raising or lowering the prestige of individuals and families—everybody is feverishly intent on making money or, if already rich, on keeping his wealth intact."

I do not, as I say, deny either the primacy or the directness of economic factors in inflation. Important, though, as these are, they take on their full significance only in social contexts. It is inconceivable that the economic conditions of inflation would exist, would be allowed to exist, in the unprecedented intensity we know today were it not for the development during the past quarter of a century of precisely the kind of society that Tocqueville believed to be inherent in mass democracy, with its breaking down of class ties, its debasement of standards, its constantly rising economic expectations, and the by now built-in agencies of government which by their nature cause economic inflation.

Economic inflation—and this point must be emphasized—is but one form of inflation going on in Western society at the present time. There is also to be seen inflation of language, the arts, science, morality, and all that is associated with these. Think only of the vital sphere of education! During the past two or three decades we have been seen a striking inflation in the residual values of education at all levels. Everyone knows that, whether in elementary school or the university, inflation of grading has been endemic. Work that once fetched a failing grade is now passing; grades of A and B are now widely given—compulsively given, it would seem—for performances which, but two decades ago, would have earned lower grades. No one aware of this inflation argues that students are brighter or better prepared. Growth in the educational sector—that is, of mind and work—is no more apparent at the moment than economic growth. The unblinkable truth is that the currency of grading has been severely inflated.

Nor is it different in other areas of the academic world. Think only of the increases in salary of the professoriat, with, however, constantly declining teaching and administrative responsibilities. Think of the fantastic accruals of luxury in architecture, services, benefits, and other aspects of the educational world. If it could be seriously argued that either research or teaching had increased at a rate to match the increase in rewards there would be no problem. Obviously, that argument cannot responsibly be made.

Precisely the same kind of inflation is to be seen in other spheres of life, ranging from welfare to such august professions as law and medicine. Nowhere, however, has inflation taken such toll as in leadership, language, and the arts. I turn to these now.

LOSS OF THE HERO

It is almost universally conceded that ours is an age of singular mediocrity in its leadership—a word I use to include spheres beyond politics alone. Rare is the American historian who, as our Bicentennial approaches, does not contrast the present paucity of commanding minds in American society with the relative abundance two centuries ago. Tocqueville, who had great admiration for the men who had led the American Revolution, regarding them indeed as representative of the very best Western society had ever yielded, thought a decline in the quality of national leadership had already begun when he was in America during the Jackson administration. The reason for this, he thought, lay in the already-advanced decline of the cultural contexts in which greatness is nurtured.

Although—as is often the case with Tocqueville's predictions—the period immediately following his visit produced contrary evidence (recall only Jackson and Lincoln among politicians and the literary renascence of the 1850s!), more recent history has probably tended to confirm him. Certainly, no one would argue that the present century, and especially the past half-century, has been a fertile period in most areas. There is a good deal of reason to believe we are running out of both heroes and the popular capacity for hero-worship, which Carlyle properly saw as vital to any genuine civilization.

In the Greek, *heros* refers to the perfect man, the expression of the highest ideals of the community from which he springs. Heroes are as diverse as the communities which produce them. War, religion, politics, science, the arts, and sports are all, from the most ancient times rich in individuals whom annalists and chroniclers have pronounced heroes. Promethus, for the Greeks, was a special kind of hero—a culture hero. He it was who brought fire to mankind and thus made possible all the other arts. For his great daring, in stealing fire from Olympus, his fate was eternal punishment by the gods; but torment, hardship, and even death are the common fate of heroes.

The earliest literature of which we have record is concerned, basically, with heroes. All the great epics, whether Persian, Greek, Roman, or Germanic, recount the exploits of individuals whose uncommon bravery, fortitude, and valor brought great rewards to their peoples. And whether in the *Iliad*, the *Aeneid*, or *Beowulf*, the hero's deeds represent the highest exemplification of the society's sacred values; he fulfills rather than transforms them.

Religion is preeminently the place of heroes. We are more likely to think in terms of prophets and saviours when we have religion before us, but these are only special examples of heroes. Moses, Jesus, Buddha, and Mohammed are without question heroes; for all early instances of the hero were touched by the divine, and it was a very thin line indeed between heroes and gods. Each of the great religious prophets bore hardships and suffering beyond normal human capacity and gave to his people far more than ordinary individuals could possibly have given. Martyrs, saints, great church leaders, and theologians belong to the ranks of heroes.

War is a natural sphere of heroes because of the privations it demands and the opportunities for courage and daring it affords. It is almost second nature for Westerners to think of events such as Thermopylae, Actium, Tours, Bunker Hill, and Gettysburg and of individuals like Hannibal, Alexander, Caesar, Cromwell, and Napoleon as examples of heroism. So does revolution produce authentic heroes, in modern times at least. The almost perfect hero is the militarist-revolutionist: Cromwell, George Washington, Napoleon, Mao, among others.

Other areas besides religion and war have produced many heroes in history. Politics is undoubtedly first after religion and war in this respect. This explains why history-writing was for so long overwhelmingly political in character, often appearing to be little more indeed than an account of the adventures, exploits, and accomplishments of kings, princes, and other rulers of state. Pericles, Augustus, Frederick II, Cromwell, Washington, Napoleon, Bismarck, Lincoln were quite literally folk heroes all over the West down until very recently. A classically rigorous school curriculum helped in this regard, to be sure, but there was much more to it than that. Politics was, from the time the Greek *polis* took shape, a sphere in which herosim comparable to that of religious saints and prophets and military leaders was readily recognizable, believed in, almost taken for granted. Some of the popular attribution of divinity to early kings and emperors communicated itself for a long period to other kinds of political leaders—presidents, governors, and legislators. But awe of office and of political personage manifestly has hard going in our day.

There are still other areas of the heroic. Navigation during the Renaissance assuredly yielded popular heroes, a number of whom have lasted down to our own day—Marco Polo, Columbus, Magellan, Vasco da Gama, Drake being but a few. It is a chastening thought that while the identity of a Columbus is still vivid in our minds, most of us cannot remember the names of those who, less than a decade ago, went to the moon. Spectacular as that accomplishment was, its human quotient was somewhat overshadowed by the impersonal technology that alone made it possible.

It is unlikely that science will yield us many more heroes like Galileo, Newton, Darwin, and Einstein, whose reputations reached most households not only in the West but indeed in other parts of the world. So long as science was the preserve of individuals working more or less alone, as Newton, Darwin, and Einstein did, it was possible for fields as austere and remote from popular knowledge as theoretical mechanics and evolutionary biology to produce from time to time genuine heroes. In our age of mass science and technology, with thousands working where only a tiny handful did once, and with the characteristic scientific discovery today the product of at least four or five, sometimes a dozen and more, individuals working together in a team, it is unlikely that individual heroes will emerge again from the mass. We have become so inured by now to science and technology, their vast and constant budgets, their immense apparatuses of equipment and human beings, and their occupation of social space, that the difficulty will be to keep science and technology from seeming banal and anti-heroic.

Neither does the economic sphere produce heroes, not at least for very long. There was a short time in the nineteenth and early twentieth centuries when the names of Rothschild, Morgan, Rockefeller, Ford had close to heroic status in Western, especially American, households. Hero-worship of the businessman probably reached its peak during the Coolidge administration in America. But that ended abruptly with the Depression, and I see little evidence, even during the astonishing business prosperity and national affluence we have known since World War II, that any heroism will again emerge from the ranks of businessmen. Between the heroic and the economic there has been fundamental opposition, it would appear, since the beginnings of human history, and however much we may relish and depend upon the contributions of the economic sphere, there is little of the hero-making in these contributions and their protagonists. For some time now the names of Rockefeller, Ford, Harriman, *et al.* have been primarily associated with political, diplomatic, and charitable achievement, not business.

For a long time the theatre, and more recently the movies, supplied us with heroes. From the time of David Garrick in the eighteenth century down to the Age of Stars in Hollywood, which occupied most of the first half of this century, there were vivid exemplars and models in the world of entertainment. With only a little exaggeration the Chaplins, Barrymores, Pickfords, Swansons, Gables, and Bogarts were referred to in this country as our substitute for aristocracy or royalty. What such individuals said and did, how they bore themselves in public places as well as on the screen, clearly mattered a great deal to Americans and, for that matter, to many millions of others in the world.

I would not argue that first-rate actors, or movies either, have disappeared. They have not, though they do not exist in as great number, what with the altered role of the movies in popular culture. But what is only too evident is that our actors, first-rate or other, male or female, do not have the commanding position in mass society that they once did. Their image is different. They are technicians in a trade or profession now; they are not the public eminences with power to affect styles of life, speech, and thought that they once were. A Brando or Newman or Streisand may be an accomplished performer, but none of them is cast in the heroic mold as literally dozens of their predecessors were.

Crime was once the source of heroes of a kind. The so-called social bandit, the Robin Hood, who supposedly robs only from the rich and gives to the poor, is the most obvious type, and for a long time in the Western states in America there was a kind of pantheon of bandits and robbers and gunmen, with a Jesse James regarded in some circles as almost the equivalent of a Robin Hood. So did heroes of a certain breed emerge in the Prohibition twenties in America, with Al Capone undoubtedly foremost in the public mind. Gangster wars and the occasional war between police and a given mob in Chicago, New York, or elsewhere, not to mention at St. Valentine's Day Massacre, could push individual names into a perverse heroism. The sheer efficiency, the bureaucratization, and the passion for anonymity in organized crime today make the appearance of heroes here in the future exceedingly unlikely.

Sports today offer a great many conditions for heroism, though present tendencies toward super-commercialization may result in the destruction of the sports hero. But for the recent past and the present it would be foolish to deny the degree to which sports—certainly more than in scholarship and science very recently—have brought the nation heroes of consequence. Babe Ruth, Jack Dempsey, Red Grange, Bill Tilden, and Bobby Jones survive in the public mind as sports heroes even today. Not a little of the blacks' cultural emergence in American life is the result of their being at last accepted in the performing arts and in major league sports. Paul Robeson, Marian Anderson, and Harry Belafonte have been authentic heroes in the black community, as have Joe Louis, Willie Mays, Jackie Robinson, and Jim Brown.

I am inclined to think that professional sports in America take a great deal of the load off war as the source of release to a bored, increasingly tension-ridden population. Teams are combat units, and there is much in common psychologically between the team in the field and the actual fighting unit, the squad or platoon or company, in wartime. (That there is some awareness of this in the public mind is attested to by the growing tendency of commentators to employ openly military terms—"bomb," "blitz," "trench war," for example—in describing field play in football.) Anyone who hates war must dread the day when athletics, amateur and professional, loses its present capacity for mobilizing aggressive forces on the field and thrilling large audiences.

Whether sports can survive the present headlong rush toward huge profits, enormous individual contracts carefully negotiated by batteries of lawyers for individual stars, and the growing image of each of these same stars as businessmen—owners of hamburger or bowling alley chains, with names prominently displayed—is still uncertain. Given the clear incapacity of business and the economic sphere to produce heroes, an incapacity rooted obviously in the nature of the economic incentive, it would not seem likely that heroes will be produced by sports for very long. One more Mark Spitz, we are inclined to say, and the age of sports heroes will be gone forever!

But if the need for heroes cannot much longer be gratified by sports that have become a mere aspect of the economy, where can it be gratified? In literature and the arts? Not on the present evidence of our seeming incapacity to shore up as heroes even writers, artists, and composers who only a few decades ago were thought to be immortal. If an Eliot, a Joyce, and a Yeats show signs, as they emphatically do, of fading quickly from heroic status, their ashes not yet really cold, on what basis can we expect any of our present luminaries to preserve it?

In a charming preface to one of his little volumes of essays, Max Beerbohm wrote that among his reasons for retiring from the scene, young though he was, was that he wished to leave the field clear to those who had "months of success" still ahead of them. Perhaps there is a clue in Beerbohm's wit to understanding the present literary scene. Manifestly we have a substantial number of writers who have not only months but years of success assured by the ever-reliable reviewing machinery in the dailies, weeklies, and other sources of literary reputations. We do not, however, associate heroic status with "success," whether financial or personal. Hardly a week passes but what the term "brilliant" is applied to a given novel, play, or piece of reportage, thus assuring the author the feeling of success of some kind. But "brilliance" is hardly the word we would use for a Sophocles, a Shakespeare, a Goethe, a Melville, or a Hawthorne. Dickens was, and remains in some degree, a hero, but this has nothing to do with any presumed "brilliance" or "success" in Dickens' life and works. The qualities we seem to cherish today in the literary world are actual obstacles, it appears, to the creation of heroism.

Nor can the desire for heroes be met in the academic areas, present tendencies continuing for very long. The decline of the university or college president is conspicuous. It is hardly possible that any president today, however able, could speak on either educational or public issues with the kind of authority possessed by such past presidents as Charles Eliot, William Rainey Harper, Nicholas Murray Butler, and Benjamin Ide Wheeler, among others.

Down until about World War II what a university president had to say, especially if he were in a major university, mattered. It doesn't today.

The same erosion of place in national esteem has affected the faculty member, the teacher and scholar, with little likelihood of early change. But what is in some ways more consequential is the disappearance of the hero-teacher and hero-scholar from the campus itself. Obviously, splendid teachers and scholars still exist. That is not the point. There are simply none around whose heroic presences in lore and legend grow in the minds of other faculty, of students, and of alumni.

Clearly, in area after area we have been stripped of heroes, which means men and women with luster in the public mind, which in turn means leadership in some degree. Between heroism and modernity there has been a fateful conflict. The acids of modernity, which include equalitarianism, skepticism, and institutionalized ridicule in the popular arts, have eaten away much of the base on which heroism flourished. Technology's reorganization of the world has brought with it a certain built-in disenchantment. Ordinary work is less likely to fetch us folk heroes of the kind we knew or used to know in the legends about John Henry, Casey Jones, Tom Dooley, Steve Brody, and others.

Unless there is a potential for some degree of enchantment in each of us, there is little likelihood that heroes will come into being, for there has to be some enchantment in the regard we hold for great individuals and extraordinary acts. There was assuredly enchantment present in the relation between the American public and Red Grange, Babe Ruth, Greta Garbo, Clark Gable, and scores of others, whether in the popular arts or in the higher reaches of culture.

Hardly a day passes but what we mourn the lack of individuals in public office of the stature of Washington, Lincoln, Wilson, and FDR, or of Churchill and De Gaulle on the world scene. But great as these individuals were, they had *audiences* of greatness, that is, individuals in large number still capable of being enchanted. How, in all truth, in an age when parody, self-parody, and caricature is the best we have in literature, could any of the above names rise to greatness? As Yeats observed long ago, the instinct to mock at the great, the good, and the wise is built into this age.

THE VANISHED VILLAIN

The essence of the hero, I have suggested, is possession of qualities regarded widely as being beyond the ordinary human dimension, touched indeed with the divine. Commonly in history, where there are heroes there are also villains: individuals to whom are ascribed qualities also beyond the ordinary human dimension, but qualities of evil instead of goodness. Just as we seem to have lost heroes in contemporary Western civilization, so in all probability have we lost villains; that is, persons regarded, not as sick, disturbed, victims of social injustice, or delinquent, but as outrightly and incorrigibly evil, base, devoid of any element whatever of virtue, deserving in their own interest and society's of swift and complete punishment.

To read about the great villains in the epics, melodramas, and tragedies of other ages is to be put in touch with the same greatness that we get in the great heroes, but of treachery, lust, dishonor, instead of virtue. Villains, like heroes, are made of different clay, and therefore deserve different treatment. A villain is by nature villainous, as the hero is by nature heroic, and throughout history we find, in art, literature, and religion, that in his own way the villain is just as important a symbol in human life as the hero. As the one is, through unique possession of virtue and strength, an exemplar of good, a spur to achievement, and thereby a vital source of creative meanings, the other becomes for us a model of all that is ultimately destructive of the fabric of morality. By that fact, the villain in his way serves the social bond, for it is when enormities take place that we are most likely to be reminded of the values which have been flouted or betrayed. In the often terrible punishments which were the lot of evil men there was for the community a sense of reaffirmation of the good along with a certain spiritual cleansing. Throughout most of history the function of punishment has been to avenge the social bond for what has been done to it by villains. Thus the existence of villains requires the same fundamental contexts which serve heroism: moral norms and ties of trust so real, so widely accepted and understood, as to make identification of the heroic and the villainous possible.

We live in a culture characterized, as Philip Rieff has insistently reminded us, by the "triumph of the therapeutic." In an age that is nearly saturated by variations on the word "sick," we tend to feel embarrassed by the use of such words as "evil" and "wicked." Without doubt the cause of the humane and merciful has been served by the therapeutic view of life. But a major problem nevertheless arises: that of being able to reaffirm the good through appropriate action against the evil. Samuel Butler, in *Erewhon,* had murderers and robbers and other criminals placed in hospitals for therapeutic care rather than on the gallows or in prisons. But it should be noted that Butler did not leave a vacuum. The gallows and prison remained in Erewhon—but for those who got sick, especially with communicable diseases.

We are without real power today to assimilate, to identify, even to find words for crimes like the Kennedy assassination, the Manson murders, the Houston murders, or the unprecedented corruption of office that Watergate has revealed. A generation under the spell of liberal humanitarianism, through which all evil is dissolved into sickness or social maladjustment, is without power, really, to cope in moral terms with either horrors or disasters, much less ordinary crimes.

Unless there is a clear and utterly unabashed sense of what is good, absolutely good, there can be no heroes; for how would we recognize them? And unless there is a sense of evil, absolute evil—

not just sickness or socially caused delinquency—there can be no villains. Heroism and villainy are two opposing aspects of the same basic cast of mind.

ESCAPE FROM CULTURE

In the strict anthropological sense there cannot of course be any escape from culture, for no human behavior is imaginable, however "natural" it may seem, that is not rooted in the totality of norms, ideas, techniques, skills, and values, transmitted socially from generation to generation, that is the substance of what we call culture. There are nevertheless significant variations among ages in history with respect to the relationships which exist between individuals and their cultures.

The nineteenth-century social philospher Saint-Simon, in reaction to the unilinear idea of progress, suggested that history can be seen as divided into "organic" and "critical" ages. In the former, a high degree of consensus is to be found, a preponderance of universals over alternatives in the moral sphere, and a commonly close relation between individuals and the constitutive norms of the social order. Dogma, ritual, tradition, convention, all tend to be present in high degree. In "critical" ages, Saint-Simon writes, we find innumerable expressions of the bizarre and the rebellious, and dislocation from established conventions. Disorder is rife, there is a perceptible alienation of the spirit in the art and literature of such ages, and unreason becomes a veritable cult, with a widespread turning to the occult, the primitivist, the archaic, and the futurist, as well as to other forms of conscious or unconscious flouting of cultural authority.

Quite evidently ours is one of Saint-Simon's critical ages. Granted that there is not the total chaos of values and the subversion of tradition and authority attributed to the age by some of its most formidable critics, there is no mistaking a good many of the stigmata of decadence and decline which attend history's occasional periods of twilight. Revolt, anomie, alienation, and other expressions of individual dislocation in the cultural realm are apparent enough, the subject of countless appraisals and analyses. The uprooted or lost individual is surely the dominant figure of contemporary art, letters, and philosophy.

The late Bronislaw Malinowski, perhaps the preeminent anthropologist of this century, wrote at length and in detail of the indispensable role of culture in the shaping of those personality characteristics which are at once safeguards of the social order and the individual ego. "Culture entails deep changes in man's personality; among other things it makes man surrender some of his self-love and self-seeking. For human relations do not rest merely or even mainly on constraint coming from without. Men can only work with and for one another by the moral forces which grow out of personal attachments and loyalties."

Malinowski is of course quite correct about social order resting on constraints coming from within personality. Unless and until a degree of internalization is achieved that makes one's conduct seem almost totally self-willed, cultural processes cannot be said to be working very effectively. And yet, this said, there is no avoiding the fact that the elements of culture, including the very deepest ones, are in fact outside the individual, waiting, as it were, to become, through complex means of interaction, constitutive parts of mind and personality. And in all this coercion, authority, discipline are crucial, in whatever degree they may operate. No one knew this better than Freud. Despite the vast amount of nonsense written about Freud and "repressions," he was fully aware of the vital necessity of authority and discipline in the individual's life, of, in sum, the coercive effect of culture. It is not hard, on the basis of his own writings and Sir Ernest Jones' masterly biography of him, to imagine Freud's revulsion from so many of the eruptions of the primitive, the "natural," and the obscene which have been given near-cult status in recent times and regarded as the measure of our liberation from authority. To explore, as Freud did, the profound and complex sources of culture in human life, to call attention to the components of coercion and constraint which can underlie the individual's relation to culture and morality, is not to declare such components superfluous.

What I wrote above about heroes and villains is pertinent here. Precisely as we lack surpassingly good men (and evil men, strictly defined) in public life, so do we lack them in literature and the arts—in what we call high culture. For a long time it has been evident that conditions no longer exist in the West in which a literature of tragedy can be written, by virtue of spreading disbelief in the reality of the kinds of individuals alone capable of being endowed with tragic being. What is now becoming evident is a lack of conditions in which serious literature of any kind is possible. To try to imagine novels and dramas being written today in which the kinds of characters and events are present which fill the pages of Melville, Hawthorne, James, Dreiser, Faulkner, and Hemingway is not easy. Our imaginative literature is, as more than a few critics have recently told us, increasingly one of self-projection, more and more of self-parody.

The reason is not far to seek. A culture is required for great individuals, good or evil, in life or art, to flourish—a culture in the literal anthropological sense; that is, composed of themes, patterns, and perspectives of meaning rich enough to evoke response, universal enough to encompass writer and reader alike. The basis of any culture is the presence of values which have external force in the individual's life, which reflect a power greater than anything that lies in the individual alone. In the fusions of such values we get the "patterns of culture" the late Ruth Benedict wrote of so eloquently, patterns which are to be found both in the ordinary lives of human beings and in the highest artistic, religious, and moral reaches of culture.

As the function of culture is, in Malinowski's words, to force the individual to "surrender some of his self-love and self-seeking," so the function of high culture, of art and science, is illumination of what is involved in this complex, often agonizing process. Great literature, as Tolstoy told us, though with unfortunate exaggeration, brings to superlative intensity emotions and experiences which are elements of the human condition everywhere and which assume constitutive place in all cultures. It is in this sense that art so often in history carries with it a social function scarcely different from the sacred. Art, like religion, binds, integrates, creates the sense of community. And it can do this only when it possesses an authority that is recognized in language, forms of reason, and in signs, images, and forms. Culture, where it is strong, *is* community: of norms and ideas and symbols. Only when the onslaught of the two great revolutions at the beginning of the nineteenth century seemed to be annihilating this intellectual community did such writers as Coleridge, Carlyle, and Matthew Arnold develop the modern sense of culture as community.

But, as Lionel Trilling has made profoundly evident, modern artists and intellectuals have nurtured an adversary spirit that has grown steadily more intense and sweeping. It is fitting that the author of the classic study of Matthew Arnold should be the one to highlight this adversary mentality, for it was Arnold himself who, in *Culture and Anarchy*, foretold it. Whatever else "philistinism" is for Arnold, it implies escape from culture and its inevitable coercions.

And, as Arnold realized with striking clarity, where there is escape some form of attack usually follows. If culture in the traditional sense comes more and more to seem an intolerable set of traps and toils, fetters on the free imagination, one will seek not only to escape it but to assault it. Escape was evident enough in Arnold's day; as witnessed and recorded by Newman, Kierkegaard, Burckhardt, and Nietzsche, among others. Assault has been largely reserved for our day.

The inherently adversary cast of mind that, as Trilling has written, was the mark of the artist and intellectual from almost the moment that the tides of political and economic modernity washed over the European landscape, was, for a long time, restrained by conventions and codes made powerful by many centuries of history. Some degree of conformity was the price exacted by these conventions and codes even from such geniuses as Cézanne, Stravinsky, Joyce, Yeats, and others early in this century. "Conformity," as I shall explain in a moment, is not quite the proper word, for a significant degree of relation with traditional values was a cardinal part of the creative act in each of these minds. I am only trying to indicate here the continuing role and influence of tradition in the West even as late as the early twentieth century, even in minds as original and powerful in influence as those I have mentioned. It is to the backwaters of the turn of the century that we must go, to those of small light who consecrated the eccentric and pathological as ends in themselves, if we would find art that is all escape. So much of what we associate with the *fin de siècle* in the way of eccentricity and the pathological, cultivated infantilism, irrationalism, and experience-destroying subjectivity, is, all too plainly, part of the present cultural scene. It is, alas, often confused with cultural creativity.

Genuinely creative work, however, in the arts, in letters, and also in the sciences never cuts itself off from tradition. It reworks tradition, evolves new forms out of old elements, and even then only with a distinct sense of trying to accomplish some highly concrete result, abandoning tradition only when the result cannot be attained otherwise. I believe that everything we know in both artistic and scientific achievement is proof of this point. I offer two examples.

One of the greatest instances of originality, of significant break with the past and the conventional, in the history of painting is the efflorescence in the nineteenth century of the Impressionists in France. Not, we learn, in more than two centuries in Europe had so momentous a change in the fundamental elements of painting taken place. What Monet and his fellow Impressionists did was virtually revolutionize the uses of color and line in their quest for visual reality. This is all well known and requires no elaboration here. What is less well known, however, is the degree to which such painters as Monet, Degas, Manet, and Renoir were superb craftsmen in the traditional art of the time, and, indeed, the degree to which they respected the best of it. It was the search for refinement and improvement of elements of that best which led them into their now historic experiments with light, perspective, and color masses. Far from celebrating any spirit of escape, the greatest of the Impressionists were in fact escaping nothing; they were simply seeking highly concrete, specific ways of dealing with visual reality.

Nor in the beginning did the Impressionists—who scarcely knew each other then—seek to identify themselves as a separate group, least of all a rebelling group. It was only after repeated rebuffs of their work in the established galleries and museums that they were led to become, after a fashion, a self-conscious group of artists. And even then their solidarity did not last very long—very possibly to the detriment of continued originality of creation, for the history of art, like that of letters and of science, is very clear on the positive function exerted by the tiny communities in which creative minds are so often to be found at one or another point in their careers. The essential point here, however, is the utter necessity of tradition and authority—if only to revolt against, if only to supply necessary background for a genuine *avant-garde;* and their absence from consciousness in the arts is indeed responsible for the infantilism and endemic mediocrity of what passes for the creative impulse in our art and letters, and for disappearance of a true *avant-garde.*

Precisely the same is true in the sciences, for there is no significant difference between the creative impulse as we find it in science and in the arts. Techniques vary greatly, but the psychology of discovery is the same. Tradition and emulation matter as much in physics or biology as in literature and painting. Werner Heisenberg, one of the most original of modern physicists, tells us, in *Physics and Beyond: Encounters and Conversations*, that even in respect of the quantum theory, commonly regarded as the greatest single advance of this century in physics, tradition and the desire to work within it were signal factors in Max Planck's eventual arrival at the quantum theory. Far from wanting to break with the past, with classical physics, Planck made, Heisenberg writes, explicit efforts to solve a certain problem in energy that had come to his mind through "conformity with all the established physical laws, and it took him many years to realize that this was impossible. Only at that stage did he put forward a hypothesis that did not fit into the framework of classical physics, and even then he tried to fill the breach he had made in the old physics with different assumptions. That proved impossible, and the consequences of Planck's hypothesis finally led to a radical reconstruction of all physics."

Even then, however, as Heisenberg reminds us, classical concepts remained, just as they do today, unchanged, as valid in context as they ever were. The point is, even a mind as original in result as Planck's recognized traditional physics, was indeed steeped in it, and sought with determination to solve a new problem in the terms of the traditional. In Einstein, Planck, Bohr, or any of the other great presences of the new physics in this century, we shall look in vain for any sweeping spirit of escape or rebellion, much less a declaration of the "bankruptcy," the "sickness," or the "moribundity" of the established.

I do not think things are different in other spheres of the imagination. Comparative study over a long period convinces me that the so-called golden ages of civilization—Athens in the fifth century B.C., the Rome of Lucretius and Vergil, Dante's Italy, Elizabethan England, and others—are evidently ages of tradition and community. They are ages also of individuality, diversity, change, and mobility. That goes without question. But the important point is that these luminous qualities exist and take on their significance and excitement only within a structure of values, beliefs, and meanings common to a great many persons. Traditions are questioned, are abandoned by the bolder minds, and old idols often destroyed. But these states of mind are rarely if ever ends in themselves, only stepping stones to new beliefs and illuminations. And it is well to remember that the principals of these ages were not only unafraid to concern themselves with great areas of experience and understanding, but were also constantly seeking to make themselves understood by the people in their cultures.

We can settle for a good deal less than a golden age in our time. Our problem is not the absence of great culture, but absence of any culture whatever in the higher reaches of imagination and learning. Given the near-century in the West during which the adversary mentality has widened and grown deeper among intellectuals, with ever-greater applause for what Richard Poirier has called "the performing self," with spreading emphasis upon the subjective and the internal, and with more and more calculated assault upon the norms and disciplines of traditional art and literature, it would be extraordinary if such culture existed.

Richard Poirier's "performing self" is the pathetic degeneration, really, of what Quentin Anderson has called the "imperial self," and each is a manifestation of that continuing emphasis upon the individual, his emotions, desires, and cravings, that is to be seen, though in varying intensities, in the West from the Renaissance on. From the beginning, and nowhere more vividly than in the writings of the Italian humanists, escape from culture, to take refuge in feeling and awareness, has been a dominant aspect of the Western tradition. But for a long time feudally derived habits, powerful traditions and structures established in the medieval age, succeeded in restraining the more extravagant efforts at escape and in maintaining a solid core of cultural authority that has only threatened to come completely apart in our own day.

Culture is inherently feudal. There is no other way of describing its sectors and strata of privilege, rank, power, and wealth. The Eliots and Faulkners are given a deference that once was enjoyed only by the highest-born in feudal society. Nor is the matter different in pop culture where the Beatles or a Bob Dylan can know adoration and veneration, along with immense wealth and power, that would once have gone only to landed barons. In the sciences and in the world of scholarship the same fundamental, feudal principle is to be found, and woe betide the tyro or the mediocre or dispossessed talent that fails to pay, in approved ways, proper deference.

It is both good and necessary that culture should be feudal in character. The trouble is, the political consciousness of the modern intellectual, formed in the Enlightenment, leaves him in a state of unease about this feudalism that he is all too aware of. Not often is he as consistent and resolute as Rousseau, who knew that of all spheres that of the arts and sciences is the most given to galling inequalities and who not only indicated the arts and sciences in a famous discourse but actually recommended their abolition in substantial degree. The contemporary intellectual, unable to muster up this kind of strength of will, is more likely simply to assault the coercions, disciplines, and canons of traditional culture, combining an equalitarianism of political mind with devotion to subjectivist retreat from culture and assault upon its constraints.

It is hardly a matter for wonder, therefore, that what we see around us at the present time is fragmentation into tiny coteries and elites, each with its own claque, each seeking fusion of a radical equalitarianism in politics with aristocratic pretensions in arts and letters. And below this collection of coteries is the immense, sprawling mass culture of the Jacqueline Susanns and Harold Robbinses. Precisely the same great division exists, in short, in the cultural community as in the political, where "imperial" and "performing" selves also bestride a more and more alienated mass.

In no respect is escape from culture at the present time more manifest than in the general loss of confidence in *knowledge:* the knowledge that is associated with scientist as well as scholar, humanist, and imaginative artist. Would anyone think of turning today to the novel or poem or other work of art for the wisdom it might cast, for the illumination it might offer of either the setting around us or the condition of man? We turn to these for diversion, yes, for titillation, for the occasional shock of recognition in some artist's meandering through his own consciousness or awareness of self, but where it is the "performing self" that is being presented, and also adored, we are hardly likely to look for any part of the kind of revelation that human beings were once able to find in art, as in religion. Thus the artist's own escape from culture is inevitably followed by the escape of audience not only from the artist's escape, but from art generally. What, fundamentally, does art have to offer in our day that is significantly above what the nightly television programs contain?

But such escape is only a part of the situation that prevails. Who, we are obliged to ask, looks with respect any longer to the professional man of knowledge: whether scientist or scholar? I shall come back to this point shortly in another context, that of the degraded position of the university, but it has its pertinence here also. There is a progressive loss of confidence in knowledge, in the capacity of the scientist—physical or social—to come up with a solution to a problem that does not create more problems than existed in the first place. In part this is the consequence of the preposterous inflation of the function of science and scholarship that occurred during and right after World War II. It is hard to forget the litany—one joined in by university presidents, trustees, legislators, foundations, even, to their shame, scholars and scientists themselves—that went somewhat as follows: *we have the knowledge, oh Lord; we need only the will to accept.* To accept, that is, the knowledge that, it was never doubted, lay in the minds of the scientists and scholars.

There is still the effort made occasionally by the intellectual from the academy to declare that such knowledge does exist and that only bigotry and special interest in the public prevent its magic reconstruction of environment and society. But the effort is not made very often now. For it has become evident to all that the social sciences are hollow sciences, with only a vagrant insight to offer here and there for the most part. The contrast between what is actually present in the social sciences and what was so grandly claimed for them in the 1950s is entirely too great to be other than the subject of disillusionment or farce. Against the almost total impotence of economists in our present combined recession and inflation lies, by way of background, the almost aristocratic assurance they possessed only a few years ago. The blunt fact is, they—and other social scientists—know very very little. That is no sin. But pretension to omniscience in the clear awareness of ignorance is very much a sin!

The physical sciences are not much better off at the present time. Here too there has been hubris and escape from the ethical demands of scientific culture. In the aftermath of the immensely popular atom bomb, scientists were only too happy to wear the mantle of greatness, the hood of the Grand Inquisitor. Merely give us the problem! Supply us with money! We Can Do! So went *that* litany.

We hear it less today. Memory is only too sharp in the American public, and among disillusioned ranks of scientists and engineers themselves, of promises made and unkept—in realms ranging from cancer research all the way to seat belts and pollution-emission devices. As I write these words, the papers are filled with the bitterness and strife among scientists in connection with the so-called war on cancer, one that produced a scientific bureaucracy that would have given joy to a Byzantine administrator, one that, through countless announcements of "discovery," built up a huge volume of expectation, one, however, that we now know to have accomplished very little.

The scientific community, once honored widely and deeply in the West, has fallen victim, it would appear, to mass production of results—so few of them, alas, of extraordinary consequence, so many at the level of mere cookbook contrivance or of ordinary gadgetry. The feverish desire to get first into print, the increasing approach to scientific problems, however small, through committees and research groups (hunting problems down in packs, as someone has put it), the whole frenzied air of accomplishment at whatever cost, all of this has produced, as is a matter of newspaper record, signal instances of corruption of mind and research. Such corruption is of course escape from culture.

The trivialization of science—nowhere to be seen more vividly than in some of the huge institutes under HEW—has also been, at bottom, an escape from the culture of science. How can science, or any body of knowledge, long maintain majesty when it becomes associated every day, through incessant news-release, with every imaginable exigency of human life? If today it is avoidance of cyclamates that is solemnly prescribed, tomorrow the "discovery" will be announced that cyclamates have been found to be preventives against sexual impotence or hair-loss.

Is it, then, a matter for wonder that where but a few years ago there was keen youthful interest in the social and physical sciences and in the central areas of humanistic scholarship, there is today a widening flight from these: one more instance of escape on the part of a public or audience that has been itself precipitated by escape from intellectual responsibility, that is, from *culture*, on the part of the sages. Scholars and scientists of true stature, still obedient to the inherent demands for both modesty and free-roving exploration, untarnished by the kind of hubris that is itself a mark of escape from culture, would have been appalled by the thought of assuring legislators, Supreme Court judges, presidents and governors, and the public that they possessed the knowledge not only to explain but to remedy the ills of ethnic relations, poverty, economic depression and inflation, war, alienation, and all the other dislocations and breakdowns to be seen on the social map. We—meaning here scientists, scholars, and teachers—are paying for this today in the widening disillusionment with which knowledge of any kind is greeted by the public, especially the young.

Such escape from culture, in all the manifestations which I have noted here, is in considerable part a consequence, I believe, of the politicization of culture that began in this country in the 1930s and that has had two or three distinct phases. Politicization of the mind is itself a form of escape from cultural responsibility, and one that clearly breeds dismal results. In the 1930s two quite distinct expressions of this politicization could be seen. On the one hand there was the radical and liberal affirmation by so many intellectuals, deeply influenced by Marxism and by certain other currents of European thought which had been in existence for nearly a half a century—currents which scholars of the order of Max Weber and Emile Durkheim had warned against, but without much effect— that the highest function of culture is political. That is, good art is art that serves mankind, defined variously as the working class, the proletariat, or the People. Art that is "reactionary" or that does not address itself to the needs of the oppressed is by definition bad art, even antisocial art. So went the catechism on the left. That the genuinely great artists of this century—such minds as Eliot, Yeats, Pound, Joyce, among others—were, with only the rarest of exceptions, distinctly *not* oriented toward the People or the advancement of mankind toward socialism did not seem to matter. If one was an artist or intellectual, he must therefore be political; or else be ground into dust.

That is one major instance of the politicization of culture in the 1930s in this country. It was shortly followed, perhaps accompanied indeed, by another, quite different form of politicization: the gradually increasing subsidization, and hence direction, of scientists, artists, and intellectuals by the national government. What we can today look back on as Depression-spawned "writers projects" under some such organization as WPA can also, with the advantage of hindsight, be seen as the beginning of a procession that would in time include the multitudinous bureaus, agencies, foundations, and projects pertaining to the arts and sciences which have occupied a substantial part of the political history of the United States since World War II. Defend or justify it as we will, the incontestable fact is that scholarship, art, and science have undergone a degree of politicization by government—invariably, to be sure, at the behest of the scholars and scientists!—that is without precedent in history, save possibly in the Byzantine Empire.

Both types of politicization have been manifestations of escape from culture and both have, on the record, been responsible for the vastly greater escape that is evident today in the appalling works which pass for literature and, often, scholarship and science. It has been proved, has it not, that the most trivial, inane, meretricious of ideas or proposals can be rewarded by Almighty Grant? The power of politics to sterilize otherwise first-rate minds has been demonstrated over and over again in history. And it does this through precisely the two forms I have described here: the inculcation of the political-adversary spirit in art and literature, making culture the pawn of ideology, and, on the other hand, the subsidization, direction, and management of culture through bureaucracy. Each *is* escape; each *breeds* escape.

THE CORRUPTION OF LANGUAGE

In no single respect is escape from culture more manifest at the present time than in language, and this appears to be true equally in written and spoken language. Of all forms of authority and indeed of community, that which is embedded in language is probably the most important. We know what happens to an economy under the erosive influences of inflation and recession alike. Much the same happens to a culture when its linguistic values become inflated on the one hand and impoverished on the other. On the testimony of many observers, both inflation and impoverishment are to be found in our linguistic resources, and the general result is a contraction of the importance of language to the social order.

No real community, no culture, can exist above the most primitive level without language and the subtle judgments and prejudgments which are incorporated in its syntax and vocabulary. Language need not be entirely verbal, of course. There is what the anthropologists call silent language: the language of gesture, of facial expression and bodily movement that can convey so many, often complex, meanings. And there are music, painting, sculpture, mathematics, and other forms of nonverbal communication among members of a community. Nevertheless, verbal language is crucial, and it is a fact of highest importance that in all the great ages of culture known to us, the role of language in the ordinary sense has been profound. One need but think of the ways Greek philosophers and poets of the sixth and fifth centuries gloried in, loved, caressed, and explored words in the fashion of lovers. It was not different in the later periods of cultural growth in the West. Experiments with words and structures of syntax are legion in these periods, but underlying them all is the spirit of advance and of progress in language.

As there are ages of growth in language, so are there ages of decline and sterility. Twilight ages have a number of linguistic traits in common. There is a kind of retreat from the disciplines and complexities of language. Often it is more than retreat; it is actual repudiation of language and of the modes of thought which are inseparable from language of high order. Corruptions abound, along with cultivations of feeling and emotion in which language, as such, is regarded with disdain, as a positive barrier to expression of what is important. The discipline of language comes to seem little more than sterile coercion. Under the guise of search for the simple and the universal, or the colloquial, there is almost a sabotage of language's authority. I do not question that something akin to sabotage of the old is to be found in the linguistically creative ages, for language grows and prospers on what it casts aside as well as on what is added. But escape from the old or sterile in the creative ages is invariably set in the larger pattern of quest for new structures, words, phrases, metaphors, and other meanings. In the twilight periods, casting-aside becomes its own justification. In such ages there is commonly a turning to the child, to the "noble savage," to the barbarian, to the demented, to all those for whom language in any rich sense is yet to be achieved or to whom it is in some manner denied. An emphasis grows, even in literature and philosophy, upon the special kinds of wisdom which are thought to lie in the preliterate or semiliterate.

These traits are certainly not lacking today. In its more extreme forms during the past couple of decades, the political left has often made direct assault upon language a primary object, for linguistic authority is a foundation of other types of social and cultural authority. The so-called Free Speech and Filthy Speech movements which got international attention in the 1960s would be no more than the flotsam and jetsam of a stormy decade were it not for the fact that their essence—that is, a flouting and corruption of the community of language in the larger social order—continues to exist. This, by the way, is another respect in which the radicalism of the recent past and the present differs from that of earlier periods. No mean lovers of language were the Jacobins, the revolutionists of 1848, the anarchists who followed Proudhon, and the socialists who followed Marx, down through the 1930s. I am not claiming felicity, much less distinction, of style in all or most of these radical movements, but there was without doubt a certain respect for language, a manifest willingness to engage it, rather than deliberately repudiate it, in the cause.

But it would be absurd to imply that all degradation of language in our age comes from the left. The left's calculated attack upon language would leave no trace were it not for the erosions of language which are to be seen on the right and in the center as well. Linguistic corruption and primitivism are a general disease in our time, especially in politics, as the late George Orwell, and before him Tocqueville, realized so well. Tocqueville—who as usual was speaking for the future more than for his own age—thought that the spread of linguistic obscurity, in its several forms, was endemic in modern democracy. Among its politicians he was struck by the

cultivation of the orotund, the pompous, and the inflated—all manifestations of the obscure in speech. He was struck too by the inflation of language in modern mass society, the incessant ballooning
of the meanings of ordinary words, the striking of new words for
the express purpose of giving inflated ideas and values. Not least,
for Tocqueville, was democracy's passion for the abstract. Democratic peoples, he wrote, are "passionately addicted to generic
terms and abstract expressions."

"These abstract terms which abound in democratic languages,
and which are used on every occasion without attaching them to
any particular fact, enlarge and obscure the thoughts they are intended to convey; they render the mode of speech more succinct
and the idea contained in it less clear. But with regard to language,
democratic nations prefer obscurity to labour."

But this is not all. Those who live in the democracies "are apt to
entertain unsettled ideas, and they require loose expressions to convey them. As they never know whether the idea they express today
will be appropriate to the new position they may occupy tomorrow, they naturally acquire a liking for abstract terms. An abstract
term is like a box with a false bottom; you may put in what ideas
you please, and take out again without being observed."

We may think Tocqueville unfair, even negligent. For in both
America and Europe the period immediately following Tocqueville's visit to this country is rich in the cultivation of new and lasting forms of speech—a cultivation, as Mencken has shown us in detail, well under way on the frontier while Tocqueville was in
America. In England, France, and elsewhere novelists of the stature of Dickens were clearly giving added wealth to national language. And the impact of the two revolutions in economy and polity in the nineteenth century alone brought with it scores of new
words and forms, many of which were to remain in both speech
and writing. Even so, in this as in so many other respects Tocqueville must be seen as prescient so far as the mainstream is concerned.

In our own day no one has expressed or developed Tocqueville's position more eloquently than George Orwell, who, himself a master craftsman, in an essay on language and politics written just after World War II, wrote:

> This mixture of vagueness and sheer incompetence is the most marked characteristic of modern English prose, and especially any kind of political writing. As soon as certain topics are raised, the concrete melts into the abstract and no one seems able to think of turns of speech that are not hackneyed: prose consists less and less of *words* chosen for the sake of their meaning, and more and more of *phrases* tacked together like the sections of a prefabricated henhouse.

Orwell also wrote: "Political language—and with variations this is true of all political parties, from Conservatives to Anarchists—is designed to make lies sound truthful and murder respectable." He made Newspeak the foundation of his totalitarian world in *1984*. What gives Newspeak its special fascination and horror, and this of course is true of so many of the elements of the society Orwell portrays, is the ease with which we can see Newspeak as a continuous development of political language in our own day, not only in the totalitarian countries but, more ominously, in the democracies.

In the preceding chapter I referred to "government as deception" and to the seemingly ingrained practice of lying to the governed that is so vivid in recent political history in America and Europe. That lying would not be as rampant, would be far more difficult to bring off, if erosions in language, the spread of empty abstractions, the widening of the inflated and of the primitive at one and the same time, and outright attempts to corrupt language were not so widespread in the popular language of the age—in the press, on television, in the theatre, even (and perhaps especially) in the school and university. It is not difficult for governments to conceal, indeed to efface complexities with bland, rounded, simplisms for the benefit of populations which contain in rising number graduates of schools and colleges where simplified, "managed" versions of classics are used and where textbooks for courses are the products of an assembly-line system of writing that had its beginning in the magazine *Time* but that has by now both widened immensely and become vulgarized far beyond anything that the founders of *Time* could have foreseen.

From one point of view, and a not insubstantial one, the crowning evil of Watergate is the language which, as the tapes have made forever evident, clothed the thoughts and decisions of the principals. The vulgarity, the primitivism, the lack of meaning or referent, the groping for expression of the simplest ideas, quite apart from the monotony of the most unimaginative obscenity are all fit accompaniment to the political and moral substance of Watergate— accompaniment and also vehicle. Such is the symbiotic relation of idea and word that it is almost possible to believe that vulgarity and primitivism of native language in the White House helped generate the fact of Watergate.

Here again, though, we are obliged to consider background. It is of course possible that had tapes covered all conversations in the White House and Executive Office Building by Presidents Kennedy and Johnson, their language would be more precise, expressive, and lucid, and also free of the dreadful overtones of banality and vulgarity in the Nixon tapes. It is possible, but, on evidence that keeps increasing all the time, supplied by intimates of these two predecessors of Nixon, hardly likely. The fact is, degradation of language in White House and government generally has been an almost constant process for the last three decades.

Nor is the profanity or vulgarity the worst aspect of this degeneration of official language. I rank obfuscation, whether deliberate or from carelessness and cynicism, as by far the greater evil. And who today, studying the speeches and official pronouncements of Kennedy and Johnson on the whole complex of domestic and foreign matters that concerned them, can doubt that the art—if that is the word—of obfuscation was reaching constantly new heights in Washington prior to Nixon and Watergate.

But very little of this would be possible in a culture that did not widely embody, in its ordinary speech and in its writing, most of the same qualities. The plain, unblinkable fact is that language in our culture has receded considerably from the position it once held. It is no longer the profoundly important tie among us that it once was; nor is it honored, respected, and loved as it once was. This judgment is not a mere opinion. It is certified by studies of the size of the average person's vocabulary today as compared to a generation ago, by the statistics of failure in college entrance examinations in English, by the turning of more and more publishers to simplified and "managed" textbooks, for college as well as secondary school, and by simple comparison of newspapers and magazines today with those of a generation or two ago.

George Steiner, in *Language and Silence*, following a detailed account of the degree to which language—that is, verbal language—has contracted over the last two or three centuries as the result of expansions of other forms of communication in mathematics, science, and other areas, gives specific emphasis to the situation that prevails today. He suggests, acknowledging the difficulties inherent in any estimate, that as much as 50 percent of modern colloquial speech in England and America comprises only thirty-four basic words; "and to make themselves widely understood, contemporary media of mass communication have had to reduce English to a semi-literate condition."

"Semi-literate" is, alas, the condition of language in all ages that are characterized by escape from culture and by ever-new expressions of despotic power. There is a kind of functional relation. Degradation of language, by virtue of its weakening of the social bond, makes political or military power inevitable, and the spread of such power necessarily extends the degradation of language.

THE FALLEN MUSE

The full significance of the university's sudden change and strikingly diminished place in the social order has not yet been grasped by scholars, intellectuals, and other guardians of culture. It is thought, even by those most sensitively aware of the nature of the change, to be a phenomenon largely confined to the area of higher education, without significant impact upon other areas of society.

This is anything but the case. To a degree unknown in the ancient classical world or in any other civilization, western culture since the medieval period has been profoundly dependent upon the university and the set of values that it embodies: reason, the free spirit of inquiry, devotion to knowledge as an end in itself. Such values have existed in other places; but nowhere else have they been given institutional structure as they have in the Western university, and nowhere else has the number of persons exposed to them—brought up, so to speak, within the disciplines of these values—been so great as in Western populations. The relation of these values, and of the individuals to whom they are important, to the political community and its own fabric of values and incentives is very close. And more than a few of the motivations which have been commonly ascribed to the middle class, to Protestantism, or to other sources, are better ascribed, I believe, to the university and its distinctive culture—one that has had continuous existence for at least one eight hundred years in Western society.

The genius of the university lies in its capacity to bring its unique values and disciplines to what is potentially the most creative part of any society: youth. As is well understood, it is in adolescence and early adulthood that the mind is most receptive, that mental powers are most buoyant; and the Western university, by virtue of its influence over this group, or a part of it, has obviously had extraordinary opportunity to communicate its values, its culture, to other areas of society, state, and economy.

I am well aware of the substantial body of intellectually creative minds in the West that has remained outside academic walls. Nor do I forget that there have been times when the universities have been in such a state of desuetude that the larger debt by society was owed to minds for whom any thought of university service would surely have been repugnant.

But it should not be forgotten that these minds outside the universities were all able, inspired, to work in a culture whose central intellectual values were shored up by the literally hundreds of colleges, schools, and institutes which, from about the twelfth century on, formed a unique part of Western society. It is impossible to imagine the high status formal education at all levels has had apart from the commanding effect that universities and university scholars have exerted for just under a thousand years. Essentially, the curriculum of the whole educational system has been shaped—at least until recently—by the criteria of intellectual excellence which flourished in the universities.

And as curriculum was shaped, so was the intellectual core of Western culture shaped. The kinds of incentive, motivation, theme, value, and end we find in the literature and learning of the West during the last several hundred years, manifest in all the different sectors of cultural creation, did not come out of a vacuum, nor have they ever existed in one. In all truth, they are incomprehensible in their intensity and extent except in a context so strong, so secure, and possessed of such unbroken continuity that an audience, a public, for the results of learning and of the creative imagination generally, could in some degree be counted upon. Until fairly recently, the great themes of literature, philosophy, and art, even at times of the sciences, were closely related to a core of knowledge that was classical at root and that depended for its vitality upon an educational system in the West that was in very large degree dominated by the university.

But what was really central was not classical learning or classical value; if that had been the case, we should probably never have gone beyond Greek and Latin and what was associated with these two languages. What was central to the university, and then in widening circles to much larger areas, was what can only be called the dogma of knowledge. The word "dogma" comes from a Greek root that means "to seem good." When something attains dogmatic status it is regarded as good, or true, or beautiful in and for itself, without reference to other value or authority. Almost anything, seemingly, can become a dogma in a given people's system of belief. Equality, freedom, justice, democracy, all of these are dogmas for us today, just as the Trinity, Resurrection, and Eucharist were (and still are) dogmas for the Christian community. We could not live without dogma in some degree, in some areas of life and thought. Ages vary, however, in the extent and intensity of dogma, and it is one of the characteristics of twilight periods in history that in such times ancient dogmas tend to become weak, to disappear, with new ones too indistinct to be helpful. What I noted above about escape from culture is often, at bottom, escape from dogma, a process that can of course be beneficial and stimulating at times, but only when such escape is not an end in itself but a quest for new anchors or belief.

It is one of the most distinctive features of Western civilization, ever since the ancient Greeks but particularly since the Middle Ages brought the monasteries and universities into being, that knowledge has been a dogma, and with it reason. That is, the belief—axiomatic in its character—that *knowledge is good*, knowledge for its own sake. Dogma, more than any principle of utility, has made it possible for many centuries for the theologian, the philosopher, the artist, the writer, the pure scientist to hold the high status that each has had for the most part, in varying degrees at different times, in Western culture.

I do not think I exaggerate here. In a true and important sense, knowledge, as such, has had, for a long time, a sacred position. It is interesting and illuminating to reflect on the fact that in the beginning the most important knowledge in society was knowledge *of the sacred*, the knowledge possessed by the priests, sages, scholars, and other guardians of the sacred. Insensibly, gradually, the idea of knowledge of the sacred became converted into that of *the sacredness of knowledge*, which came to include, of course, a great deal more than what is commonly involved in the sacred. Only, I suggest, in a civilization where knowledge in almost any form could attain the luster of sacredness, of dogmatic importance, would it have been possible for the kind of continuing, ever-enlarging stream of inquiry, enterprise, analysis, and synthesis we have known in so many intellectual areas to have begun at all.

To argue, as some have, that a principle of utility operated here, that there was recognition, even dimly, of the practical value in the long run of knowledge, misses the point. For until a few years ago, the larger prestige among intellectuals as a class was possessed by those, such as artists and philosophers, in whose works little in the way of utility either existed or was ever claimed. Within the living memory of many of us, the highest positions of status in a university were occupied not by engineers, lawyers, or scientists, but by men and women in the classics, in literature, philosophy, and history. The aura that originally overhung knowledge of the sacred continued over the whole domain of the humanities. To have asked for demonstration of the practical value of any part of this realm would once have seemed not merely irrelevant and banal but heretical.

The university has not been for everyone irrespective of mental gifts, and it is absurd to pretend that it should be. There are types of mentality for which the university would surely be constrictive and sterile. It is not easy to imagine the works of Shakespeare, Goethe, Mozart, and other geniuses being created in the corporate atmosphere of the university. And it is chastening to recall the opposition from universities faced by creative minds in the physical and social sciences.

But all of this, while true, does not offset the immense and even determinative function of the university in the rise of the kind of public among whom the achievements of a Shakespeare or Goethe could be regarded as important. Not for some time, as we know ruefully, were the works of these minds allowed into the curriculum of either school or university; but there is much reason to believe that had they not gotten in at some point, their luster today would be a great deal less, their public even smaller, than it is.

Is it likely that *books* could have attained the special significance they have known in the West during the past few centuries apart from their central position in university libraries and classrooms? Religious books could have, no doubt, but I think it questionable that other books could have acquired the rank they did as icons of culture apart from their commanding position in school and university. In an age such as ours when the book has undergone striking loss of status, among educated and uneducated alike—as the result of many factors, mostly technological—it is instructive to recall a time not very far back when the colloquial phrase "I read it in a book" could oftentimes end all argument. And this kind of almost religious regard for the book, as such, was bound to have had great stimulus both in the schools and toward the founding of an ever-larger number of schools and colleges. It is very hard to imagine the numerous substitutes for books around us today—the micro-copying techniques, for instance—ever arousing anything of the veneration for knowledge and reason that could once be aroused even (often especially) among the uneducated as well as the educated.

The relation of the university, or similar associations, to the liberal political community was well understood by the Founding Fathers. We need merely think of Jefferson's tireless effort in the founding of the University of Virginia, or the establishment by John Adams and Benjamin Franklin of societies for the cultivation of the arts and sciences in Boston and Philadelphia respectively. Granted that the colleges which came into being in the eighteenth and nineteenth centuries had for the most part a religious and also professional character, their mission largely that of educating for the clergy, still we would not see the special affection that political and business leaders had for a Harvard, a Yale, or a Princeton if there had not been values cultivated and disseminated which went far beyond profession. The Founding Fathers knew how fragile liberty was and would always be, and how closely related it is to the constraints which reason exerts. Thus the efforts most of them made to help establish associations of whatever kind in which the values of reason, or knowledge, and of humane as well as practical learning would be made manifest to the entire population.

It is an interesting fact that Tocqueville, who saw so much during his nine months in this country in 1830–31, missed entirely the colleges, the old ones like Harvard and Yale, and the new ones so rapidly coming into being at that time. He can perhaps be forgiven, for none of these, not even the old ones, could have seemed very imposing to any visitor from Europe who had grown up in the presence of a University of Paris. All the same, had Tocqueville noticed the colleges, he might have extended his notable prescience to the role they, and later the universities, were to have in offsetting that overpowering interest in the merely practical and technical which he thought endemic in the democracies.

For it is an often-overlooked fact that the development of the liberal arts in the United States—by which I mean literature and the fine arts as well as scholarship—has been deeply dependent upon university or college centers. If one takes the towns and cities in which efflorescences in literature and art are most notable—Boston, New York, Chicago, San Francisco, to name perhaps the four greatest—it is a fact of at least some importance that in each a college or several colleges nearby contributed sustantially to the effective setting. The "flowering of New England" took place, as we know, in the culture of Harvard, Yale, Bowdoin, Trinity, and other colleges. The burst of literary and artistic excellence which later took place in such cities as San Francisco and Chicago has to be seen against a background in which the University of California and Stanford University could exert immense influence upon the former city and the University of Chicago upon the latter.

But this profoundly creative role of the university in Western culture may well now be coming to an end. I do not think many sensitive observers have missed the recent fall of the university from the status it knew for many centuries. University presidents complain that they do not command the kind of respect nationally that their forebears did. So do university faculty members. In that class of fallen heroes I referred to above, whose reduced status gives such a melancholy cast to our age and makes so difficult the whole problem of leadership in all areas, university personages have their due place. No one would argue that the university scholar walks as tall as he once did in either American or European society. The fact is, the university and college are fast becoming expendable in the minds of a growing proportion of the Western population.

In some degree this is explainable, no doubt, by the rise of other and competing spheres of deep personal interest: health, environmental reclamation, the position of the aged, social security—all requiring today shares of the public purse and of public regard once not required. It is explainable in part also by the envelopment of culture by television which, with its instant availability and low intellectual quotient, can make school and college seem less and less necessary. But I am inclined to think that most of the explanation for the low and declining esteem not only of the university but of all formal education today resides in the transformation of the university that commenced in the United States right after World War II, and that has spread by now to many areas of the West.

I refer to the transformation of the university from a community founded upon the academic dogma that knowledge is good in its own right and must be the core of any academic community to an organization that bears less and less resemblance to community of any kind and more and more to factory, office, and marketplace. Institutions thrive when their functions seem distinctive and important; and they undergo decline and death when their functions have come to seem more or less indistinguishable from those performed by other institutions. So long as the university and college did what no other institution in the social order did—add to knowledge in the humanities and the pure sciences and diffuse it through teaching—they had, and could hold, the respect of the public and of generations of students.

Once, however, the universities succumbed, as they did just after World War II, to the view that there was no limit to what they could do in and for society, the destruction of their own unique mission had begun. In the process of becoming all things to all people—at once research capitalist, bastion of political power, undiscriminating humanitarian, adviser of the rich and powerful, pretended healer of all psychic wounds, and redeemer of society's ills and discontents—the university lost its unique authority in culture, its own distinctive community.

It is still argued by many that what brought the universities down to their present level in Western countries was the rash of student riots and rebellions which took place in several Western countries, including, as will not be forgotten, our own, during the 1960s. Some of these rebellions show an occasional sign of persistence, though not many. But it was not the student revolution that brought down the university's system of authority; it was the prior collapse, or grave weakening, of that authority that brought on the student revolution. In this the university does not differ from institutions like family, local community, and church. As we have seen, contemporary revolts against these or alienations from them also must be seen against a background of prior dislocation of function, earlier loss of legitimacy of authority.

There is more than coincidence in the simultaneous decline of the political community and of the university in the West. In striking degree the university has been the chief nurturer of the values of disciplined freedom, of language and culture, and of other intellectual and moral elements vital to a liberal democracy.

THE TRIUMPH OF THE SUBJECTIVE

"Ages which are regressive and in process of dissolution," Goethe said to Eckermann, "are always subjective, whereas the trend in all progressive epochs is objective." Twilight periods are commonly rich in manifestations of subjectivity, and our own is no exception. The retreat to inner consciousness that began in literature at the very beginning of the century, but which was offset for a long time by still-powerful currents of objectivity, has become a major phenomenon in the cultural setting of the present, and may be seen not only in literature and the fine arts, but in substantial areas of the social sciences, philosophy, and, variously, in the wide range of popular therapeutic explorations of self. This subjectivity would be less significant if it were not associated with what has become an enlarging distrust of reason and science in some of the areas of inquiry which only recently have become accepted in the terms of rationalism. Nor can we properly overlook in this context the whole effusion of the occult in its many forms.

Sir Gilbert Murray, in his *Five Stages of Greek Religion*, has given us insight into another twilight age, that in ancient Greece which led up to the rise of Christianity. He writes, "Anyone who turns from the great writers of classical Athens, say Sophocles or Aristotle, to those of the Christian era, must be conscious of a great difference in tone. There is a change in the whole relation of the writer to the world around him." We find a general indifference, Murray observes, toward matters that had fascinated an earlier age in Greece: the nature of the cosmos, the structure of the good state, man's reason and the relation of this reason to the outer world and problems of human justice, rights, freedom, and welfare. Such topics had appeared during Greece's great age of rationalism—a rationalism that had room in it for the religious, as we know from Plato's *Dialogues*, and for the drama and art of the fifth century B.C. But now, Murray writes, everything about the individual's relation to world and society is different. We are confronted by

> a period based on the consciousness of manifold failure, and consequently touched with both morbidity and with that spiritual exaltation which is so often the companion of morbidity. It not only had behind it the failure of the Olympian theology and of the free city-state, now crushed by semi-barbarous military monarchies; it lived

through the gradual realization of two other failures—the failure of human government . . . to achieve a good life for man; and lastly the failure of the great propaganda of Hellenism, in which the long-drawn effort of Greece to educate a corrupt and barbaric world seemed only to lead to the corruption or barbarization of the very ideals which it sought to spread. This sense of failure, this progressive loss of hope in the world, in sober calculation, and in organized human effort, threw the later Greek back upon his own soul, upon the pursuit of personal holiness, upon emotions, mysteries, and revelations, upon the comparative neglect of this transitory and imperfect world. . . .

In a phrase that was to become famous and widely used, Murray epitomized the age as one of "failure of nerve." It was in fact, a failure of the rationalist imagination, of the disciplines of reason, to attract any longer the philosophical minds in the schools and academies. These, as the record makes evident, preferred ideas which became steadily more mystical, solipsistic, and which often were linked with the occult. Popularly, it was an age of widespread superstition and of a turning to literally dozens of bizarre forms of faith, many imported from the East. If there is a single word that well describes this renunciation of government, society, of the external world in general, it is "subjectivity."

The Greece that Murray writes of is only one of the twilight ages in which a retreat from mind and its disciplines is evident in Western history. There is the Rome of the war-ridden decades leading up to Augustus and the Emperorship, the later Rome of Augustine's *City of God*, the period we know conventionally as the Renaissance but that is better thought of, in Huizinga's phrase, as "the waning of the Middle Ages," and, as I have noted, the *fin de siècle* at the turn of the present century, limited in scope though it was. In all of these periods there is a great deal of the kind of mentality that Murray finds in post-Peloponnesian Athens: a courting of the irrational, the occult, the bizarre, and, above everything else, the internal, the *subjective*.

Plainly, that word also describes an imposing section of the contemporary mind, intellectual and popular. As so often happens in history, art pointed the way. What had been specialized, limited to a handful of writers, painters, and sculptors in the early part of the century—epitomized, in the novel, by "stream of conscious-ness"—suddenly occupied a great deal of the intellectual landscape. Literature plunged deeper and deeper into the recesses of the self—the writer's self—and conventional narrative rapidly retreated to novels and stories of the most popular kind, though even here, in some of the new mass-circulation magazines, the subjective was taking hold.

By the end of the 1950s, preoccupation with self, with the pre-rational, with awareness, and with internal consciousness gener-ally, had come to the social sciences, even to political militance. If there is one overriding difference between the New Left that flourished in the 1960s and the Old Left that had been spawned in large part by the rationalist systems of Marx and Freud, chiefly the former, it lies in the value given the subjective by the New Left. And with this went an attack upon objectivity itself, which, largely by virtue of its association with large-scale science and science's own linkage with modern industry and government, could seem to be the essence of the detested Establishment. The kinds of books that mattered to substantial numbers of young Americans on the left included Theodore Roszak's *The Making of a Counter Culture* and Charles Reich's *The Greening of America,* which quite frankly put conventional rationalist liberalism in the camp of the enemy. So cryptic, often downright obscure, a psychiatrist as R. D. Laing could become, for a time at least, virtually a hero for his praise of states of consciousness derived, in his words, from "our looking at ourselves, but also by our looking at others looking at us and our reconstitution and alteration of these views of the others around us." The eminent sociologist Alvin Gouldner, long a master of ob-jective sociology and protagonist of the Old Radicalism, in his best-selling *The Coming Crisis of Western Sociology* now wrote of the new sociology that he wished to herald: "The ultimate goal of a Reflex-ive Sociology is the deepening of the sociologist's own awareness, of who and what he is, in a specific society at any given time and of how both his social role and his personal praxis affect his work as a sociologist." That kind of self-consciousness would only have offended a Marx or a Durkheim, but it clearly did not offend a large number of young sociologists in the period right after the book was written.

Some of the works which flourished a few years ago are undoubtedly already fast becoming forgotten. It is always this way. What is important is not the identity of this or that work, or its duration as a best-seller, but the whole state of mind that is fed by it. If that state of mind were to be described solely by the word "subjective," we might be able to give it less attention. But, as I have suggested, contemporary subjectivity in art, philosophy, and social science is set in a context of widening regard for the mystical and the occult, of communal forms of association which have quite frankly withdrawn from the society around them, of novel forms of religious faith—some profoundly fundamentalist, some drawn from Eastern creeds—and, towering over all these, of increased attack upon reason as the proper vehicle for our understanding and control of the world.

What Lionel Trilling has written in his Jefferson Lecture, "Mind in the Modern World," is instructive. The new irrationalism, he notes, "stipulates that only those things are real, are true, and then to be relied on, which are experienced without intervention of rational thought. And it is on the basis of this judgment that the contemporary ideology of irrationalism proceeds, celebrating the attainment of an immediacy of experience and perception which is beyond the power of the rational mind. The means to this end are not new; they are known from old. They include inspiration, revelation, the annihilation of selfhood perhaps through contemplation but also through ecstasy and the various forms of intoxication, violence, madness."

I do not pretend, nor does Trilling, that these last are practiced by more than a rather small minority in our society. Numbers, however, are not an infallible guide to historic impact, as revolutions teach us. In any event, we cannot be blind to the larger setting in which such a minority exists and takes on importance. And this setting is, as I have emphasized, one of increasing preoccupation with self, ego, and identity in popular literature as well as elsewhere in contemporary thought and writing.

Nor do I imply that in this twilight age of ours, as in other twilight periods of history, subjectivity cannot occasionally produce literary and philosophical works of genuine worth, taken in themselves. It is entirely possible that the best, the most sensitive and probing minds in such ages are the most likely to be attracted to this cast of thought and imagination. There is certainly nothing that is intrinsically wrong with exploration of one's self in its relation to others.

But when subjectivity is a pervasive state of mind in arts, letters, and philosophy, in the social sciences, and even in social protest, it is bound to rank high among the forces which have negative impact upon not only culture, reason, and the whole sense of membership in a social order, but the political community itself.

Once again we see a force inimical to the liberal political state that has been in substantial degree created by the form of power that lies in the state. The Western state, which has been so instrumental in the formation of the idea of the discrete individual, possessed of his own rights and liberties, is also, I would argue, the principal cause, when it reaches the degree of centralization and aloofness of power that has been so evident in recent times, of an intensification of individualism that is manifested by subjectivity. It was Simmel, above any other observer at the turn of the century, who saw the degree to which modern political society, through its destructive impact upon local communities, through its absorption of values previously resident in these communities, becomes the means of turning individual consciousness back upon itself. The late George P. Adams was but echoing Simmel when he wrote in *Idealism and the Modern Mind:* "It is not strange that this self-discovery and self-consciousness of the individual should have steadily mounted higher as the environment of individuals more and more takes on the form of an impersonal, causal, and mechanical structure."

The political state quite as much as technology and mass industry has been a primary force in the creation of this environment of subjectivism.

THE LURE OF
MILITARY SOCIETY

I BELIEVE THAT everything around us at the present time suggests the rising influence of the military, its roles, coercions, and symbols, in civil society in the West. This has less to do with any aggressive intent on the part of the military, which is, after all, professional at its core, used to the limits of elites, and inherently ungiven to Faustian ambition, than it does with the mounting concern on the part of government and society that apart from military dominance of some kind, the texture of social order will not be maintained. The recipe for militarism in a society is basically twilight of authority in the civil sphere.

It was this way in the ancient world, in Greece and Rome; the Alexanders and the Caesars sprang out of political and social breakdown. So too, after the waning of medieval society, do we see in the Renaissance the rise of military monarchies and princedoms, all in the setting of dislocation and decay of accustomed authority. Always, it would seem, the onset of widening perceptions of breakdown or corruption in the nonmilitary areas of life is followed by the enhanced position of the military, as the result of the ever more likely turning by increasing numbers of people, and also, as I shall stress at some length later, by intellectuals fascinated by the uses of power in times of crisis, to the military and to war. One of the surest indicators of twilight ages in history is the pervasiveness and intensity of war, and also of military types of mind in high political places.

The likelihood of militarization of Western countries in the years immediately ahead is of course greatly increased by two prominent aspects of the world scene. First and greatest is the kind of military socialism Russia and China have brought to the level of super-power. To pretend that these and other national socialisms are any-thing but military in essence and structure, ideology notwithstand-ing, is naive. It is, unfortunately, a widespread naiveté, especially among those professors and reporters who are seemingly enchanted by China and Maoism. No nation could be as thoroughly saturated by military discipline, regimentation, and the symbolism of war as are Russia, China, and other, smaller countries, and not be a threat to the rest of the world. Militarism supplies its own momentum; also, as I shall indicate, much of its own necessary ideology.

The second great force in the world scene that is bound to accel-erate the process of militarization of not only Western but other societies is terrorism. If terror, as manifested by such groups as the PLO and the IRA, increases by the same rate during the next de-cade as it has during the past decade, it is impossible to conceive of liberal, representative democracy continuing, with its crippling pro-cesses of due process and its historic endowments of immunity before, or protection by, the legal process.

My interest, though, in this chapter is solely the relation of the military to civil society in Western, especially American, society. It cannot be denied that the size, reach, and sheer functional impor-tance of the military are all vastly larger today than ever before in our history except for the short periods of actual warfare as during World Wars I and II. Given this immensity it is inconceivable that the military's influence would not mount steadily in all spheres—political, civil, cultural, and social as well as economic. To imagine that the military's annual budget of just under a hundred billion dollars does not have significant effect upon the economy is of course absurd, and it may be assumed that with respect to the military as with any other institution, beginning with the family, what affects the economic sphere also affects in due time other spheres of life. It is often said by those seeking to rationalize the existence of a large military establishment that its budget has not risen as sharply, is indeed not as large as, the total "social welfare" budget at the present time. This is quite true. But the affinity between military expansion and expansion of what in ancient Greece and Rome was called the corn dole—supplemented in imperial Rome by the circuses—is nothing new. In remarkable degree the two types of public enterprise go together.

Nor is the sheer bulk of the military in contemporary American society due to Pentagon alone. Organizations like the CIA and FBI are by now essentially paramilitary organizations, more like the army in important respects than like civil organizations. If we are interested in assessing the comparative significance of the military at the present time in American society we need only go back half a century. Then, despite the fact that we were but a few years away from the First World War, with all that it had meant in the way of reorganization of American society, the military was tiny in size and virtually devoid of influence on either Congress or the Presidency. There was of course no CIA or any cognate organization, and the FBI was but an infinitesimal acorn in the Department of Justice.

How very different the present scene! I repeat: I am not suggesting anything in the order of a military design that would contemplate domination of government and society in this country. That would be fatuous and irresponsible, even though we are living in a world where country after country is to be seen passing from civil to military rule, irrespective of the covering ideology, whether "left" or "right." But the fact remains: we have at this moment a vast military establishment, taking it as we are obliged to in the full sense of the term, and it is sheer fantasy to suppose so vast an organization, governed necessarily in ways which are the very reverse of those of civil society, is without constant and significant effect upon the social order.

I do not doubt that if our political government were as strong and as productive of patriotic allegiance as it once was, if our economy were not the relatively fragile thing a combination of inflation and recession has made it, and will continue to keep it, so far as we can see, and if our fundamental social institutions were not in a condition of decline, the military organization, for all its present bulk, would be rendered more or less sterile so far as influence upon civil society is concerned. But, as I have indicated in the two preceding chapters, we live in an epoch of decline of authority, of profoundly diminished confidence in political and social structures, not to mention political and social leaders, and everything we have learned from comparative history tells us that such a period is ripe for both war and for military dominance. Nor can we overlook the striking fact that in poll after poll at the present time the military is revealed to possess more public confidence than any other class—business, political, academic, or religious—in our society.

It was the military philosopher-strategist Clausewitz who, in the aftermath of the Napoleonic wars, laid down the vital principle that modern war demands a large-scale reconstruction of the society that participates in it. Such reconstruction, Clausewitz did not hesitate to proclaim, includes a great many measures we have subsequently come to identify with the welfare state, not least those pertaining to the spread of the equalitarian ethic. I suggest it is possible to add a corollary to Clausewitz's dictum: that the kind of reconstruction envisaged for military purposes by this great strategist tends by its very nature to increase the attractions of war and of war society. My reasons for this will be set down in some detail in the remaining sections of this chapter. For the moment only the high correlation between democratic war and democratic society during the past century needs to be stressed.

The age of the mass democracies has been, only too clearly, the age of mass wars. This is a truth first uttered, so far as I know, by Taine:

> One war after another and the institution becomes worse and worse; like a contagion, it has spread from State to State; at the present time, it has overspread the whole of continental Europe and here it reigns along with its natural companion . . . its twin-brother, universal suffrage, each more or less conspicuously trotted-out and dragging the other along, more or less incomplete and disguised . . . : the one thrusting a ballot into the hands of every adult, and the other putting a soldier's knapsack on every adult's back: with what promises for the twentieth century.

For a long time in the United States the military fell into desuetude after each war. It was unsung, unhonored, avoided indeed by the major talents of any generation, which went instead to business, government, or one or other of the professions. The last of those periods of desuetude, however, was that between 1920 and 1940. Since World War II the military has not been other than prominent and, in its higher reaches of command, exceedingly lustrous, with occasional, brief periods of moderate decline to be of course kept in mind. Viet Nam and the draft, falling as they did upon white, middle-class youth that had been reared in the unprecedented affluence of the aftermath of World War II, profoundly affected three governments, those of Kennedy, Johnson, and Nixon, but it is a point too little noted that in no *significant* way did the military itself, as an establishment, suffer. Fury was turned on civil government, on White House occupants, primarily, not on the military. Nothing even approximating the disdain and contempt for the military this country had manifested at earlier times was to be seen in the 1960s. There were even one or two generals with broad popular appeal, at least as measured against the low esteem in which three successive Presidents were held. And, as will be remembered, it was to a four-star general that President Nixon turned to become chief of White House staff when, as the result of Watergate, demise of his administration had become inevitable.

There is nothing so constrictive of freedom, of creativeness, and of genuine individuality as the military in its relation to culture. This has always been true. Granted that ages of sudden onset of strong personal military-political power, like the ages of Alexander in Greece, of the first Caesars in Rome, and of the military despots in Renaissance Italy, can be rich for a time in creative personalities, all the evidence shows this time to be very brief. As soon as the special character of military power begins to envelop a population, its functions, roles, and traditional authorities, a kind of suffocation of mind in the cultural sphere begins. Nor is there any evidence that military power, even when its onset has been welcomed, is ever loved by those under it. Populations, on the evidence, quickly become restive unless the strongest and most formidable measures are taken by military authorities to curb them; unless propaganda, force, and even terror become almost incessant. Even then, as the recent history of Russia has demonstrated, restlessness in the population, especially among the more buoyant and creative minds, is evident. Of all forms of despotism, that of the military is harshest, for under the military the social order is scarcely more than permanent garrison. Even so, we must understand the military's appeal.

WAR AND WESTERN VALUES

Western civilization is no stranger to war and to military values. Nowhere else has the martial had the same symbolic effect for so many lives in so many different kinds of situations. Overwhelmingly our political pantheons are occupied by military figures, and Western languages are filled with metaphors and images of military origin. In the West it is almost instinctual to apply to ordinary civil problems or difficulties the images of war. Thus we do not simply try to solve the problem of poverty; we must have a "war against poverty." Words like "battle," "attack," "conquest," and "mobilization" are strewn all over the political scene, revealing clearly enough the appeal that war exerts upon the conscious and subconscious mind.

It is fair to say that there have been more large-scale wars in Western civilization during at least the past three thousand years, more armies on the march, more battles, more lives lost through armed combat, more land devastated, more civil populations terrorized and subjugated, more governments destroyed, more governments founded as the direct result of war, than in any other civilization known to us. And, flowing in inevitable consequence from all of this, more sheer *thought*—political, economic, social, even philosophical and literary—has been given to war and its values in the West than anywhere else in world history.

To declare this is not to impute a unique instinct for war to the many races which have migrated over the millennia to the promontory of Eurasia that is Western Europe. If there is a single factor at work, it is not germ plasm but geography—the study of which is singularly and lamentably absent from most of the historical and social sciences today. Western Europe quite simply cannot be improved upon as a geographical setting for war. Its climate, terrain, ease of access from the East, abundance of resources of every kind, have made it a rich prize for many a people on the move for one reason or other from Eastern and Central Asia. Contact, then conflict, among peoples on the promontory of Western Europe was inevitable.

We do not know how many thousands of years have been occupied by the migrations and counter-migrations of peoples into Western Europe, but the number is very large, and the efforts of Eastern peoples to subjugate large parts of the West did not really terminate until well into modern European history. If so much of

Western literature, from the Homeric epics on, has been preoccupied by war, the reason is not far to seek. If Western morality has tended above most world moralities to prize those virtues which are inalienably associated with war and its demands, the explanation is obvious enough. William James, in an essay titled "The Moral Equivalent of War," did not exaggerate in his stress upon the degree to which Western values have been permeated by the incentives of war.

But what I want to point out in this section is the vital affinity between war and the Western state. The state is born of war and its unique demands. Those social evolutionists who have tried to derive the political state as a development from kinship—that is, as an emergent of household, kindred, or clan—have simply not recognized the issues involved. The first political figure in history is not patriarch but *military leader*. The history of every people of which we have record demonstrates that the first and greatest of all role-conflicts in history is that between head of household and clan on the one hand and, on the other, military chieftain. For the only times in which authority over sons passed out of the hands of the house-father, the *paterfamilias* in Roman history, and into hands alien to the family line, was during times of war, when a totally different set of needs and values came suddenly into existence along with a totally different kind of leadership. The kinship group and the militia were thus set into complete and unremitting opposition so far as their aims and needs were concerned.

It is a truism that the political state arose first in precisely those areas—so often seaports and river valleys, but wherever geography created a natural setting for contacts between peoples—where the traditional kinship and religious system of a given people broke down as the result of strains imposed by warfare. It is equally a truism that all of the great world religions—I mean the so-called universal religions—had their origins in exactly the same kind of setting. For it is the essence of the universal religion that it makes its god available to all who pledge their worship to him, irrespective of racial, kinship, or local background. There is thus an affinity between universal religion and the rise of the political state. For the military-political ruler could not help but acquire assistance from any religion that, by its very devotion to a single, transcendental god open to all peoples, was driven just as was the political state itself to assault upon ethnic, local, and class ties.

From the beginning the state was nothing more, basically, than an institutionalization of the war-making power. If war is, as Randolph Bourne put it, "the health of the state"—and it is, at least as far as the functions and powers of the state are concerned—this is demonstrably one of the most ancient of political facts. Inherently and primordially military qualities such as centralization of command, unremitting discipline, a chain of power from military chief straight down to individual soldier, even communalism were in the course of time transmitted to the political state. That the state slowly takes over many of the functions previously resident in family, religion, guild, and other social institutions—to become, as in our day, an economic, social, moral, and intellectual Leviathan—in no way offsets the fact of its origin in war or its recurrent expansions of function and power in times of war.

Even democracy is closely related to war. It was Condorcet who declared the rise of the infantry to be the first significant step in the modern West toward political democracy. It is, characteristically, within circumstances of outright war as well as revolution that the modern democracies have come into being. Whether we take France or America as our model in this respect, it is a fact worth emphasizing that during the seminal revolutions in both countries at the end of the eighteenth century, the needs of war were as basic in the refashioning of popular convention and government as were the more strictly ideological elements of political and social revolution. Most of the major advances in what we think of as the democratization of the West—the reduction of the powers of class and wealth in politics, the leveling of traditional ranks, and the endowment of the people as a whole with greater and more direct powers, rights, and freedoms from economic or social oppression—have taken place in times of war.

James, in "The Moral Equivalent of War," took note of the paradox that war represents in the human mind. On the one hand its violence and awful cost in human life and property are deplored, but on the other hand certain values closely associated with war are among the most deeply respected in civilization. James thought that something short of war in the form of a mission or crusade might be established, around which these values—valor, fortitude, leadership in a cause, and also the sheer historical pageantry of war—could cluster and thus maintain their integrative importance in human society. It is doubtful, though, that anything ever really substitutes for war in social and psychological terms. I am not suggesting that war, in organized, mass form certainly, is instinctive in human beings or that peoples cannot live without it. Some peoples seem to have lived for long periods without it, and among many peoples the incidence of war has been slight by modern Western standards. But considering our civilization, where warfare has been nearly continuous for many hundreds of years, where large institutional structures exist whose primary function is military, which possesses, as I have already indicated, a vast folklore and literature in which the martial is ascendant, and which repeatedly turns to war as the accepted means of resolving diplomatic, political, and economic crises, we would do well to regard war as a kind of universal, a deeply rooted incentive or potential incentive to action.

Hateful though war is in its violence, bloodshed, and devastation of landscape, it has, alas, historical attributes, by no means absent today, which give it—especially in time of domestic crisis, economic or other—a profound appeal. I think it worthwhile to describe briefly the essentials of this appeal, not only in the West but elsewhere in the world, past and present.

Change. War brings relief from the tedium, the fixity and routine, and the monotony that so often characterize life for all but a minority. Fixity, not change, is king! "When it is not *necessary* to change, it is necessary *not* to change." These words, uttered by Falkland during the English Civil War, are an admirable generalization for human history with respect to change. Change is very rare in the life of any society; it too often produces inconvenience, hardship, and bewilderment. Eric Hoffer correctly refers to "the ordeal of change." Habit is our adaptation to uncertainty. No one familiar with the role of the rebel, the heretic, and the deviant in most of man's history will doubt the immense power of tradition and of persistence in society or the monumental difficulties encountered by the genius, the prophet, or the individual simply seeking escape from the stifling atmosphere that tradition and conformity can sometimes lead to.

And yet, for all the difficulties put in the way of change by the ordinary character of human behavior, for all the stress upon conformity and convention, there is every reason to believe that change—if only in the sense of variety, new experience, fresh observation, and release from the fetters of habit and custom—is welcome to many persons from time to time. Here, plainly, is where war can be, despite its tragedies and devastations, attractive to those of buoyant, innovative, or venturesome nature eager to find relief from boredom.

Boredom is, as we know, a problem for man; it has proved one of the by-products of a central nervous system as highly developed as man's is. Ritual, drink, drugs, and sex have all been means for escaping the monotony of so much of human existence—especially before the twentieth century's consciously built-in diversions and releases from boredom. Now, war can be a wonderful means of releasing the buoyant and assertive individual from the tyranny of tradition, from what Walter Bagehot called the cake of custom, and from the gnawing, even agonizing, boredom that must always beset the energetic or creative in conditions of stationary culture. If even in our day the phenomenon of the bored individual, especially among the young, turning for release to combat and violence if not to drink or drugs, is not uncommon, it is easy enough to imagine the lure of war in earlier ages. One thinks of the horrors of the Civil War battlefields in America, the *known* horrors, but also of the unending line of the young and the bored, as well as of the patriotic, reaching from the American village to those battlefields. It was always thus, we may be certain.

War, then, offers change, and passion for this change can burn strongly in a great many of us from time to time. If loss of life is a possible consequence, well, that is but one risk as against abundant and guaranteed gains. And no one lives forever! How much better, in any event, the quick and possibly heroic ending of one's life than the inching away through tedious old age and senility. War, in sum, breaks down social walls, releases individuals from the monotony of the traditional and the tyranny of the predictable, and sets up the possibility of new experience and change.

War also creates opportunity for what can only be called "licensed immorality." War, after all, is the supreme manifestation of violence, and no people is known to us that does not relish the sight of violence in some form and degree. I cannot say that during my Pacific Theater experience in World War II I ever encountered soldiers who actually enjoyed every moment of direct combat experience—indeed, who did not in some way fear it. But I knew many who were chronically restless in garrison and who were, and knew they were, at their peak in a great many phases of battle. It used to be said that there was a good deal in common psychologically between the kind of soldier who could win a Congressional Medal of Honor or even a Silver Star and the kind of individual we label psychopath in civil life. In each there is a strong relish for violence. In the former, exercised by artillery, machine gun, rifle, or grenade, it is licensed violence.

So is there fascination with war's violence in civil populations—along with fear, to be sure. It is impossible to doubt the widespread thrill of violence experienced vicariously through the media, especially television. Tens of millions of Americans watched the war in Viet Nam every evening. And it has been correctly said that World War II is the longest running movie of all time. War movies and documentaries retain their appeal for all ages.

But there is a different kind of licensed immorality that comes with war, and that has still wider appeal inasmuch as it exists on the home front as well as in garrison and on the battlefield. I refer to the whole area of sexual conduct. Mars and Venus have ever been close companions. It was under the steady impact of the Roman Republic's wars, first foreign, then civil as well as foreign, that the destruction of the Roman family system gradually began. It was not easy for young Romans, after a number of years in the field where every form of violation of the canons of continence was scarcely more than routine, to return to the iron morality of the traditional Roman family system, with its built-in coercions, constraints, and subjections to patriarch and matriarch. The great wave of immorality that hit Roman society in the first century B.C., so well attested to by contemporary essayists, and that the Emperor Augustus strove valiantly to terminate through laws and decrees, had its origins in war.

I do not think it extreme to link the breakdown in moral standards in all spheres—economic, educational, and political, as well as in family life— to the effects of two major wars—celebrated wars!—in this century. What is in the first instance licensed, as it were, by war stays on to develop into forms which have their own momentum.

Progress. I refer to notable advances in level or quality of human culture and to significant improvements in standards of social organization. Such advances and improvements have nothing to do with any built-in trajectory of development of a people, and they are not the consequences of genetic fusion of racial stocks, as some of our biological and physical scientists continue to believe. Spurts of progress in culture are the results of fusion of idea-systems, of mixture of values, and of the stimulus to individual creativity so often occasioned by such fusions and mixtures. It is character-istically where peoples meet, repeatedly and diversely, that we find the major settings of intellectual and cultural progress in history, as in Athens during the fifth century B.C., Rome in the first century, Paris in the twelfth century, London in the sixteenth and seven-teenth centuries, and so on. There is nothing linear or continuous about progress; it is always to be found in spurts, with definite, as-certainable conditions.

Like it or not, war has been the commonest occasion in history for these spurts and for the fusions of values and idea-systems which underlie them. I do not deny that peaceful migration, trade, and commerce have also brought peoples together, with creative results on occasion. But such is the power of conservatism in kin-ship and in traditional society, such is the tendency of this society to confine the individual and to punish deviations from tradition, that for the most part simple migration and commerce are not enough. They are too easily contained within the structure of kin-ship and tradition. This is why we are so often obliged to look to the kinds of crisis generated by war alone for explanation of the sig-nal release of individuals during spurts of intellectual progress. What we have just noted about the dependence of much change in history upon war holds equally for cultural advance: the kind of ad-vance we find in the so-called golden ages. The fifth century B.C. in Athens began and ended in major wars, and there was not a year in between when the Athenians were not profoundly occupied by the needs of war. Yet this century was, as we know, very probably the greatest single century of creative efflorescence known to mankind. The same forces which liberated soldiers and politicians also lib-erated—in each instance from fettering convention and use and want—the great artists and philosophers of the century, who were much freer to brave the hazards of novelty in their works in time of crisis than they normally would have been.

Particularly impressive is the historical record of the relation of technical inventions to war. If invention is indeed mothered by necessity, then military necessity is supreme, for when else is survival so closely and so often wedded to the inventive faculty, a faculty always difficult to stir? No one acquainted with the uneven history of inventions in technology can be blind to the high correlation between periods of invention and periods of war. If even in our invention-oriented technology today in the West, war is indisputably the greatest stimulator and accelerator of technological invention, it is easy enough to imagine the role of war in earlier times.

Nor, finally, can we overlook the high correlation between war and the adoption of social measures intended to ameliorate poverty, discrimination, illiteracy, and inequity in the social order. Each of America's great wars has been associated with adoption of such measures at home—for the short-run purpose, no doubt, of welding the people into greater unity through greater participation in society's distribution of its wealth, but with the long-run consequences to be seen in continuation of the social security systems, improvements of education, and civil rights measures begun under the crisis conditions of war. It is probable that far more of the social gains prized today in Western populations have been the direct result in the first instance of the needs of war than of the ideology of socialism or social democracy—though, as I shall note shortly, there is a close relation between war and socialism.

Community. Human nature seemingly cannot tolerate a moral and social vacuum; hence the abiding quest for community—kinship, political, military, or other. One of war's greatest functions is giving a sense of community to those on each side. This is as true of a civil population as of those linked closely in military combat. What the English philosopher L. P. Jacks called "the spiritual peace that war brings" is well known in history. At a stroke, the ordinary factionalisms, the gnawing conflicts and competitions of the marketplace, and the ideological divisions of politics become muted, even dissolved. In their place is the kind of moral and social and political community that war can bring to a population which feels it is engaged upon some kind of mission or crusade. Millions of Americans and Europeans learned of this kind of community during the two world wars of this century. The effect of war can be, and has been, to endow with welcome meaning or purpose activities that all too easily come in ordinary times to seem lacking in either.

Moral values untested, unchallenged by evil, can easily become stale and flat. One of the great appeals of war in the modern world especially has been its capacity to effect moral crusades on the grand scale, with the enemy seen, or made to appear, as the embodiment of evil and the challenger of all that is good. It was the French Revolution that first moralized military operations in a large sense. For attack upon or defense against the nations surrounding France could and did seem suffused with a transcendent morality, one that was rooted in the goals of the French Revolution and the people. No one who has experienced the major wars of this century will have forgotten the mobilization of moral community as well as of armies in these wars. Again it is important to be reminded of the extremely unrepresentative character of America's war in Viet Nam. Better to use the position of Israel in the hostile Middle East, with all that is involved morally, psychologically, and socially, as a paradigm of war's capacity for creating moral community.

So is community a vital aspect of the military group itself. I learned this directly in World War II. No one could have disliked war, our intervention in that war, or the intrinsic character of military life more than I did. Three years as an enlisted soldier in the Pacific did not much change these sentiments. But there was hardly a moment during that period when I was not conscious of the intensity of the ties among soldiers, especially those in combat units. Formal studies of combat have documented what soldiers have known from the beginning of history, that armies tend to fight on the basis of these ties more than anything else when it comes to the actual rigors of combat. The announced objectives of a war may be of the greatest interest to the people and press at home; but they were of little if any interest to the soldiers in World War II, so far as I could see; what mattered was the intimacy and cohesion soldiers knew in their squads, platoons, and companies. To be separated, even briefly, from one's outfit was to know the feeling of isolation with peculiar intensity.

Our major values—love, protection, courage, honor, loyalty among them—were all nourished originally in the small contexts of human association: family, neighborhood, small community. For individuals who find the search in our large-scale society today for these contexts and values difficult and frustrating, the experience of war and its community known at first hand in the squad or platoon can be memorable. Not a little of what the French call *nostalgie de la guerre* is based precisely upon this poignant sense of community gained in war and community lost in peace.

Revolution. War is by nature revolutionary in its impact upon a people. How could it be otherwise? Its values, or rather those of the military units fighting the war, are antithetical in the extreme to the values of kinship-based society with its consecration of tradition, conventionality, and age or seniority. Everything that makes for the breaking of the cake of custom and the weakening of social walls also makes, as we have noted, for the release of energetic, talented, and ambitious individuals, usually young. Youth rises faster in crisis than under ordinary circumstances. So do other sections of a population: intellectual, economic, social, and ethnic. What we call the secularization of culture is a common phenomenon in wartime; moral rigidities are loosened and the line between good and bad becomes ever more indistinct.

Hence the appeal of war to revolutionaries—the successful ones at any rate. It was Lenin, well before the onset of World War I, who expressed most brilliantly this appeal in his famous attack on the pacifism of certain German Marxists and in his declaration that national wars are virtually made to be turned into revolutions. But the affinity between war and revolution had long been known in Western society. It was, after all, largely within the New Model

Army of the Puritans in the seventeenth century in England that radical equalitarianism, expressed in literally hundreds of tracts, took shape in modern thought. The Jacobins later were superb at exploiting war in the name of revolution and revolution in the name of war. Napoleon was the perfect exemplar of revolution as well as of war, not merely in France but throughout almost all of Europe, and even beyond. Marx and Engels were both keen students of war, profoundly appreciative of its properties with respect to large-scale institutional change. From Trotsky and his Red Army down to Mao and Chou En-lai in China today, the uniform of the soldier has been the uniform of the revolutionist.

Many of the basic values of war and revolution are identical. In each there is legitimization of violence in the name of some moral or social end that transcends violence. The appeal in each is overwhelmingly to youth—its unique energies, strengths, and also values, the latter so often subordinated in peacetime to the values of the older and the established members of the social order. In both war and revolution there is an emphasis upon loyalty, honor, and cause that is all too often difficult to find in ordinary political and economic society. Even the disciplines of war can be compared with those of the revolutionary crusade. No one today can be oblivious to the appeal exerted upon radical youth, even idealistic youth, by the spectacle of a China where uniformity and discipline are the symbols of escape from the frustrations and torments of a social order that can so easily come to seem moribund.

Not only is revolution allied psychologically to war; so is the whole communist ethic in history. Max Weber tells us that the idea of communism was born in the military association. "The primeval way of creating trained troops—ever ready to strike, and allowing themselves to be disciplined—was *warrior-communism.*" In the primitive war band, not in the primitive kinship community, lay the first and practical expression of "from each according to his abilities; to each according to his needs." The first assaults in ancient Rome upon the traditional *patria potestas*, which was basically the authority of the corporate family over its members and all their property, came from military leaders, beginning with Gaius Marius and continuing fatefully through the Caesars, in the name of soldiers understandably resentful of taking themselves and their booty back to fall under the traditional authority of the family. Whether we think of imperial Rome as a quasi-socialism or a state capitalism, there is no question but that its far-reaching social bureaucracy, its vast system of welfare to the masses, had its beginnings in military assault on traditional society.

There is much in common between the militarist and the revolutionist in the view each takes of traditional civil society, its privileges, immunities, and conventional authorities. To both mentalities this society, especially in its modern capitalist form, can seem egoistic, venal, needlessly competitive, often corrupt, and fettered by privilege unearned. Careful reading of the memoirs of the great generals in history will, I am sure, reveal as much distaste for all this as one finds in the memoirs of revolutionists. There is also likeness between the distinctive type of following the revolutionist and the militarist, when successful, have among the masses. It was Gaius Marius in the final century of the Roman Republic who gave the lesson: in military victory coupled with a certain degree of generosity with the spoils a revolutionary thrust is inevitably involved. Julius Caesar and then Augustus were only following—the second with utter success—the lessons Marius had taught nearly a century earlier.

Nor can we miss in our century the linkage between the military and revolutionary styles in the totalitarian states. How quick the revolutionary orders, so called, are to take on the habiliments of the military, complete with ostensible austerity, privation, and summary punishment of the wrongdoers or counterrevolutionaries. Stalin, the early Tito, Mao, and Castro, all revolutionary ideologists, have been quick to assume the uniform and the manner of the successful marshal or general. Note too how, beginning with Russia in the early 1930s, "soldiers" as a word was joined to "workers and peasants" on banners and in official speeches. It was the Red Army that became the single most celebrated element of Soviet Communism in the 1930s, and it is the army that remains the absolutely vital element of all revolutionary countries at the present time. Nowhere is this fact more evident than in Maoist China. The blunt and inescapable fact is that more than a million members of the army have no other duties than those of civilian governance: they are to be found holding key positions in all of the communes, in village councils, in ostensibly civil ministries, in the universities—*especially* the universities—and in each of the major spheres of social, cultural, and intellectual activity. A great many of these army members wear civilian clothes; but their military identity is rarely a secret. And there is abundant testimony to the effect that in Maoist China today the People's Liberation Army is, in the eyes of youth, the supremely elitist organization in all society, the ideal place in which to begin any type of career. Mao, very astutely, is commander-in-chief of the armed services as well as head of the political party, with party and military coming more and more to resemble one another.

I do not suggest that all war, or perhaps even most war in the modern world, satisfies those impulses which range from the revolutionary to the reformist. And it is hardly necessary to underscore here the blights which war brings in the way of devastation and despotism. I suggest only that in a great many modern wars, certainly in those of the present century, there is a strong undercurrent of hope to be seen, of action taken, with regard to social and economic improvement within the nations involved. In war alone lay the opportunities which such individuals as Lenin and Mao seized, and on a smaller scale there are others who have followed almost identical courses. Solzhenitsyn tells us that Lenin referred to businessmen, landlords, and peasants as "harmful insects." Lenin did not, however, include soldiers in this epithet. Trotsky's love of the army was, of course, passionate.

But, as I have indicated, we do not have to go to the military socialisms for evidence of the larger point, which is the compatibility of sustained national war and what is widely denoted social progress. The histories of the Western democracies are rich enough in their own exemplifications of this compatibility. One does not have to love war and the military to know that great enterprises in a score of sectors can take place in wartime, and that these are generally the longest remembered by populations.

THE ROMANIZATION OF THE WEST

It would be difficult, I think, to account fully for the high incidence of war in Western society and for the effect of military elements on civil society without reference to Roman Law and the whole view of society contained in its basic principles. This great system has always appealed to the centralizing despots, those engaged in converting civil life into war society. The reason is not far to seek. Roman Law as we know it in the Institutes of Justinian is preeminently the law of a strongly military state. Given final codification by Justinian's scholars in the sixth century, its fundamental legal and political elements are the products of the imperial Rome that began with the Caesars.

Rome is not the first great state in history to have depended heavily upon the military; there had been the Persia of Darius and the Greece of Alexander. But Rome is without question the first state in Western history in which incontestably military values became building blocks for an entire political order. I refer, of course, to the Empire, not to the Republic. From the time of Augustus—*Imperator Caesar divi filius Augustus*—who attained first the principate, then the emperorship, solely by virtue of his position of military commander, militarism acquired a leading role in the shaping of society. All the centralization of command that was basic in the Roman military, everything that made the individual rather than the family the fundamental unit, everything that put a premium upon contractual rather than ascribed relationships, became constitutive in the system of Roman Law we see developing in the imperial age.

Roman Law, then, is the law of a military state. I do not question its manifold uses in commerce and trade, its pertinence to any society characterized by a high degree of centralization and by large masses of individuals, but the fact remains that the Roman Law of the Empire is at bottom the law necessary to keep armies constantly in the field, properly supplied and replenished in the battles which were fought at every outpost of the greatest political organization—in size and sheer administrative architecture—that the world had ever seen, or was to see again prior to the formation of the British Empire.

I give here a brief account of the significance of Roman Law because it became, following the so-called Dark Ages during which its concepts were dim, a major foundation of the Europe that sprang from the ashes of the Middle Ages. It is no exaggeration to say that Western society has been twice Romanized: first in ancient times, second during the late Middle Ages and the Renaissance. In striking degree the effects of war and of the military on modern society have been registered through a political and legal system constructed out of Romanist elements.

"At the end of the Middle Ages," wrote F. W. Maitland, that most eminent of legal historians, "a great change in men's thoughts about groups of men was taking place, and . . . the main agent in the transmutation was Roman Law." Elsewhere Maitland refers to the "pulverizing" and "macadamizing" effects upon Western society of the kind of military centralization that was inherent in the Romanist system.

It would be hard to account for the distinctive character of the modern Western state, which has been from the start a process of institutionalized revolution in its effect upon family, class, estate, church, and other social institutions, except in the light of the basic concepts incorporated in the idea of the state by scholars, intellectuals, and technicians who, in Europe's universities, starting in medieval times, revived Romanist principles of law.

Roman Law in the form it took following this revival was, as Maitland's contemporary Paul Vinogradov wrote, "bound to appeal to the pioneers of the state conception, to ambitious emperors, grasping territorial princes, reforming legists, and even clerical representatives of law and order." Whether to the political ruler eager to break through all the intermediate authorities that the Middle Ages were so richly endowed with, the businessman equally eager to escape the network of restrictions laid upon him by the Church in matters of trade and finance, or the military leader seeking release from the multitude of contemporary religious and philosophical limits to warfare, Roman Law offered a great deal. It offered precisely the combination of political centralization, a sovereign defined as being not under the law but its very source, contract rooted in will or volition in place of ascribed and fixed status, and, far from least, a conception of society composed of atomlike individuals rather than of impenetrable social groups and associations that, in fact, has proved to be the framework of modern warfare, capitalism, and nationalism.

It is one of history's numerous ironies that the ultimate weapon of destruction of the medieval social order should have arisen in the first place as one of the central elements of an institution medieval to the core. I refer to the university. It was in the corporate, communal university which began to proliferate in the twelfth and thirteenth centuries that Roman Law and all the principles associated with it became an object of study which, though at first purely theoretical, entirely academic, became increasingly practical and applied in character.

When we speak of the faculties of law in the medieval university we are generally more apt to have in mind canon law than Roman, religious rather than secular. And I do not deny that canon law held a superior place in the university for a long time; it was intimately fused with the larger curriculum of theology. But even so it would be a great error to underestimate the appeal and the power of the *Corpus Juris Civilis,* the codification of Roman Law that had been brought into being by order of the emperor Justinian in the Eastern Empire in the sixth century, chiefly through the labors of Trebonian, the greatest legal scholar of his day. Copies of the *Corpus* were not difficult to come by, and once the revival of towns and cities in the West again permitted the growth of an intellectual class, largely resident in the universities burgeoning all over the West, it was not long before the study of Roman Law began to match in intensity the study of theology, canon law, and medicine.

The largest impact of the principles of Roman Law following its revival came on the Continent. The exact degree of influence of this law on English polity is still a matter of dispute. Once it was thought that Roman Law had had no effect at all upon English legal and political institutions. That extreme view has, however, been put to rest. It would be extraordinary indeed, given the constant mobility of scholars, legists, and others throughout the Middle Ages, if ideas popular on one side of the Channel had not somehow reached the other side. Yet, without question, it was on the Continent, and above all in Italy, at Bologna, that the study of Roman Law produced a large number of minds deeply consecrated to the special perspectives of the *Corpus Juris Civilis.*

Such minds were bound to make their way to positions in politics and business where their knowledge could in time be put to practical, eventually military and revolutionary uses. No social order, however organic and well-articulated it may be, is ever free of elements—oftentimes generated and nurtured by that social order—which by their very function militate against it. The pluralism, localism, regionalism of the Middle Ages, together with the almost total lack of the idea of secular sovereignty and its correlates, constituted anything but the kind of society in which Roman Law had germinated in the first place—that is, imperial Rome with its military centralization of power vested in the emperor. How, then, could there not have been deep conflict in the Middle Ages between, on the one hand, the large body of customs and traditions which surrounded the major institutions of the time and, on the other, a body of principle which could only find this body of customs and traditions repugnant in the extreme, offensive to the profound rationalism and symmetry which are the hallmarks of the Roman code?

Fundamental to Roman Law is the idea of the *sovereign*, the being held to be the sole source of genuine or legitimate law and, by that token, superior to the law. Clearly there is a strong element of potential revolution in the idea of sovereignty when it erupts within a social order that has no clear conception of sovereignty or of the centralization that goes with it; once accepted, the idea of sovereignty stands as an inevitable threat to the medieval kind of pluralism. No legal understanding was more widespread in the medieval period than that which declared the ruler to be *under* the law. The Romanist idea of power, broadcast throughout the West, was a tempting weapon indeed to all those—emperor, king, prince—who were eager to enhance their power over those immemorially protected from such a doctrine by medieval custom and writ.

The second important principle was Roman Law's notable doctrine of *concession*, under which no group or association, however deeply rooted in history and tradition, however profoundly structured in human allegiances, could claim to have legal existence, legal reality indeed, except insofar as this existence and reality had been conceded by the sovereign. Clearly the effect of this principle was to make precarious the existence of all those intermediate associations and communities which had been the very substance of medieval society. A great deal of modern political centralization in the West is the consequence of application of the Roman Law idea of concession to those social unities—guilds, village communities, monasteries, and other groups—which stood between the king or other sovereign and the mass of individuals claimed as subjects.

The third principle emphasized by Roman Law was *contract*, found primarily of course in the economic and civil sections of the

Roman Law texts. It rests upon the fiction set forth by the Roman lawyers from earlier times in the Empire that the whole of government, including its most stringent powers over individuals, is the product of an aboriginal contract between the people and their ruler. As eventually cast into natural law terms, this idea was to become a potent influence on the theory of the Western state in the seventeenth and eighteenth centuries.

But what I am concerned with here is not so much this aboriginal notion of contract as the highly concrete and substantive ideas on contract in Roman Law which affect the interpersonal relations among citizens. The Roman doctrine of contract says that no relationship among individuals, however ancient, however sacred in tradition, however useful, can claim the sanction of the state unless it is shown to have emanated from the willing assent of free actors. The essence of the doctrine was emphasis not so much upon written instruments as upon the highly individualistic idea of volition and will.

Now the overwhelming number of medieval relationships were founded in status rather than contract; in ascribed traits arising from age, sex, and ethnicity; in traditional arrangements which by their very nature could claim no origin in legal contract; and in the functional solidarities in which medieval society abounded. The Roman idea of contract was as foreign to the realities of medieval life as was the idea of the sovereign being above the law. How, then, could such a doctrine *not* have had a destructive effect upon all those communal, hereditary, and traditional relationships?

It would not be easy to enumerate the groups, guilds, and communities which, beginning about the fifteenth century, suffered dissolution and dismemberment through application of the Romanist principles of sovereignty and contract. Such entities had nothing but memory and tradition in most instances to vindicate their right to their being and their holdings, land included. Never mind the diverse motives behind enclosures and other acts of expropriation; these ranged from capitalist cupidity to political aggrandizement.

The important point is that such acts were legitimized, often even inspired, by principles of Roman Law. The historic passage of Europe from *Gemeinschaft* to *Gesellschaft* could never have taken place had it not been for instruments of law first fashioned in the imperial despotism that was Rome under the Caesars.

It is worth emphasizing that this change is first to be seen in the military in the late Middle Ages. Marx himself was struck by the fact that the earliest manifestation of the capitalist wage system lay in the kinds of military organization which succeeded the knighthood. The downfall of the traditional knighthood itself took place, as its historians have stressed, in the conversion from ties of fealty to those of, quite literally, cash. The first significant presence in the modern West of what Carlyle was later to refer to as "the cash nexus" occurs in the military. The model the military provided industry and state alike in its regimented masses of individuals, its use of barracks, its ingrained discipline, its secularism, and its whole envisagement of society as a kind of inverted pyramid of power was made all the easier to communicate by the residual concepts of Roman Law, a law admirably constructed for the purposes of military commander, despot, and industrial titan.

Further, I think it would be impossible to account for that whole distinctively Western—modern Western—idea that law, far from being simply a reflection of social reality, is a powerful means of *accomplishing* reality, that is, of fashioning, making it. As is well known, throughout history in all major areas known to us, civilized as well as primitive, law has for the most part been something that is either given directly by divine spirit or else has grown up over a long period through use and wont. The idea of actually creating a law, and with it a new form of social behavior, is a very recent one, with only a few exceptions in the past. The ancient Greek *polis* knew in some degree what it was to create law: that was the business of its government. Even there, however, the relationship between law and religion was close. Not really until the class of Roman jurists rose, to flourish as they never had before, did the conception of law as an instrument of social change become clearly conceptualized. The conversion of Rome from republic to empire could not have been accomplished except by means of explicit legal decree buttressed by the doctrine of imperial sovereignty.

This notion of positive, creative law faded with the Empire, to be succeeded—with only the rarest and faintest of exceptions—by the idea once again that law and tradition are inseparable, that law is never made, only discovered. The first great function, for example, of the English Parliament—and this was true of other parliaments in Europe in the Middle Ages—was judicial, not legislative. The assembled lords and masters were seeking to restrain royal prerogative through interpretation of laws which, it was believed, the king was obliged to respect once Parliament had made them evident. Parliament, in short, was basically a court. Only later did the idea of its actually creating laws become accepted and even then only hesitantly.

There have been periods of waxing and waning of the idea of prescriptive law, of using statutes to effect social, economic, and political changes. Even after the concept of prescriptive law was well known and utilized, judges, as we know, made tradition—above all, precedent—vital in the judgements they issued. The struggle between monarch and judiciary, between aggrandizing kings like Henry VIII and some of their judges—duty-bound, as they saw it, to respect the established law—makes a luminous chapter in the history of modern liberty. Without question, law can be even today a symbol of traditionalism rather than of social change, much less revolution.

Yet it is with a perception founded in part on historical awareness that today more and more individuals dedicated to social change are turning to the legal profession, properly seeing in law, prescribed law and interpreted law alike, a powerful weapon for accomplishing reforms and changes hardly short of revolutionary. Major ages of social change and mobility almost always involve great use of law and of litigation. In such ages ordinary customs and traditions either become dislodged by prescriptive law or else elevated to legal, sovereign status.

Above all other historical forces, the revival of Roman Law based on rationalism, calculated achievement of ends through volition, and charged with the vision of central power extending to all areas, is the real source of the strain of modernism which seeks constantly to make and remake the world around us. From the class of scholars steeped in the principles of Roman Law that assumed such intellectual prestige in the Europe of the late Middle Ages and was able to supply to princes and merchants alike indispensable principles of legitimacy for what interest impelled them to, down to the thousands of lawyers today who at times appear to wish to convert every ordinary relationship in the social order to a legal relationship, there is a straight path. Even in our day the Romanization of Western society proceeds apace.

The full significance of the Romanist stress upon the individual legal actor and upon individual volition, interest, and motivation, with society envisaged much less as community than as an aggregate of individuals bound together only by the ties of contract and by the will of the sovereign, goes well beyond the legal and political domains. It is hard not to conclude that a great deal of the stress we find in modern art, philosophy, and literature on the individual conceived as a discrete being, whether as hero or villain, man of faith or of reason, Apollonian or Dionysian, objective or subjective in disposition, springs from a social setting that has existed in the West since the waning of the Middle Ages, a setting in which individuals have in fact taken on increasing identity, in countless spheres, *as individuals*. We may not at first thought consider Roman Law a shaping force in the subjectivism that, allowing only for periods of waxing and waning, is so fixed a part of the Western mind. But Roman Law's stress upon will and volition, its emphasis upon a remote, aloof sovereign possessed of ultimate authority, and its envisagement of the social order as a kind of sand heap of legally discrete individual particles, is bound to give the individual mind a sense of separateness from social and moral tradition that is not to be found in, say, the common law.

There is another aspect of Roman Law that is pertinent to our time. It gives a primacy to the magistrate that is virtually unique in the world's law codes. In Roman Law and in codes founded upon Romanist values the judge holds a singular degree of authority. He is, in fact, more than judge in the ordinary common law sense; he is something of legislator, executive, monarch—conceived, in historical fact, much in the image of the Emperor. Interestingly, it was directly from Roman Law that Jeremy Bentham—who loathed the common law and, with it, the jury system—acquired his ideal of an all-powerful Magistrate ruling directly with the theoretical consent of the mass of people, with all intermediate bodies such as parliaments, assemblies, parties, and juries obliterated, and with no check upon him except his own understanding of the people's will and a scientifically contrived code of justice.

That Benthamite being has not yet come into existence in the Western nations, but few observers have missed the rising importance of judges, courts, and judicial decrees in the American political, social, and economic orders. Even today we tend to think instinctively of the judiciary as a check upon legislative and executive powers, and of course it is. But it has become more: something that falls between the executive and legislative branches, participating in some degree in each of these but possessed of a constitutional autonomy that allows it to exert itself without check save only that inherent in itself. Judicial is hardly the word for this new assertion of role.

I see nothing contradictory between this new (by traditional, common law standards) conception of law as a positive force in the remaking of the social order and a setting that is more and more dominated by the coercions and symbols of war, as is the case in contemporary Western society. The increasingly Romanist character of law and the judiciary in the United States, the spreading appeal it has to minds eager to indulge in permanent revolution without fear of reprisal, and the whole, fateful conversion of so many once-social or once-customary relationships to those now of over-whelmingly legalist character, all of this is a perfect accompaniment of the kind of society that the inherently dislocative impacts of war and the military bring about, and also the kind of corporatism that sustained military influence give to a society thereafter.

Rightly did students of Roman Law in the later Middle Ages see it as a lever with which to move vast areas of historically accumulated traditions and rights. Rightly did they see too the immense appeal this form of law would have to all military minds, to minds bent upon eradication of the customary and traditional and upon centralization of power. For it was in circumstances of war that Roman Law was born and has ever since flourished.

WAR AND THE INTELLECTUAL CLASS

From at least the time of the ancient Greek Sophists, there has been a striking affinity in the West between war, its symbols, roles, constraints, and objectives, and a substantial part of the intellectual class. I refer to those—artists, writers, philosophers, rhetoricians, teachers, and others—who are by nature or profession engaged seriously in what might be called the representation of society through idea and image. It is the common character of intellectuals to take what is at the least a detached view of the human condition, one that easily become a critical, even adversary stance. I do not say all intellectuals are critical or adversary. There are indeed conservative, traditionalist intellectuals.

By and large, though, it is the mark of the Western intellectual, and has been, as I say, at least since the Sophists, to take the role of teacher, critic, and polemicist, in some degree at least. There is commonly too a utopian element in the intellectual; I mean a vision of the good and an explicit contrast between this good and what lies around him in society. By nature concerned to render, through idea or image, the human condition, the intellectual is more given than most persons to an interest in the unusual, the striking, the dramatic; in change, tension, and conflict. He may seek, as did Plato, to end strife and disruptive change, to provide a vision of the timelessly good, true, and beautiful. He may, like Hobbes, reach in due time a solution involving almost total repression by the state. It does not matter. One does not have to be a revolutionary intellectual to be obliged, by the nature of one's role, to take a more than ordinary interest in all that breaks routine and dissolves tradition. It is worth noting that even Burke, generally regarded as the source of modern philosophical conservatism in politics, gave strong support to the cause of the American colonists, and also the causes of the Irish and the inhabitants of India in their relations with Great Britain.

An interest in war and in the uses of war and of the military is a vivid characteristic of the intellectual mind in Western history. So is an interest in politics and the uses of power for the achievement of moral ends. The state originated in circumstances of war and has never been very far from the planning or the execution of war. Politically minded intellectuals have been perforce military intellectuals in substantial degree, a fact sufficiently attested to by a long and imposing line of Western intellectuals that includes Plato, Machiavelli, Hobbes, Rousseau, and Marx. War, like revolution, is crisis, and crisis is always an opportunity for a break with the despised present, for liberation from the kinds of authority which are most repugnant to bold, creative, and utopian minds.

As one scans the works of the great political intellectuals, it is apparent that while none of them could be properly accused of warmongering, there is an abiding fascination with the kinds of leadership, heroism, and unity we are more likely to find in war than in peace. Few prescriptions by out-and-out militarists have exceeded Plato's *Republic* in devotion to military values, though it would be unfair to say that Plato loved war as such. Few intellectuals do. It is that they hate other things more: economic phenomena like profits, competition, and all the tensions and conflicts which threaten constantly to erupt from the marketplace. Economic values, so antagonistic, as I noted above, to heroism and great leadership, tend to be despised accordingly by writers, artists, and other intellectuals.

Most of the great military-political personages in Western history have surrounded themselves at one time or other with intellectuals, often to the considerable profit of their cultures. We may be certain that Aristotle was not the only philosopher close at one time to Alexander; earlier Plato had associated himself with Dionysius the Elder, military tyrant of Syracuse. Augustus, we learn, saw much of Rome's historians, philosophers, and rhetoricians. Charlemagne's court was resplendent with scholars, teachers, and artists. It is impossible to miss the intellectual cast of the courts of such notable military leaders as Frederick II, the divine right monarchs, or most of them, and Napoleon. In our day there is a high correlation between the appearances of war-presidents in the United States and the flocking to Washington of large numbers of intellectuals.

There is a natural crisis-mindedness, I think, among intellectuals generally; a fondness for the great changes and great decisions which the crisis of war makes possible. It is not that writers and artists and professors love the carnage of war, or even the military as such, though they seem to prefer the military to businessmen. It is simply that when it comes to a choice between the banality and anti-heroic nature of the marketplace and the heady opportunities of crisis, especially military crisis, the decision is not hard to make. Most certainly when there is an Augustus, Cromwell, Napoleon, Churchill, or FDR to serve!

It may fairly be said, I think, that the American intellectual's romance with war and with the kinds of structures and processes which attend war began under President Wilson in World War I. Being himself an academic man, Wilson had the fealty of the intellectuals, for the most part, from the beginning of his first term in office. But it was only when he made the fateful decision to plunge the United States into the war raging in Europe that his affinity with the intellectual and academic class reached its zenith. Wilson badly needed the assistance of the intellectuals, for opposition to American entry was formidable in almost all parts of the country. To have waged war with volunteers only, with business as usual at home, with the social and cultural pursuits of the American people untouched, was, as we know very well indeed today, utterly out of the question. If an army was to be manufactured for export to Europe in a war that a very large number of the American people considered none of America's business, then a new nation had to be manufactured: economically, politically, culturally, and, not least, psychologically. Elementary social psychology dictated that if war enthusiasm among Americans was to be generated, then a whole new set of mind must be created on a mass level. And if popular consciousness was to be transformed, there must be superbly articulated instruments fashioned for this herculean labor. Who but intellectuals could have fasioned, could have *become*, these instruments?

To this day I think few people, even American historians, have an adequate conception of what took place in the intellectual class, and between the intellectual class and the American public, from 1917 to about 1920. With but the rarest exceptions, *trahison des clercs* was the rule of the day. George Creel, one of the most gifted architects of propaganda, of manufacture of public consciousness, that has ever lived, was put in charge of mobilizing artists, writers, actors, musicians, and scholars. The bond between Creel and Wilson was almost absolute; there is no record of Wilson's ever questioning, much less reproving, any of Creel's extraordinary invasions of civic morality. And overwhelmingly the intellectuals—novelists, poets, musical composers, dramatists, performers, clergymen, and, well toward the front, university and college professors—allowed themselves to be, nay, demanded to be, willing manipulators of the public mind. In America, not Russia or Germany, were first to be seen "artists in uniform."

With the enthusiastic compliance of intellectuals, indeed with their leadership, nearly a hundred thousand "Four Minute Men" were organized; their job was to infiltrate every public gathering of any kind with the objective of delivering four-minute speeches in celebration of the war, the Allies, and, far from least, Woodrow Wilson himself. Their canned speeches, filled with references to traitors and enemies of the sacred war effort, to cowards, draft-dodgers, and wearers of the white feather, as well as to those making the supreme sacrifice, could be counted upon, as time passed, to generate a whole spectrum of home-front atrocities that ranged from the excision in public libraries of stories and songs composed by Germans all the way to the public pillorying of those with German names or family ties in Germany.

Helping to supervise or otherwise engage in this vast propaganda enterprise with its frequent uses of intellectual and moral, if not physical, terror, were artists of such national fame as Charles Dana Gibson, Montgomery Flagg, and Joseph Pennell; such writers as Booth Tarkington, Saumel Hopkins Adams, Mary Roberts Rinehart, and Ernest Poole. Historians of the stature of Guy Stanton Ford, Stuart P. Sherman, Carl Becker, and Frederick Paxson also wore the invisible uniform of war.

There were performers galore: musicians, actors, comedians, singers of every kind, mobilized to whip up through ballad, jingle, and anthem hatred of the enemy and of the home-grown isolationist or pacifist. The motion picture industry was of course taken into tow. The pulpit became ferocious in its militance.

Nothing like this mobilizing of intellectuals and artists for national war purposes had ever been known before—anywhere in the entire Western world. I am not suggesting that European intellectuals did not rally to the support of England, France, and Germany. But the spur of the war was sufficient there—together with the memory of old nationalist hatreds. The United States, however, was thousands of miles distant; it had prided itself for generations on its isolation from the antagonisms of the old world; and a very large majority of the American people was all too clearly opposed to America's entrance right up until 1916. Indeed Wilson was reelected on the campaign slogan "He Kept Us Out of the War." For America to have moved from a position of isolationist pacifism so suddenly to the kind of passionate intensity of collective purpose that was so evident by 1917 can be explained only by, first, devotion of a great many intellectuals and artists themselves to war and, second, by their unique capacity for whipping up similar devotion on the part of ever larger aggregates of the population.

Again it is necessary to emphasize that such passion and devotion to the war did not arise from any perverse love of carnage and devastation. That President Wilson's academic-intellectual articulation of war aims would be attractive to intellectuals goes without saying. No modern political leader in the West has matched Wilson's command of abstractions in public oratory and in crucial documents, or his genius for making familiar words and their sounds convey meanings that would only be assimilated by public consciousness after it was too late.

World War I was America's first plunge into a form of socialism or near-socialism (or, as many astute and informed minds came to realize later, after the word had become available through Mussolini's Italy, Fascism or near-Fascism), and it may be assumed that opportunities were abundant for intellectuals. Wages, prices, profits were controlled by the national government for the first time in history. Mines, railroads, and other great industries were taken over by the Federal government; so were the telephone and telegraph, and, far from least, the use of the Atlantic cables. Workers' councils came into being in many large industries; for the first time in many areas rigid controls were set up affecting hours, wages, and working conditions, but also the freedom to strike, even to organize in traditional ways. World War I was, in every sense of the word, a crusade, and in many ways its least important aspect was the actual war in Europe, except insofar as it supplied the motive power, the organizing myth, for the far more intoxicating crusade at home; one in which old social roles, traditional social authorities, and accustomed autonomies and immunities were in large measure slipped off for the duration and new, much more exciting roles and collective participations were adopted—for the duration in theory, but for a much longer time, as it transpired, in memory and nostalgia.

To be sure there was a price of sorts to be paid for this heady spirit of socialism in the intellectuals' America. There was the frightening spirit of repression that sprang up in many parts of America. Under the sedition act that was passed, nearly 1600 persons were arrested for what was no more than exercise of free speech; many thousands more were certainly restrained from free speech by this act and fear of imprisonment. Not all of our intellectuals (only the great majority) gave themselves to the war, and there was a small minority that suffered substantially—oftener from erstwhile intellectual friends now at war, we read in memoirs, than from police or judiciary. Eugene Debs, very probably the greatest labor leader in our history, went to prison for his refusal to support the war, and such was the bitterness on Wilson's part— and on the part of a good many close to Wilson—that he steadfastly refused clemency of any kind for Debs and the other opponents of the war after the Armistice came. It was left to the Republican Warren G. Harding to pardon Debs and most of the others who had been convicted under America's first national sedition act.

And of course there was the draft! Not for a moment did Wilson and his close advisers think to depend upon any voluntary system. We learn that detailed draft plans had been prepared, and dispatched in strictest confidence to state and municipal governments, even before America's official entry into the war. "Draft-dodger" became as feared an epithet in this country—and for the first time in our history—as "pro-German." Every possible effort was made to strike fear into the hearts of the large number of Americans who had opposed, and in their minds continued to oppose, American participation in the European war across the Atlantic. It has been estimated that around 175,000 men were arrested and disciplined, often by jail sentences, invariably by a whipped-up public scorn that could ruin business careers and family lives.

I believe it no exaggeration to say that the West's first real experience with totalitarianism—political absolutism extended into every possible area of culture and society, education, religion, industry, the arts, local community and family included, with a kind of terror always waiting in the wings—came with the American war state under Woodrow Wilson. That very substantial transformations of European states, on both sides of the war, took place is not to be doubted. But, as I say, in these there was the direct experience of the war to stimulate patriotic energies. Much was required in the United States, and supplied by intellectuals, to substitute for that directness.

Wilson was, of course, an almost perfect type to create the sense of war-crisis among American intellectuals. He was, after all, a scholar himself. Deeply, passionately, committed to whatever cause he took up, whether the reform of Princeton, the declaration of war on Mexico—which he characteristically saw as a protection less of American border interests than of mankind's conscience—or the cause of the Allies against Germany, he succeeded in infecting a whole generation of intellectuals with the sense of cause, of mission, in the moral sphere, to be accomplished only through the power of the national state he came close to worshipping. His hatred of those who opposed him in however small a degree was religious in intensity.

World War I influenced the American intellectual mind as no preceding war or major event ever had. We know how little impress the Civil War made, with rare exceptions, upon writers and artists and other intellectuals. For the national popular mind, it became almost obsessive; but writers seemingly were unable for the most part to assimilate war into their art forms, their styles and vocabularies. Very different in this respect was World War I. Almost from the beginning it permeated every crevice and corner of

American intellectual life; and this condition lasted for a full decade afterward.

So did World War I affect the minds of social reformers. A great deal of the spirit of localism, of grass roots, and of pluralism that had characterized so much American reform thought, ranging from anarchist utopianism to the special form of socialism that characterized, for example, Eugene Debs and the editors of *The Masses*, disappeared with the war. A very different spirit, rooted in the centralized power of the national government and which in a sense took war-society minus war as its ideal of planned economy, replaced the older one. It is easy to see this new intellectual pattern developing slowly through the 1920s.

It was, however, the Depression that led to a maturing and intensification of this spirit. "We planned in war" became a cherished rallying cry in the early 1930s. There is thus little wonder that when the New Deal began to take shape so much of its administrative shape resembled that which American society had known between 1916 and 1920. So many of the New Deal's boards and agencies were designed in the image of those which earlier had been part of the war effort. It was no doubt in perfect keeping with this that Hugh Johnson, who had presided over the military draft in World War I, should have been chosen by FDR to head the NRA, which, with its industry-dominated political councils given absolute power over prices, wages, and profits and its power to replace by administrative fiat all ordinary market mechanisms, was America's first experience with Fascism, though it was not seen in precisely that light by most liberals at the time; indeed when it was declared unconstitutional by the Supreme Court, most of the response of liberal intellectuals consisted of verbal assault on the Court and, then, an almost monolithic willingness to endorse FDR's effort to pack the Court.

To a large degree the so-called New Deal was no more than an assemblage of governmental structures modeled on those which had existed in 1917. The extraordinary likeness between the New

Deal, so far as governmental structures to combat depression were concerned, and Nazi Germany stems entirely from the fact that, ideology and spirit aside, each country was doing little more than drawing upon experiences it had known in World War I in order to combat the depression. And it has to be admitted that in the United States it was those aspects of the New Deal—NRA, AAA, PWA, and the CCC among them—with the most overtones of war-inspired militance, of centralization and collectivism, that clearly had the greatest attraction for our intellectual class. Anyone who today thinks the American nation in the 1930s did not make use of war symbolism during the largely unsuccessful effort of the New Deal to meet the depression, should go back to illustrated magazines of that time. In terms of frequency of use of such symbols by the national government not even Hitler's Germany outdid our propagandists. And in the universities and colleges still another large wave of social scientists formed a part of the tidal movement which, for want of a better phrase, can be called the "We Planned in War, Why Not Now?" crusade.

Add to the effects upon the American intellectual mind of World War I and the New Deal the World War that America entered in 1941, and it is evident enough why one does not need to scratch too deeply to find the military in a large section of our academic and other intellectuals today. If it is said that Marx has to one degree or other shaped the conscious mind of this class of intellectuals, I suggest that it is to a Jomini or Clausewitz that we should turn for the shaping of the unconscious mind in this class.

The novel effect of World War II was the creation of formal, official—and lasting!—union between the intellectual and the national government, at least when the latter could be thought of as in trustworthy hands, like Wilson's or FDR's. The liaison between the intellectual class and the national government to which we have by now become accustomed in this country had its major impetus from the experience that tens of thousands of academics and other intellectuals came to know and to cherish between 1941 and 1945.

The marriage of university and government took place then; the Manhattan District that produced the atom bomb was but the most sensational result. (Interestingly, I felt more of a martial atmosphere, more pressure of war-values, while on the faculty at Berkeley from 1939 to 1942 then I was to feel during the next three years out in the Pacific as an enlisted soldier. Even the appalling act of expropriating, exiling, and interning tens of thousands of Japanese-American citizens did not raise a liberal-intellectual hackle anywhere.)

The Cold War followed World War II, and the marriage between intellectuals and national government became a firm tie. Now an even larger number of scholars and scientists became involved in projects under the grant system which were funded not only by the Federal government but, in a large number of cases, by the Pentagon, AEC, CIA, and other war-related agencies. It was a lonely scientist, physical or social, who did not have, in the late 1940s, the 1950s, and the early part of the 1960s, a Federal—commonly military-sponsored—grant for his research. One does not like to think of the number of faculty members in the top universities for whom regular, and often confidential, trips to Washington, D.C., for consulting at the Pentagon and its military analogues were common practice. Inevitably in the 1950s, academic consulting at Defense or State had much more prestige than at, say, Commerce or Labor.

There was thus really nothing astonishing about Project Camelot, which surfaced to Congressional and national attention in late 1965. The world was treated in grim detail to the clandestine operation that had been going on for two or three years, in which a substantial group of social scientists, nominally working for an institute in American University in Washington, D.C., were revealed to have been engaged in planning secret surveillance missions into foreign countries for the purpose of aiding the military in identifying revolutionary and counter-revolutionary elements in these countries. It was only when one of their number eventually fled the operation, turning over to friends in Chile—where Project Camelot was to have had its first rehearsal—the crucial details, that the whole matter was reported, first in a Washington newspaper, then officially through a series of Congressional hearings. Project Camelot, which had been funded from the start by the Department of the Army, suddenly came to a halt.

Two aspects of it stand out lastingly. There was the apparently widespread view among members of the project that the Army was an ideal instrument for bringing reform, humanitarianism, and democratic culture, to the underprivileged abroad. To be sure, these members were in historical step with their intellectual predecessors, from the Sophists down to a great many French and German socialists of the early twentieth century. Second, the outrage of the social science world, after Camelot had been publicized and ended, was directed far less toward either the Camelotians or the Army than it was toward the State Department under Dean Rusk for its efforts to prevent future Camelots.

Nor can we overlook the American war of ill-fame in Viet Nam when we think of the fondness of the intellectual for military pursuits. How else are we to account for entry into war without so much as a bow in the direction of Congress, without initiative or enthusiasm from the professional military, or for that matter from the old-line professional politicians in Congress, and least of all from the major economic interests? None of these issued the decisive counsel to President Kennedy that resulted in the dispatch of 16,000 uniformed soldiers to Saigon under a four-star general or the later counsel that led President Johnson to escalate that contingent to something of the order of a half-million soldiers. Nor did any of these groups plan the unseating of Diem in South Viet Nam, the act that made American participation irrevocable and which also had the enthusiastic support of intellectuals in this country at the time.

It is the intellectuals—the Hillsmans, Bundys, Ellsbergs, Rostows, Schlesingers, Rusks, and McNamaras, and so many others

like them, at all levels—that we see when we look at the precipita-
ting conditions of America's crusade in Viet Nam. Nor, of course,
can we omit the intellectuals who were not actually in the government writing memorandums in behalf of "piece meal" entry in the
fashion of an Ellsburg, but who, whether in the press or on television or in Rand-like "think-tanks" or university institutes ever in
search of funds, did their substantial share to either support war in
Viet Nam after 1960 or at least seek to dissolve opposition to it
from Congress, business, and most of the American middle class.
Think only of what David Halberstam and his fellow press-in-
tellectuals managed to accomplish along this line by virtue of their
boundless hatred of Diem and his government and their strategic
efforts in Saigon to improve our war-making.

All of this, that is, down to about 1964, after we had become
hopelessly committed (if only, as I say, by virtue of our planned
unseating of South Viet Nam's government in 1963) to the war. By
late 1964 the student riots had begun, the New Left was exerting
an almost magnetic effect upon old-line intellectuals, the war was
clearly unwinnable save by recourse to the unthinkable, the
country was deeply agitated, Kennedy—whom intellectuals had
loved above all White House predecessors—was gone, his royal
presence succeeded by President Johnson, and things were, in
short, generally in a mess. The result was foreseeable: intellectuals
began washing their hands of the Intellectuals' War by the hundreds, then thousands. The question, though, that has to be asked
is: would this hand-washing, this collective self-purification, ever
have taken place had there been no New left? I am wholly skeptical
that it would.

Why did sophisticated, graceful, brilliant, and press-pleasing
types such as those I have mentioned—the Bundys, Rostows,
Goodwins, Schlesingers, and McNamaras—put President Kennedy in the position of commencing war in Viet Nam, as earlier
they had helped involve him in the disaster at the Bays of Pigs and
then the deadly missile confrontation with Russia over Cuba? Be-

cause of ingrained love of combat and of the military as such? Hardly. This is but one more instance of the fondness of intellectuals for crisis which can be seen recurrently throughout Western history. The desire to be close to the seat of power, to seek with every means to expand that power, to make it as concentrated and personal as possible, and to extend it over as wide a field, domestic and foreign alike, as possible, was as strong in the Rome of Augustus as in the Washington of Kennedy. The deep dislike of the economic—not of great wealth (especially inherited wealth) but of the ordinary businessman's regard for profits, wages, and prices—can be justified and given practical effect by the use of power made immaculate through avoidance of such regard.

Above all, though, there is the intoxication of participating in great decisions—"eyeball to eyeball," as the now famous phrase had it in Kennedy's Washington—and of feeling free of all ordinary constraints of caution, convention, routine, and form. What I described earlier as the dislike of *forms* in modern democracy, a dislike that reached such dangerous intensity in Nixon's government, is easily exploited by those who do not actually hold power but sit at its right hand. What matters is "resolute action without fear of domestic upheaval," to use the phrase supplied wistfully by a young intellectual, Benjamin Stein, in a recent evocation of the Cuban missile crisis; he referred to his own sadness that "such decisive days may never come again."

Almost certainly, they will! The Age of Wars we live in, and have lived in since 1914 in the West, is scarcely over, and Presidents are beginning to discover that one of the necessities for maintaining the image of commanding leadership in high government officials is the presence of young intellectuals to provide brilliant rhetoric and constant encouragement. Even Nixon, as we know, turned almost instinctively to intellectuals when he entered the presidency in 1968.

If, as our experience with Viet Nam suggests, the political intellectual is rarely firm in his loyalties, seldom willing to live long with his own decisions and advice given, often much more interested in celebrity status than in his job, and a sayer rather than a doer—why this is a character that goes back at least to the Sophists.

There will always be intellectuals, from the academy, from institutes, foundations, and from freelance ranks, to take the places of those who may defect. If wars in the twentieth century have tended to become longer, more destructive, and more total in relation to the rest of society, not all the fault can be laid at military and political doors. Without slogans, manufactured ideals, the rhetoric of crisis, and, most important, the moralizing, rationalizing, and ideologizing mind of the intellectual in government, warfare in this century would surely have been very different.

THE IMAGE OF WAR SOCIETY

What is central, though, is not any historic affinity between the military and the intellectual classes, vital though the latter have been in shaping—often brilliantly, even profoundly—patterns of assimilation of war in the public mind. What is central is the image of war, and of the military, in a society that is beset by agonizing, even insoluble, economic problems, by boredom with normal cultural pursuits, and by alienation from the normal authorities of government and society.

That war is the hell—in direct battlefield experience, at least—its generals have so often declared it to be, that the military can be, has often been, the harshest of despotisms, goes without question. Man's war on man, killing, wounding, torturing, imprisoning, and devastating, is, as we know, a form of behavior unique to the human species, as is, indeed, man's war in one form or other upon other species. Even in the best light, war is man's greatest folly and also sin.

But it is also, on the evidence in the West for some three millennia and in other areas as well, one of man's most constant practices. It used to be said that democracy, and socialism, were the proper antidotes to war; each has in fact only made war a more massive enterprise on the planet, and also more sustained, intense, and imperious as a value. As I have stressed, it is in the context of political and economic socialism that our largest and most formidable military states are to be found today. The militarization of nations in this century is one of the clearest of international processes. Area after area of the earth's surface has fallen under forms of government which are military to the core, no matter what their ideological vestments may be. To suppose that this process will stop at the threshold of the West, or go no farther than it has already gone in the West, is to indulge in fantasy. One need but think of Greece, Chile, Cuba, and, as I write, Portugal—with the already-uttered prediction that what has started in Portugal will spread as a plague of red militarism all the way across the southern flank of Europe, with government after government taking recourse in armies and generals as a means of at one and the same time effecting revolution, or the illusion of revolution, and providing some kind of order, however harsh, where only the void is now to be perceived by a rising number of minds. I believe that only events presently unforeseeable in nature and scope—perhaps those constituting a major religious movement of worldwide proportions—could possibly arrest the present drive of militarism in the Western world or for that matter the world at large.

War and the military are, without question, among the very worst of the earth's afflictions, responsible for the majority of the torments, oppressions, tyrannies, and suffocations of thought the West has for long been exposed to. In military or war society anything resembling true freedom of thought, true individual initiative in the intellectual and cultural and economic areas, is made impossible—not only cut off when they threaten to appear but, worse, extinguished more or less at root. Between military and civil values there is, and always has been, relentless opposition. Nothing has proved more destructive of kinship, religion, and local patriotisms than has war and the accompanying military mind. Basic social institutions can, on the incontestable record, survive depression, plague, famine, and catastrophe. They have countless times in history. What these and related institutions cannot survive is the transfer of their inherent functions and authorities to a body such as the military, which has, as I have suggested in this chapter, its own dominant values, symbols, constraints, and processes of consensus.

Yet, evil as war and the military are as the pillars of society, there are, in ages of twilight such as our own, worse afflictions, at least in the imaginations of those who feel threatened by breakdown, corruption, moral erosion, and downright physical danger. War society, with its promised protection from these, its proffer of security to civil populations, its guise of revolutionary achievement, as in China, Russia, Cuba, and many another nation, its repudiation of all the economic and social values which have become repugnant to people under depression or inflation, its manifest means of relieving the terrible weight of boredom that modern democratic and industrial populations increasingly find themselves enduring, and, perhaps foremost, its sense of mission or crusade—can be, indeed already shows vivid signs of being, almost redemptive in appearance.

The proper image of war and of military society should never be an America in Viet Nam. That was, in the light of American history and its several wars, sheer aberration, so far as the relation between the war and the domestic population was concerned. The bumblings, downright stupidities, and miscalculations—which really began, as I have noted, in the Kennedy administration, to be greatly expanded, of course, in the Johnson presidency—coupled with the unalterable logistical nightmares and unprecedented exposure to the spotlights and floodlights of the media which attended this unhappy military adventure are not likely to be repeated. Nor is the confluence of revolutionary agitation by a segment of youth on the campus, a major civil rights thrust by a large minority, and a given war—all of these within the same decade —likely to again occur.

The proper image of war, of military, and of war society should be, by all that is attested to in our two hundred years of history, an American war of independence from England, a Civil War, a Spanish-American war (one of America's all-time great national thrills!), a world war for democracy or a world war against fascism. Or, for present purposes, the war of a courageous, beleaguered, American-supported Israel.

If our problem were *only* a world scene increasingly dominated by the military socialisms or *only* a domestic setting of combined political centralization and social erosion, there would be reason for doubting that America will, like other Western nations, turn increasingly to a variant of the war state. But the fact is, *both* of those conditions are present, and in mounting intensity, and against them any thought of arresting or reversing the processes of militarization of society seems rather absurd. The industrial-academic-labor-military complex President Eisenhower referred to in his farewell remarks has become vastly greater since his presidency, and the military's ascendancy in this complex becomes greater all the time, though not, as I have noted, without much assistance from each of the other elements.

THE NEW SCIENCE
OF DESPOTISM

WHEN THE MODERN political community was being shaped at the end of the eighteenth century, it was thought by its founders that the consequences of republican or representative institutions in government would be the *reduction* of political power in individual lives. Nothing seems to have mattered more to such minds as Montesquieu, Turgot, and Burke in Europe and to Adams, Jefferson, and Franklin in this country than the expansion of freedom in the day-to-day existence of human beings, irrespective of class, occupation, or belief. Hence the elaborate, carefully contrived provisions of constitution or law whereby formal government would be checked, limited, and given root in the smallest possible assemblies of the people. The kind of arbitrary power Burke so detested and referred to almost constantly in his attacks upon the British government in its relation to the American colonists and the people of India and Ireland, and upon the French government during the Revolution, was foremost in the minds of all the architects of the political community, and they thought it could be eliminated, or reduced to insignificance, by ample use of legislative and judicial machinery.

What we have witnessed, however, in every Western country, and not least in the United States, is the almost incessant growth in power over the lives of human beings—power that is basically the result of the gradual disappearance of all the intermediate institutions which, coming from the pre-democratic past, served for a long time to check the kind of authority that almost from the beginning sprang from the new legislative bodies and executives in the modern democracies. The eighteenth-century hope that people, by their direct participation in government, through voting and of-fice-holding, would be correspondingly loath to see political power grow, has been proved wrong. Nothing seems so calculated to ex-pand and intensify the power of the state as the expansion of elec-torates and the general popularization of the uses of power.

Even so, I do not think we can properly explain the immense power that exists in modern democracies by reference solely to the enlargement of the base of government or to the kinds of parlia-ments Sir Henry Maine warned against in his *Popular Government*. Had political power remained *visible*, as it largely did down until about World War I, and the manifest function of legislature and ex-ecutive, the matter would be very different. What has in fact hap-pened during the past half century is that the bulk of power in our society, as it affects our intellectual, economic, social, and cultural existences, has become largely *invisible*, a function of the vast in-fragovernment composed of bureaucracy's commissions, agencies, and departments in a myriad of areas. And the reason this power is so commonly invisible to the eye is that it lies concealed under the humane purposes which have brought it into existence.

The greatest single revolution of the last century in the political sphere has been the transfer of effective power in human lives from the constitutionally visible offices of government, the nominally sovereign offices, to the vast network of power that has been brought into being in the name of protection of the people from their exploiters. It is this kind of power that Justice Brandeis warned against in a decision nearly half a century ago: "Experience should teach us to be most on guard to protect liberty when the Government's purposes are beneficent. Men born to freedom are naturally alert to repel invasion of their liberty by evil-minded rulers. The greatest dangers to libery lurk in insidious encroachments by men of zeal, well-meaning but without understanding."

What gives the new despotism its peculiar effectiveness is indeed its liaison with humanitarianism, but beyond this fact is its capacity for entering into the smallest details of human life. The most absolute authority, wrote Rousseau, "is that which penetrates into a man's inmost being and concerns itself no less with his will than with his actions." The truth of that observation is in no way lessened by the fact that for Rousseau genuinely legitimate government, government based upon the general will, *should* so penetrate. Rousseau saw correctly that the kind of power traditionally exercised by kings and princes, represented chiefly by the tax collector and the military, was in fact a very weak kind of power compared with what a philosophy of government resting on the general will could bring about. Tocqueville, from a vastly different philosophy of the state, also took note of the kind of power Rousseau described. "It must not be forgotten that it is especially dangerous to enslave men in the minor details of life. For my own part I should be inclined to think freedom less necessary in the great things than in the little ones, if it were possible to be secure of the one without the other."

Congresses and legislatures pass laws, executives enforce them, and the courts interpret them. These, as I have said, are the bodies on which the attentions of the Founding Fathers were fixed. They are the visible organs of government to this day, the objects of constant reporting in the media. And I would not question the capacity of each of them to interfere substantially with individual freedom. But of far greater importance in the realm of freedom is that invisible government created in the first instance by legislature and executive but rendered in due time largely autonomous, often nearly impervious to the will of elected constitutional bodies. In ways too numerous even to try to list, the invisible government, composed of commissions, bureaus, and regulatory agencies of every imaginable kind, enters daily into what Tocqueville calls "the minor details of life."

Murray Weidenbaum, in an important study of this invisible government, *Government Mandated Price Increases*, has correctly referred to "a second managerial revolution" that is now well under way in American society. The first managerial revolution, described originally by Berle and Means in their classic *The Modern Corporation and Private Property* and given explicit identity by James Burnham, concerned, as Weidenbaum points out, the separation of management from formal ownership in the modern corporation. The second managerial revolution is very different. "This time," writes Weidenbaum, "the shift is from the professional management selected by the corporation's board of directors to the vast cadre of government regulators that influences and often controls the key decisions of the typical business firm." Weidenbaum concerns himself almost entirely with the business sector—pointing out incidentally that this whole cadre of regulation is a by now deeply embedded cause of inflation—but the point he makes is just as applicable to other, non-business areas of society.

In the name of education, welfare, taxation, safety, health, and environment, to mention but a few of the laudable ends involved, the new despotism confronts us at every turn. Its effectiveness lies, as I say, in part through liaison with humanitarian rather than nakedly exploitative objectives but also, and perhaps most significantly, in its capacity to deal with the human will rather than with mere human actions. By the very existence of one or other of the regulatory offices of the invisible government that now occupies foremost place, the wills of educators, researchers, artists, philanthropists, and enterprisers in all areas, as well as in business, are bound to be affected: to be shaped, bent, driven, even extinguished.

Of all the social or moral objectives, however, which are the taking-off points of the new despotism in our time, there is one that stands out clearly, that has widest possible appeal, and that at the present time undoubtedly represents the greatest single threat to liberty and social initiative. I refer to equality, or more accurately to the New Equality.

THE NEW EQUALITY

"The foremost or indeed the sole condition required in order to succeed in centralizing the supreme power in a democratic community is to love equality or to get men to believe you love it. Thus, the science of despotism, which was once so complex, has been simplified and reduced, as it were, to a single principle."

The words are Tocqueville's, toward the end of *Democracy in America,* in partial summary of the central thesis of that book, which is the affinity between centralization of power and mass equalitarianism. Tocqueville yielded to no one in his appreciation of equality before the law and equality of opportunity. Each of these, he thought, was vital to a creative society and a free state. It was Tocqueville's genius, however, to see the large possibility of the growth in the national state of another kind of equality, more akin to the kind of leveling that war and centralization bring to a social order. It is only in our time that his words have become analytic and descriptive rather than prophetic.

Side by side with militarism as a force and pattern of authority in the present age is the New Equality and all that it signifies in the way of centralized, collective power. There is indeed a great deal in common between military collectivism and the kind of society that must be the certain result of the doctrines of the New Equalitarians, whose aim is not mere increase in equality before the law, or in equality of opportunity. In fact those two historic types of equality loom as obstacles to the kind of equality that is desired: *equality of condition, equality of result.* There is nothing paradoxical in the fondness of equalitarians for centralized power, the kind that the military best evidences, and the fondness of centralizers for equality. The latter, whatever else it may signify, means the absence of the kinds of centers of authority and rank which are always dangerous to despotic governments.

Equality of condition or result is one thing when it is set in the utopian community, the commune, or the monastery. The Benedictine Rule is as good a guide as we need for the administration of this kind of equalitarian order, small enough, personal enough to prevent the dogma of equality from extinguishing normal diversity of strength and talent. For countless centuries, everywhere in the world, religion and kinship have been contexts of this kind of equality; they still are in theme.

Equality of result is a very different thing, however, when it becomes the guiding policy of the kind of national state that exists in the West today—founded in war and bureaucracy, its power strengthened by these forces throughout modern history, and dependent from the beginning upon a degree of leveling of the population. We may have in mind the ideal of equality that the monastery or family represents, but what we will get in actual fact in the modern state is the kind of equality that goes with uniformity and homogeneity—above all, with war society.

Tocqueville was by no means alone in his perception of the affinity between equality and power. At the very end of the eighteenth century Edmund Burke had written, in *Reflections on the Revolution in France*, of the passion for leveling that exists in the militant and the military. Those, he wrote, "who attempt to level, never equalize." The French Revolution, Burke believed, correctly was different from any revolution that had ever taken place before. And the reason for this difference lay in its combination of eradication of social diversity on the one hand and, on the other, the relentless increase of military-political power that expressed itself in the time-worn fashion of such power. All that tended toward the destruction of the intermediate authorities of social class, province, church, and family brought simultaneously into being, Burke noted, a social leveling and a transfer to the state alone of powers previously resident in a plurality of associations. "Everything depends upon the army in such a government as yours," he wrote; "for you have industriously destroyed all the opinions and prejudices, and, as far as in you lay, all the instincts which support government." In words prophetic indeed, since they were written in 1790, Burke further declared that the crisis inherent in "military democracy" could only be resolved by the rise of "some popular general who understands the art of conciliating the soldiery, and who possesses the true spirit of command." Such an individual "shall draw the eyes of all men upon himself."

The theme of military democracy, of the union of military and social equality, was strong in certain nineteenth-century critics. We see it in some of Burckhardt's writings, where he refers to the future rise of "military commandos" in circumstances of rampant equality. We see it, perhaps most profoundly, in James Fitzjames Stephen's *Liberty, Equality and Fraternity*, though what is most evident in that remarkable work is much less the military, save by implication, than the implacable conflict Stephen could see between equality and liberty. There were others—Henry Adams in America, Taine in France, Nietzsche in Germany—who called attention to the problem equality creates for liberty in the modern democratic state. Nor were such perceptions confined to the pessimists. Socialists such as Jaurès in France saw in the citizen army, based upon universal conscription, an admirable means of instilling in Frenchmen greater love for equality than for the liberty associated with capitalist society.

It is evident in our day how much more of a force the ethic of equality has become since these nineteenth-century prophecies and prescriptions were uttered. Two world wars and a major depression have advanced bureaucracy and its inherent regimentations to a point where the ideology of equality becomes more and more a means of rationalizing these regimentations and less and less a force serving individual life or liberty.

No one will question seriously the fact that a higher degree of equality now exists in Western countries than at any time in the past. This is true not only of equality of opportunity and legal equality, each of which became a burning issue by the early nineteenth century, but of the more generalized equality of economic, political, and social condition. It is result, not opportunity, that is today the central perspective in equalitarianism; and that ideological fact is itself part of the larger reality of extraordinary achievement of equality of condition or result, at least by the standard given us by history. Nor is there anything strange in the intensification of equalitarianism in such an age as ours, for, on the evidence of the history of social movements, powerful agitation in behalf of some social or moral value comes only when the surrounding social order can be seen to reflect that value in at least some degree, commonly only recently accomplished.

Equality has the great advantage of being able to draw upon both religious and political energies. It is only in the religious and political realms indeed that the cry for equality has been heard historically—much more often in the former than the latter, prior to the Age of the French Revolution. Whatever else equality is, it is a spiritual dynamic. Major social movements require such a dynamic, irrespective of whether they are primarily religious or political at the core. It is not as much the surrounding material conditions as it is this inner spiritual dynamic that in the long run determines, though by means which are complex and still inadequately understood, what the outcome of an issue will be. I think it would be hard to exaggerate the potential spiritual dynamic that lies in the idea of equality at the present time. One would have to go back to certain other ages, such as imperial Rome, in which

Christianity was generated as a major historical force, or Western Europe of the Reformation, to find a theme endowed with as much unifying, mobilizing power, especially among intellectuals, as the idea of equality carries now.

Equality has a built-in revolutionary force lacking in such ideas as justice or liberty. For once the ideal of equality becomes uppermost it can become insatiable in its demands. It is possible to conceive of human beings conceding that they have enough freedom or justice in a social order; it is not possible to imagine them ever declaring they have enough equality—once, that is, equality becomes a cornerstone of national policy. In this respect it resembles some of the religious ideals or passions which offer, just by virtue of the impossibility of ever giving them adequate representation in the actual world, almost unlimited potentialities for continuous onslaught against institutions.

Affluence is a fertile ground for the spread of equalitarian philosophy. What I referred to earlier as the pains of affluence manifestly include in our age the pain of guilt over the existence of any and all inequalities. It is not enough, as we have been discovering, to create equality before the law—at least to the degree that this is ever possible—and to seek to create equality of opportunity. Vast systems labeled Affirmative Action or Open Admissions must be instituted. And then, predictably, it is discovered that even these are not enough.

The reason for this is plain enough. Equality feeds on itself as no other single social value does. It is not long before it becomes more than a value. It takes on, as I have suggested, all the overtones of redemptiveness and becomes a religious rather than a secular idea.

Like other historic religious ideas, and also ideas of political character, equality has an inherent drive that carries it well beyond national boundaries. The proper abode of equality, like any other redemptive idea, is all mankind,' not simply this or that parochial community. We are already in the presence of this universalizing state of mind in discussions of equality. It is not enough that classes and groups in the United States, or in the West, should become equal. The entire world, especially the Third World, must be brought in. Yet simple arithmetic suffices to prove the impossibility of either the United States or the West extending its resources to this Third World—particularly in light of the population increases which would become inexorable and, also, the present spread in these countries of an ideology, Russian or Chinese in source, that, as the present record makes only too clear, reduces what productive power is presently in existence.

But it is the nature of providential ideas like equality that they are stayed by neither fact nor logic. They acquire a momentum of their own, and I can think of few things more probable than the spread of equalitarianism in the West—not despite but because of its manifest irrationality as the sovereign objective of national and world policy.

EQUALITY AND POWER

The significance of equalitarianism in our day is made all the greater by the profound affinity that exists, and has existed for many centuries, between equality and the distinctive nature of the Western state from the time of the Cleisthenean reforms at the end of the sixth century B.C. Those revolutionary changes put an end to the inequalities of traditional kinship society in Athens and ushered in the *polis*. Excepting only, as we are obliged to here, the class of slaves, a high degree of equality was instituted among the Athenian citizens. This equality was, of course, in part a function of the central power that was also inaugurated in the *polis*, a power that cut, often destructively, through all the intermediate loyalties which had been handed down from the most ancient times. Athenian equality, in sum, is comprehensible only in light of the leveling which resulted from political extermination of the traditional kinship diversity of Athenian society.

Neither Plato nor Aristotle liked equalitarianism, though there is assuredly an equality of sorts within the class of guardians that Plato creates to govern his utopian Republic. But like it or not, both Plato and Aristotle perforce gave equality a higher place than could be imagined in the minds of earlier Greek thinkers such as Heraclitus or statesmen such as Solon. Aristotle, who disliked intensely Platonic communism, nevertheless thought that a substantial degree of equality of wealth was a prerequisite for political stability.

With rare exceptions, the Western philosophy of the political state has carried from that time to ours an imposing emphasis on the desirability of equality. The reason for this lies, in the first instance, in the nature of the power that has gone with the Western state since the Greeks. This power—sovereignty, as it is commonly called—seeks to go directly to the individual. The great difference between the Western state diring the past twenty-five hundred years and the traditional states of Asia—as Karl Marx was one of the first to note—lies in the contrasting relation they have to the individual. In China, India, and other Eastern societies prior to the present century, governments reigned, as it were, but did not rule. Their claimed powers were at times certainly as centralized and bureaucratized as anything to be found in the West, but these powers almost never touched individual lives directly. Between the power of the government and the life of the individual lay strata of membership and authority—clan, village, caste, temple—which were almost never penetrated by the ruler or his bureaucracy. It was possible, in short, for the Asiatic state to exist for thousands of years in the presence of, as a superstructure of, a nonpolitical society founded on kinship and locality that was the real center of human life in matters of authority, function, and responsibility.

Very different has been the Western state. Omitting only the Middle Ages—and even then the *idea* of the centralized state remained vivid to those acquainted with Greek and Latin—the Western structure of political power has been a process of almost permanent revolution against the social groups and authorities which lay intermediate between individual and state. By virtue of its inherent centralization, its definition in terms of territory rather than social or religious function, its prized doctrine of sovereignty through which the state's power is declared superior and supervening to all other powers, the Western state's very existence in the ancient world and in the modern since the Reformation has represented a kind of built-in war against traditional society and its ingrained authorities.

In its struggle for individual allegiance the Western state has, in a very real sense, actually manufactured individualism. It has done this not merely as a result of the negative attitude political rulers since Cleisthenes have taken toward social, religious, and economic groups which seemed to be competing with the state, but, perhaps more crucially, in the positive creation of individual rights, freedoms, and benefits. Say what one will of the unique power of the state and of its all-too familiar capacity for extending this power bureaucratically into the lives of countless human beings, creating coercions and invasions of autonomy all the way, the fact remains that the central power of the state has also been associated with some resplendent gains in liberty and welfare. It is no exaggeration to say that from the time of Pericles, through Alexander the Great, the Caesars, and down to the Cromwells and Napoleons of modern history and also the more centralizing of American presidents from Jackson to Lyndon Johnson, a great many such gains have come directly from the use of central power. It was after all the central power of the American government, not the local or regional powers of communities and states, that brought about first the abolition of slavery in the United States and then, slowly but surely, increased civil rights for blacks and other minorities.

It is for this reason, no doubt, that the state in the West has attracted to itself what can only be called a clerisy of power. I refer to the long succession of philosophers and intellectuals from Greek and Roman times to our own who have made the political state the temple, so to speak, of their devotion. Religion is the only other value system that has had its clerisy—older than the political clerisy but, in modern Western civilization, possessed of much less power and influence. No other institution comes to mind that has won itself a clerisy as have religion and politics. Not until the early nineteenth century did economists come into existence in their own right, and it is hard to find in economic writings any of the sense of redemptive passion that is so common in religious and political works. It is possible, though I am skeptical, that technology today has a clerisy in the sense in which I use the word here. There is surely no other.

Through most of the history of Western civilization the political clerisy has given itself to the needs and values of the state just as its great rival, the religious clerisy, has to those of the church. Each clerisy has produced its titans—St. Augustine, Aquinas, Luther, on the one side; Plato, Hobbes, Rousseau, on the other—as well as its vast ranks of lesser minds, its ordinary intellectuals and technicians. The political state can be seen to be a temple in Rousseau quite as much as the church is a temple in Augustine.

Not surprisingly, there are close similarities of dogma and concept. After all, the rise of Christianity, like that of each of the other world religions, was set in historical circumstances which also produced a great political structure, the Roman Empire. State, like universal church, had an abstracting, generalizing, and also individualizing effect upon human loyalties that had been for so long anchored in kinship, local, and caste contexts.

The basic perspectives are strikingly similar; in each an emphasis upon masses of legally (or religiously) equal individuals, all conceived as liberated from competing allegiances, all united in a collective crusade, or at least purpose, and all given unity by a sovereign, whether secular or sacred, or both. In the religious clerisy equality has perhaps more often been honored in the invisible than the visible community, but it is the nature of a world religion to set great store upon equality.

So is it also the nature of the political state, in the Western world at least, to effect a considerable degree of equality. I am well aware of the differences of estate, rank, and power which can accompany the Western state, in our time as in earlier ages, but the very fact that the Western state has sought to engage individual allegiances directly, to bring its power down to the level of the individual, cutting through intermediate strata, implies a leveling that forms the base for equalitarian impulses and movements. Roman Law established, as we know, different legal classes possessed of varying rights; but by virtue of its stress upon a single sovereign over the entire people, upon the idea of individual citizenship, upon contracts effected by individuals possessed of equal rights, and, not least, upon the ancillary status of all groups not of the state's making, Roman Law proved to be, in the ancient world and then in the modern after its revival in the medieval university and subsequent spread to other areas of society, a powerful force for equality.

Without exception the major political philosophers, from medieval times on, have projected a high degree of equality in their ideal states, certainly as assessed by the criteria of their respective ages. We may not think equality the outstanding attribute of Dante's *De Monarchia* or even of Hobbes' *Leviathan* a few centuries later, but as compared with the signal inequalities which existed in the social orders around them, especially Dante's, the emphasis upon equality, or at least equity, is impressive.

After Hobbes, the value of equality became, along with freedom, the great preoccupation of the political clerisy. In the eighteenth century equality was a burning issue, nowhere more spectacularly than in the writings of Rousseau, the foremost political mind of his century. Rousseau constructed a moralistic anthropology around equality in his second Discourse; a counter-cultural attack in the *Discourse on the Arts and Sciences;* and a whole social and political order rooted in the quest for equality in his *Social Contract.* To this moment Rousseau remains the greatest single theorist of equalitarianism the West has seen.

Always, however, whether in a Hobbes or a Rousseau, the idea or ideal of equality is made an adjunct of a highly centralized, collective system of power. The awful power that Hobbes gives to his Leviathan, as the only means of combating the forces of disintegration and anarchy which, Hobbes thought, dominate man's life outside Leviathan, has for its necessary consequence an elimination of all the differences and inequalities which compose the social order. The state for Hobbes is at bottom a kind of sandheap of absolutely equal particles given unity by the state's power alone.

Rousseau's famous doctrine of the General Will was oriented primarily toward achieving equality in the social order. In his first two Discourses Rousseau specifically declared inequality the primary cause of the corruption, duplicity, and tyranny which he made virtually synonymous with the *ancien régime*. Only, he thought, through the establishment of a nearly absolute equality—social and cultural as well as economic in its fundamentals—could the individual's freedom from social oppressions be secured. This in turn, as Rousseau realized full well, demanded the establishment of an absolute and pervading system of political power that would be rooted in the people, but the people conceived as having first become liberated from the corruptions of traditional society. That is the essence of the unique authority of the General Will, an authority vested equally in all citizens, but limitless in its scope.

It is, however, Tocqueville who, so far as I know, first made this relation between equality and power a principle not only of political sociology but of the philosophy of history. "In running over the pages of our history," Tocqueville writes in the Introduction of *Democracy in America*, "we shall scarcely find a single great event of the last seven hundred years that has not promoted equality of condition." The Crusades, the introduction of firearms, the rise of the infantry, the invention of movable type in printing, the Protestant Reformation, the opening of gates to the New World, all of these, Tocqueville noted, had been attended by a leveling of medieval ranks and a spreading equality of economic, political and intellectual condition.

But equality is only half the story that Tocqueville gives us, not only in *Democracy in America* but also in his classic study of the old regime and the French Revolution. The other half of the story is, of course, centralization of power. In the same Introduction he writes: "I perceive that we have destroyed those individual powers which were able, single-handed, to cope with tyranny; but it is the government alone that has inherited all the privileges of which families, guilds, and individuals have been deprived. . . ."

Centralization and equality: these are for Tocqueville the two dominant tendencies of modern Western history, with the relationship between them functional. All that has magnified equality of condition has necessarily tended to abolish or diminish the buffers to central power which are constituted by social classes, kindreds, guilds, and other groups whose virtual essence is hierarchy. As Tocqueville—and before him Burke—perceived, some degree of inequality is the very condition of the social bond. Variations among individuals, in strength, intelligence, age, aspiration, ability of whatever kind, and aptitude, will always tend toward the creation of inequality of result. Only through operation of a single, centralized structure of power that reaches all individuals in a community, that strives to obliterate all gradations of power, rank, and affluence not of this power's own making, can these variations and this inequality be moderated.

This is clearly the reason why all the great modern revolutions, with the single and mixed exception of the American, have presented the by now often described spectacle of enormous increases in governmental authority. Never mind the motivational value of the catchwords freedom and justice; the unfailing result of European revolutions, culminating in the Communist and Nazi revolutions of this century, has been immensely greater use of political power.

Not least of the reasons for this has been, of course, the role equalitarianism has played in these revolutions. For all European revolutions have been founded upon assault against the kinds of inequality which are the lineal products of the Middle Ages. The real issue was not capitalism but the lingering remnants of feudalism, even for the revolutions in this century which have taken place in the name of socialism. But the thrust toward equalitarianism inevitably led to a disintegration of old social unities, and only the power of the state was left to fill this vacuum.

The modern history of revolution is one, then, of combined intensification of power and freedom from the inequalities of feudalism, and this is nearly as true of the American Revolution as it is of the revolutions in Europe. Despite a myth of middle-class homogeneity in the American colonies, class differences were great, as were differences of legal and political right, and the war with England had the effect of loosing a great many of the tensions and conflicts which lay beneath the surface of the colonial life.

The conditions for the spread of equality as a motivating value have been very fertile during the past two or three centuries. Populations have grown hugely; local and regional boundaries have eroded away in large measure, thus exposing many inequalities which had been concealed behind these boundaries. Industrialism, with its own machine-based disciplines, has done much, as Marx realized more vividly than anyone before him had, to diminish inequalities, to concentrate them, as it were, into the single inequality between capitalist and worker. The immense spread of consumer goods, their cheapness of price, has also done much to bring about a generalized equality of patterns of living, at least as measured against earlier patterns in the West. And finally, as I have noted, there has been the incessant spread of centralized power, whether in the hands of king, military, or the people, during the past two centuries, to spread further equality by virtue of this power's destructive effects upon social and economic differentiation.

In one of his excellent essays, the British political scientist Kenneth R. Minogue refers to the "suffering-situations" which modern history so abundantly reveals. These either are in fact or can be rendered into a fairly widespread, standardized kind of situation calling for sudden and heroic action, invariably political action. I think inequality will prove to be the single greatest "suffering-situation" in our age. As one thinks of it, one sees that feudalism and capitalism were regarded in earlier times as suffering-situations by large numbers of intellectuals concerned with political power. The word "feudal" did not come into existence until the seventeenth century, and when it did it took on almost immediate pejorative significance. By almost all of the key minds of the seventeenth and eighteenth centuries, feudalism was regarded as infamous; its localisms, decentralizations, and divisions of power were made tantamount to anarchy and evil. We would not, surely, have seen the central power of the national state increase as greatly as it did in these two centuries had there not been something large and evil, by designation at least, for the state to cope with. The *philosophes*' notable liking for highly centralized political power had behind it in great part their loathing of everything that could be labeled feudal.

In the nineteenth century "capitalism" replaced feudalism as the important suffering-situation. Contemporary radicalism is to a great extent formed around hatred of capitalism, and while not all radicals, by any means, gravitate toward the national state as the means of redemption, we find just about all of them, save only some of the anarchists, profuse in their appreciation of revolutionary centralization of power. If any single thing identifies the modern radical mind, in Western and non-Western civilizations, it is the invariably negative reaction to private enterprise, profit, and competition. And just as the national state aggrandized itself in the seventeenth and eighteenth centuries at the expense of authorities which could be labeled feudal, so has the national state in the nineteenth and twentieth centuries further aggrandized itself, in powers claimed and set in bureaucracy, by virtue of the controls and restraints it has placed upon capitalist enterprise. That the controlling boards and agencies quickly become dominated by representatives of the very industries and channels of commerce they are supposed to regulate, leading to even greater exploitation of consumer and public, is a fact well attested by this time, but not one that ever enters the minds of legislators and others when some alleged suffering-situation leads to the creation of still another regulatory agency.

I am inclined to think that "capitalism" is in our time becoming as moribund, as archaic a term as "feudalism." What is surely succeeding these is "inequality," though there are some serious observers of the present scene who believe that "technology" comes very close in this respect. There is no doubt that the powers of government have become greatly increased in very recent years on the basis of undoubtedly well-intentioned proposals for the regulation of technology, which so many of poetic or romantic disposition have seen as suffocating to the human spirit. Even so, the evidence is clear, I think, that inequality is the great suffering-situation of the late twentieth century. In its name power will increase drastically; it already has!

THE SPIRIT OF ROUSSEAU

Something more must be said about the mind that above any other I can think of exerts profound influence upon the New Equalitarians in the present age. Rousseau is, as conservatives and anarchists alike came to realize in the early nineteenth century, the true founder of the special equalitarianism that is inherent in the modern centralized national state. He is, I believe, the single most radical political mind in the West after Plato—whom Rousseau adored and regarded as the first of his intellectual masters. Not even Marx exerts the kind of effect Rousseau has today upon the radical mind.

His influence is more than political in the ordinary sense. He is the real source of that subjectivism of political and social consciousness that has been growing steadily ever since the appearance of his major writings in the late eighteenth century. Not only in radical ideology but in large sectors of education, psychology, literature, philosophy, and the social sciences his distinctive blend of worship of self and of power conceived as community is only too apparent.

What gives Rousseau currency in so many areas of thought on man and the state is his extraordinary combination of individualism, emphasis upon the ego and its liberation from all social restraints, and power—the power that lies in the General Will. This is the will of the people, but only of a people that has been cleansed, so to speak, of all the corruptions and prejudices which lie in the historic social order. Equality is the very essence of Rousseau's political community; but it is the kind of equality that exists when every form of association and every social value that could possibly rival the General Will have been exterminated. Equality of result is the great and overarching aim of Rousseau's political writings. Freedom too, if we like; but, as nearly all commentators have stressed, Rousseau's is a very special kind of freedom which is virtually indistinguishable from the equalitarian political community. No one knew better than Rousseau the intensity of political power that would be required to create equality in the political order. It is in this light that one of the New Equalitarians, Christopher Jencks, writes in our day:

> If we want substantial redistribution we will not only have to politicize the question of income equality but alter people's basic assumptions about the extent to which they are responsible for their neighbors and their neighbors for them. . . . As long as egalitarians assume that public policy cannot contribute to economic equality directly but must proceed by ingenious manipulations of marginal institutions like the schools, progress will be glacial. If we want to move beyond this tradition, we will have to establish political control over the economic institutions that shape our society.

But in actuality such control will almost certainly have to go beyond strictly economic institutions and values, which are the express concerns of most proposals today for equality of condition.

For, as Rousseau realized so prophetically, once equality has been made the dominant value of a social order, it must, and will, reach toward cultural, social, educational, even psychological spheres of human life, for it is in these that the real consequences of economic inequality are most deeply felt. We have Rousseau's *Confessions* as witness of the fact that, in his own life, it was less the occasional poverty he experienced that gnawed at him than the subtler gradations of prestige, influence, and power he encountered when he made his way to the Paris of the Sorbonne, the glittering salons where brilliance of conversation was so much prized, and the *philosophes*, whose intellectual superior Rousseau was in most respects but whose general love of the *haute monde* he found repugnant.

Moreover Rousseau realized, and stated eloquently in his *Discourse on the Arts and Sciences*, that the springs of egoism, ambition, and desire for social eminence lie deep in human nature as it has been formed over the long period of man's history following the original instituting of private property and the rise of the agricultural and mechanical arts. All of man's ills, his torments and subjections to oppression originated, Rousseau tells us in the second *Discourse*, with inequality, when with private property there appeared "social interdependences" which made inequality of status fixed and inevitable. Given the length of mankind's history since the early "fatal departure" from natural equality, it is evident that corrective measures must be encompassing and powerful. Men may want equality, once its virtue is made evident to them, but more than simple popular desire by majorities is required to root equality securely in human nature. Hence Rousseau's call, in the *Social Contract*, for a Legislator, as Rousseau calls him, who will not hesitate to remake human nature itself in the pursuit of equality:

> He who dares to undertake the making of a people's institutions ought to feel himself capable, so to speak, of changing human nature, of transforming each individual who is by himself a complete and solitary whole, into part of a greater whole from which he in a manner receives his life and being. . . . He must, in a word, take away from

man his own resources and give him instead new ones alien to him, and incapable of being made use of without the help of other men.

Elsewhere Rousseau tells us with the candor that is so typical of his political writings that "if it is good to know how to deal with men as they are, it is much better to make them what there is need that they should be. The most absolute authority is that which penetrates into a man's inmost being, and concerns itself no less with his will than with his actions."

How well Rousseau knew! He records in his *Confessions* that from an early age he had become aware of the fact that men are entirely what their form of government makes them. Hence there must be no reluctance in the uses of power, the power, especially, that lies at the core of the absolute, total, and unremitting General Will. If we would have virtue, Rousseau wrote electrically in his *Discourse on Political Economy*, we must be willing to *establish* it!

Western society is rarely lacking in those who, in one way or other, religious or political usually, are obsessed by the mission of establishing virtue. Most clearly, the West is not lacking now in such individuals. And in our time, by a rising number of persons, chiefly intellectuals and politicians, virtue is defined solely and exclusively as equality; again, let it be emphasized, equality of condition or result.

And there is no want either of ingenuity or cleverness in demonstrating that virtue is equality—nothing less, nothing more. Undoubtedly the most highly praised work in philosophy of the past decade or two is John Rawls' *Theory of Justice*. Although there is excellent reason to believe that the almost ecstatic response to it will shortly abate among professional philosophers, it is certain that this book will be for a long time to come the central work in moral philosophy for those belonging to the clerisy of power. It is tailormade for the needs of those for whom equalitarianism and central power are but two sides of the same coin.

Justice, we discover, is for Rawls "fairness," which is surely a reasonable definition. What is a good deal less reasonable is the author's further conclusion that justice and fairness are—equality! And for John Rawls as for all others in the cult of equality, equality has nothing to do with historic equality before the law or equality of opportunity. Through two dubious rhetorical techniques which he labels "the original position" and "the veil of ignorance" Rawls seeks to demonstrate that all men of reason and good will, when liberated from the misconceptions and prejudices of the social order they live in, will easily reach the conclusion that society is built on the rock of equality; that is, equality of "social primary goods," the economic, cultural, political, and even psychological attributes which are so variously distributed in society as the result of equality of opportunity and equality before the law. Social primary goods, which may be made to include even "bases of self-respect," are to be made equal, or at least equitable, through what he calls "the difference principle."

This principle means simply that there shall be no inequalities of "social primary goods" in society unless it can be demonstrated that such inequalities are in the interest of the less advantaged. There must be no differences among individuals in social position, the fruits of knowledge, talent, and enterprise, as well as in income and property, except insofar as superior possession among some can be demonstrated to redound to the welfare of others. This, succinctly stated, is Rawls' difference principle.

The mind boggles at the thought of the political apparatus necessary to give expression to and to enforce such a principle. Rawls seems not to have heard of political bureaucracy, but even if he had, he would no doubt take refuge in his stated principle that the "liberty" of each individual is primary, not to be violated by interests of utility or expediency. Liberty, however turns out to be for Rawls very much what it is for Rousseau: mere equal shares of something *called* liberty which bears little relation to the autonomies and immunities which are the true hallmarks of liberty. Equality is the dominant value in Rawls.

The New Equalitarians of our day seem to detest the central elements of the social bond quite as much as Rousseau did. I refer to the whole tissue of interdependences—interactions, conflicts, coercions, conformities, protections, and disciplines—which are the molecules of social order. It is with good reason that our equalitarians detest such interdependences, for, in whatever degree or form, inequality is the essence of the social bond. The vast range of temperaments, minds, motivations, strengths, and desires that exists in any population is nothing if not the stuff of hierarchy. When associations are formed for whatever purpose, cooperation and mutual aid included, inequality is immediately apparent. Even the New Equalitarians would presumably balk at the thought of holding all musical talents to the same limits; and no doubt they would feel the same way with respect to academic and intellectual talents. It is the "economic" they have in mind. But, as I have said, it is cultural, psychological, and social inequality that galls once equality is declared the ascendant ideal. Rousseau detested the arts and sciences, just as he did all social interdependences, seeing correctly that in these areas inequality is difficult to contain.

Inevitably there is opposition to kinship. The family, final enclave of political and economic privacy, is correctly perceived by the New Equalitarians as the most powerful barrier to the redistribution of goods and statuses which is called for in their strategy. In this they are also in harmony with Rousseau, who did not hesitate, in the final pages of the *Discourse on Political Economy*, to recommend virtual abolition of the family, chiefly as a means of separating the children from what Rousseau described as the "prejudices" of the fathers. There were a number of radical equalitarian movements in the late eighteenth and early nineteenth centuries that frankly proposed that children be separated from family at a very early age and brought up in state-operated schools. Only thus, it was believed, could the family's inherently destructive effect upon the ideal of the accomplishment of mass equality be offset.

There is much less awareness of this vital necessity among present-day New Equalitarians, or, if there is in fact awareness, much less courage and forthrightness in recommending abolition of the family. It is much easier to concentrate upon private property as the target, not giving emphasis to the well-attested fact that wherever there is private property there will be a strong family system. After all, the origins of private property lie in clan and kindred; and even after the conjugal family, the household, became the chief element of kinship, its relationship to property remained very close. As Joseph Schumpeter noted in his *Capitalism, Socialism and Democracy*, it was not the isolated individual, so dear as an abstract concept to the classical economists, but the household that was the main engine of modern capitalist development. Not economic man but, quite literally, the head of the household working for the present *and future* of the members of his family, and hence saving and investing in however small degree, is the central figure in the capitalist drama, as in all earlier forms of economy.

Unquestionably it is this fact that will offer the New Equalitarians their greatest single challenge. For, although equality is a prestige-laden word in contemporary Western society, it is largely the more traditional types of equality—in law and economic opportunity—which are the referents. Individuals at all levels may at times burn with the sense of injustice where the multiple rewards of social life are involved—social and cultural as well as economic— but it is far from certain that a majority of Westerners, even if given a clear choice, would wish for a generalized policy of equality, whether of income or anything else. The realization is too strong that, given the immense range of aptitudes, desires, aspirations, strengths, and motivations in any population, any genuine effort to offset this range by a national policy of mandatory redistribution would only result in novel forms of inequality: those which result when differently endowed human beings are obliged to submit to a single measure of result. Ordinary majority will in democracy, then, can hardly be counted upon, certainly at the present time, to support and give acquiescence to the kind of equality that is dreamed of by those members of the clerisy of power who have result and condition, not opportunity, in their minds.

All of this is true; but we are living in strange and frightening times; the waning of the historic political community, founded in such large degree upon majority will, is, as we have seen, one of the major facts of our age. Whereas majority will, merely polled by Roper or Gallup, might very well even today register strong opposition to the New Equality, the blunt fact is that an operating and motivated majority will shows clear signs of becoming one of the casualties of the decline of the political habit of mind, of the revolt against politics in any and all of its forms.

The politics of virtue, from Plato to Bentham, has rarely if ever corresponded with emphasis on majority will any more than it has with emphasis on historic individual rights and immunities before the law. Plato thought majority will in the good state as absurd as in matters of mathematical truth. Rousseau made a careful, and absolutely vital, distinction between majority will as such, which he termed the mere "will of all," and the General Will which might or might not, Rousseau candidly states, be congruent with what a simple majority might wish at any given time. It is interesting to note that in *Theory of Justice*, while not actually abrogating majority will in a democracy, John Rawls has given it a somewhat lower status among the crucial verities than certain other elements of his just society.

There are also what I referred to earlier as the crumbling walls of the political community, social institutions and cultural disciplines foremost. The already well-advanced dislocation of family, locality, religion, and voluntary association in our society carries us a long way toward a political condition in which a strongly nationalized system of equality might easily come to seem a refuge.

I have perhaps given too much attention to the writings of the New Equalitarians, for, ascendant though they assuredly are at the present time in the intellectual world, and fertile though they will doubtless prove to be in the preparing of political manifestoes and platforms, there is no more reason to believe they will be crucially responsible for egalitarian tendencies in the future than their intellectual forerunners—socialists, social democrats, progressives—have been in the past.

If we plot the development of social equality in Western society over the past few centuries, we find that it follows almost perfectly the development of centralization and bureaucratization in the political sphere. Even more strikingly, the development of equality follows the trajectory of war. It is in periods of national, mass warfare that we observe the greatest advances of the egalitarian ethic in many areas. The point is that even if no egalitarian ethic existed, if there were not the vein of equality in the modern Western mind that there so plainly is, the mere existence of political and military centralization in the modern world would have brought about pretty much the same patterns of equality we see around us.

My own estimate is that a good 75 percent of all the national programs which have been instituted in Western countries during the past two centuries to equalize income, property, education, working conditions, and other aspects of life have been in the first instance adjuncts of the war state and of the war economy. Equality is far from least among the qualities which go with social and economic programs of nationalization during times of war.

"Every central power which follows its natural tendencies," wrote Tocqueville, "courts and encourages the principle of equality; for equality singularly facilitates, extends, and secures the influence of a central power." And it was Thomas Jefferson who observed that the state with power to do things *for* people has the power to do things *to* them.

I do not say that the ethic of equality necessarily leads to the demand for absolute power. Philosophers, like the rest of us, are entitled to be taken at their word, and, however naive the New Equalitarians may be in their common indifference to problems of political power, we cannot justly accuse them of wishing to bring about either military socialism or political absolutism. Moreover, there are ages in history when diffuseness of power, fragmentation, and the concomitant forms of local oppression and inequality are so great that even the most ardent libertarian could properly wish for an increase in central political power and the leveling of ranks in society that goes with it. The West has seen such ages. Nor will we soon forget the morally repugnant inequality of opportunity and legal right imposed upon the blacks right down to very recent times. I do not see how anyone who prizes a free and creative culture could oppose the extension of the forms of equality which have been, over and over, the crucial circumstances within which long-oppressed minorities have broken free and given their talents to the arts, the sciences, politics, and other areas of leadership.

But the evidence is clear enough that we are looking well beyond either legal equality or equality of opportunity in many circles today, and a very different kind of equality is becoming ever more widely prized. With it, or with such achievements of this kind of equality as have been thus far a part of the social order, goes a degree of political power and of political intrusion into once autonomous areas that a rising number of persons will, I am convinced, find odious. Ongoing experience with certain programs of equalitarianism—Affirmative Action, mandatory busing to achieve ethnic quotas, Open Admissions, among others—certainly suggests this. All other things being equal, it is more than likely that popular opposition to such programs would increase and even become successful.

Alas, all other things are not equal. For the equalitarianism of such programs is only one facet of a much larger reality: the existence of a bureaucratized welfare state that prizes uniformity above all other things and that, as a large number of recent instances suggest, will stop at nothing to enforce this uniformity. Uniformity is prized by all bureaucracies, political or other, simply because it saves bureaucrats from the always agonizing responsibility of dealing with the individuality and the complexity of real life.

There is a measure of equality without which any community must suffer. And although I would not rank equality among the very highest of the West's moral values—not as high, assuredly, as liberty and justice—its ethic is no mean one. The tragedy in our time is that what is good in the ethic of equality is fast becoming swamped by forces—of power above all—which aim not, really, at equality in any civilized sense but at uniformity, leveling, and a general mechanization of life.

There is, obviously, inevitable conflict with liberty. I mean the kind of liberty that goes with differentiation, variety, individuality, and a very wide spectrum of social and psychological traits; the kind of liberty that is involved in all creative work, whether in the arts and sciences or in the economic sphere. It is nonsense to say that the pupil in public school today has the same freedom to learn that was once present before uniform programs took command in the country, as the result of the ever greater penetration of the school system by the Federal government and its central bureaus of education. Given these and also the constantly increasing emphasis upon equal grading, or upon no grading at all, with differences between the bright and dull wiped out symbolically, how could there possibly be the freedom to learn that is always stimulated by visible incentive?

There is, to be sure, another kind of freedom that does not suffer from the spread of equalitarianism: the kind best seen in totalitarian societies; the kind that is divisible into equal shares irrespective of the talents and motivations of those holding these shares. The Russian and Chinese governments are scrupulous in their attention to this kind of mass freedom, for there is nothing to worry about in the way of consequences. What such governments do have to worry about is the kind of freedom that is simply impossible to divide equally among a people: the freedom to be creative. The problem of the intellectual, the artist, and the scientist in contemporary Russia is evidence enough of the strain presented to a social order by this kind of freedom, which is inherently incompatible

with any kind of equality except equality before the law and of opportunity.

THE SOFTENING OF POWER

It is extremely unlikely that political power could be as encompassing of life, as penetrating of privacy, were it not for certain
changes in the nature of power. If I were to seize upon a single
phrase for these changes it would be "the softening of power." The
power of the state is no less—indeed it is far greater—than it was
even during the divine right monarchies. But where the exercise of
power over individual life was then nakedly coercive, commonly
brutal in infliction, and above all direct and personal, the same exercise of governmental power is today blander, more indirect,
engaged in the immobilization of the human mind when possible
rather than in the infliction of corporal punishments. A great deal
that is commonly ascribed to popular welfare, to humanitarianism,
even to increase in individual freedom, might better be ascribed to
the softening of power, through organization, technology, social
work, psychiatry, equalitarianism, and various other techniques
and values whereby the impact of government upon human life has
been lessened in the experiencing all the time that political control
of human life has vastly increased.

We have been recently made aware of profound changes in the
nature of power in Soviet Russia. Rare today are the brutality, torture, and terror which were so manifest in the Age of Stalin. Rare
too are the public trials before state tribunals which in the 1930s
were means not only of exterminating declared enemies of the state
but of terrorizing the public at large. I think it is exceedingly unlikely that we shall see again in the world the kind of direct, naked
use of force on large numbers of persons which the governments of
Stalin and Hitler brought to such heights. Very probably Stalinist
and Nazi concentration camps, torture chambers, and death camps

represent a watershed in the history of the use of power by government over individual lives. For it is notable that even the Nazi government felt it necessary to so organize the torture and destruction of Jews and others as to conceal so far as was possible these enormities from the German public. To a lesser extent, that was true of Stalin's Russia as well. Once, in almost all nations of the world, such torture and execution, far from being in any degree concealed, would have been flaunted before the public. I am inclined to think that the advances of humanitarianism during the past century or two, together with advances in technology which have made possible a liberation, through drugs and machinery, from the incidence of pain our ancestors knew, have combined to give people a very different attitude toward the visible infliction of cruelty and brutality.

"Not many people," writes Sir Dennis Gabor in *The Mature Society*, "could stand the sight of a tumbril moving slowly through the streets of a town, with the delinquent tied to a stake, and the executioner with the brazier next to him digging the red hot poker into the screaming wretch." Indeed they could not; not today. Yet a surprisingly short time separates us from ancestors who not only could stand it but who solemnly regarded such spectacles, along with public hangings and floggings, as indispensable to the maintenance of order. We do not have to go very far back in Western history to find otherwise humane and gentle minds in perfect composure at the sight of floggings, drawings and quarterings, and flayings which it is unlikely that more than a tiny handful of the pathological could today bear the knowledge—much less the sight—of as systematic public policy.

In substantial part, as Sir Dennis observes, the changed attitude toward the more brutal uses of power by governments has come from the changed place of physical pain in almost all human lives. It is difficult, in our age of pain-preventives and pain-liberators, to realize the extent to which physical pain was once commonplace. It is rather horrifying today to read of the agony that was once the unavoidable accompaniment of a long list of diseases, not to mention injuries and disabilities of one kind or other. And, as Sir Dennis well notes, in a society in which physical pain is the common lot, there is not likely to be the same reaction to, the same perception of, pain deliberately inflicted upon individuals either for amusement's sake or for the protection of society. A social order that could, in its lower classes, find diversion in the frequent spectacle of bloody, knock-down, eye-gouging, nose- or ear-mutilating fights—among women as well as men, we read of the English eighteenth century—would not be likely to react as we do to the torturing, flogging, and hanging of miscreants.

That kind of society has almost wholly disappeared in our time, and with it the shape of punishment and of power. But such transformation of police or governmental power in no way means that such power has lessened. It can mean actual increase, especially if power is disguised as a form of therapy. The relative absence of Stalinist torture and mass murder in Russia does not mean that a power vacuum now exists. No doubt the memory in the older generation of Stalinist terror is sufficient to restrain dissident impulses, but, as we have recently been made aware, the art and technology of therapy, so called, have become in present-day Russia the commonest guise of power over the unruly or dangerously creative. Techniques lumped in the public mind under the label "brainwashing" have manifestly assumed far greater use in the totalitarian countries than would once have been thought either desirable or necessary by their rulers.

It is not as though such uses of power had not been foreseen—by Huxley, by Orwell, and before both by Samuel Butler in *Erewhon*, a utopia in which the delinquent and criminal were put in hospitals. It is a commentary on the time we ourselves live in that we are less likely to find Erewhon as humanitarian as our Victorian ancestors might have, for we are too well aware of the employment today of hospitals and other contexts of therapy for the express purposes of punishment and overt behavior control.

It would be comforting if power-as-therapy were confined to the totalitarian societies, but it is not. As I write, there has just been released a 651-page report by Senator Sam Ervin's subcommittee on constitutional rights which describes in great detail the number and variety of projects, mostly sponsored by the Department of Health, Education, and Welfare, whose essence is the control of behavior through drugs and related means. Alcoholics, shoplifters, child molesters, and homosexuals are, the report states, but a few of those on whom therapy is being used, often in clear violation of constitutional rights, as a means of alteration of mind and behavior. "There is a real question," Senator Ervin is quoted as saying in connection with release of the report, "whether the government should be involved at all in programs that potentially pose substantial threats to our basic freedoms."

Dr. Thomas Szasz, eminent psychiatrist, has been writing eloquently for years now on the extent to which legal pleas of insanity and mental inadequacy, with consequent commitment of individuals to asylums rather than jails, have intruded into the once sacrosanct area of individual ethical responsibility. As I noted in an earlier chapter, our villains have vanished along with our heroes, and each disappearance is related to a spreading state of mind that sees less and less responsibility devolving upon the individual for his acts. The same overall set of mind that snatches the chronic rapist or the mass murderer from the ranks of villainy and places him among the mentally disturbed is likely to remove the occasional great man or woman from the ranks of heroism and subject this individual instead to relentless examination of private life and to public exposure. Not a Washington or a Lincoln, surely, would have been able to maintain the image of greatness in circumstances such as those the media, the social sciences, governmental investigative agencies and committees, have created.

The greatest power, as major political theorists from Plato to Rousseau have declared, is that which shapes not merely individual conduct but also the mind behind that conduct. Power that can,

through technological or other means, penetrate the recesses of culture, of the smaller unions of social life, and then of the mind itself,
is manifestly more dangerous to human freedom than the kind of
power that, for all its physical brutality, reaches only the body. We
shrink today from the infliction of physical pain upon our contemporaries—except, that is, in time of war, and even then we prefer
the kind that is dealt out at thirty thousand feet in bombs to the
kind revealed at My Lai—but we do not shrink from projects in
government, in the social and behavioral sciences, and in the media
by which mind and spirit are invaded and thus affected by power,
in however soft a form.

Privacy is an excellent litmus test, it would seem, for the actual
state of freedom in a culture. I do not think many people would
argue seriously that the extent of individual privacy today is even
close to what it was a few decades ago. The exposure that Gover-
nor Rockefeller was required to make of economic, family and personal life—and, I think, much more could have been required
without serious outcry—during the consideration that followed his
nomination to the vice-presidency would have once been utterly inconceivable. So gross a violation of privacy would surely have converted our political heroes of the past, from Washington to FDR,
into beings of somewhat less than heroic mold. I am aware that a
strong case can be made for the propriety and safety (to public
weal) of detailed penetrations of economic and political privacy.
But we shall, I think, find that an equally strong case will shortly
be made in justification of identical invasions of sexual and other
equally intimate recesses of privacy.

Large-scale government, with its passion for equalitarian uniformity, has prepared our minds for uses of power, for invasions of
individual privacy, and for the whole bureaucratization of spirit
that Max Weber so prophetically identified as the disease of modernity. We do indeed see, and take a measure of comfort in, certain
liberties of an individual kind in the realms of the theatre, publish-
ing, and public speech which our ancestors did not know. Rights to

obscenity, pornography, public display of body and mind, and others of related character exist which were once absent. If these are in some way connected with the larger structure of freedom, especially political freedom, and might even be reckoned forces in the long run toward ending the kinds of invasion of privacy which governmental, military, and paramilitary agencies now represent, we can perhaps overlook the crudities and vulgarities which such rights so plainly carry with them.

It is well to be reminded, though, that more often than not in history license has been the prelude to exercises of extreme political coercion which shortly reach all areas of a culture. That is one observation that history makes possible. Another and related one is that very commonly in ages when civil rights of one kind are in evidence—those pertaining to freedom of speech and thought in, say, theatre, press, and forum, with obscenity and libel laws correspondingly loosened—very real constrictions of individual liberty take place in other, more vital, areas: political organization, voluntary association, property, and the right to hold jobs, for example.

I believe it was Napoleon who first sensed the ease with which, in modern society, the illusion of freedom can be created by strategic relaxation of regulations and law on obscenity, pornography, individual thought—provided it is *only* individual—and freedom of speech, while all the time fundamental economic and political liberties are being circumscribed. The real barriers to the kind of power Napoleon wielded as emperor are not individual rights so much as the kinds of rights associated with autonomy of local community, voluntary association, political party. These are the real measure of the degree to which central political power is limited in a society. Neither centralization nor bureaucratized collectivism can thrive as long as there is a substantial body of social authorities to check them. But on the other hand there is no reason why a considerable degree of individual freedom cannot exist with respect to such matters as sexual conduct, speech, writing, and religious belief without serious impact upon the structure of political power.

There are, after all, certain freedoms which are like circuses. Their very existence, so long as they are individual and enjoyed chiefly individually as by spectators, diverts men's minds from the loss of other, more fundamental, social and economic and political rights.

A century ago, the liberties which now exist routinely on stage and screen, on printed page and canvas, would have been unthinkable in America—and elsewhere in the West, for that matter, save in the most clandestine and limited of settings. But so would the limitations upon economic, professional, educational, and local liberties, to which we have by now become accustomed, have seemed equally unthinkable a half century ago. We enjoy the feeling of great freedom, of protection of our civil liberties, when we attend the theater, watch television, or buy paperbacks. But all the while we find ourselves living in circumstances of a spread of military, police, and bureaucratic power that cannot help but have, that manifestly does have, profoundly erosive effect upon those economic, local, and associative liberties which are by far the most vital to any free society. From the point of view of any contemporary strategist or tactician of political power, indulgence in the one kind of liberties must seem a very requisite to diminution of the other kind. We know it seemed that way to the Caesars and Napoleons of history. Such indulgence is but one more way of softening the impact of political power and of creating the illusion of individual freedom in a society grown steadily more centralized, collectivized, and destructive of the diversity of allegiance, the autonomy of enterprise in all spheres, and the spirit of spontaneous association that any genuinely free civilization requires.

THE RESTORATION
OF AUTHORITY

Is IT POSSIBLE to arrest, to actually reverse, present accelerating tendencies toward political Leviathan on the one hand and moribundity of the social order on the other? Can the bureaucratization of culture, mind, and spirit which assumes an ever more militant, even military cast in the West be somehow offset by renewal of the social bond and its diverse contexts of authority and freedom?

Nothing about us at the moment offers much encouragement. We live, after all, in a world that becomes constantly more militarized, more power-oriented, and hence more dangerous to America and other Western countries. The mere presence of the great military socialisms which are Russia and China, with their consecration to aggrandizement of one kind or other, is enough to create pessimism so far as our own prospects are concerned. And we have begun to see in the Western world—in Greece, Chile, and Portugal—open rule by the military in the name of one moral or political value after the other. Will this process of militarization of government in the West cease before other countries have been added to the list?

Everything suggests continuation of the trends I have described. After all, if the advancing power of centralized government could not be checked during the age of affluence that for a quarter of a century followed World War II, when Western economies, especially that of the United States, were generally strong, when recession seemed banned forever and inflation was still moderate, what likelihood exists for retreat now amidst fear of depression and inflation alike? Moreover, as I have noted, it was precisely in that period of affluence that the authority of the university, of reason, of objectivity, of language, and of culture underwent its most pronounced decline in modern times. The combination of widespread sense of corruption in society and government and of spreading psychological unease, alienation, and fear of future is in itself an admirable recipe for the spread of power in military form.

Nor is the voice of the political clerisy any less clamant today than in recent times past. To a man the veterans of the New Deal, of Kennedy's Camelot, and of the Johnson administration, those who sat at the right hand of power and relished every moment of it, preach the gospel that was first heard in this country from Woodrow Wilson, especially after America's entry into World War I. That this clerisy and this gospel have an imposing record of big budgets and bureaucracies, of adventures in what is by now a string of foreign wars, and of close to total failure in the work either of terminating depression and inflation or of creating the conditions of economic and social prosperity, does not matter in the slightest. For labor, press, the academic and intellectual world, and even increasingly for business and industry, it is this clerisy, with roots deep in the doctrines of Hobbes, Rousseau, and Bentham, that speaks most authoritatively at the present time. The ranks of those still committed to the private sector, to the social sphere, and to the individual liberties within each of these, become progressively thinner, their voices increasingly muted. The worse the conditions become which are the direct spawn of the New Despotism, the greater the cry for its intensification. After all, the huge regulatory agencies, the military, and the numberless laws passed by Congress do represent action of a sort, and in twilight ages action is king.

We are thus obliged to be skeptical in the extreme that any arrest, much less reversal, of the tendencies of political centralization and social disintegration around us is possible. It was one of the prophecies of those like Tocqueville, Burckhardt, and Nietzsche, who a century ago foresaw our time of troubles, that paralysis of the will on the part of peoples and governments would be a part of what lay ahead. Burckhardt's imagined future of military commandos ascendant in the West had no room in it, obviously, for very much of civility and culture. We live, as I have suggested, in one of Saint-Simon's "critical ages," and there is no reason to believe optimistically that we are reaching its end, with something substantially different at hand. If one were to wager, it would be sounder to think in terms of a few decades at least, perhaps another century, of continuation of present tendencies in the direction of a military Leviathan set in circumstances of social erosion and cultural decay.

But having said this, indeed taking it virtually for granted as social analyst and prophet, I would like nevertheless to turn to something very different: to some reflections on what a genuine social regeneration in the West might consist of—either as the consequence of historical factors now only dimly to be seen or foreseen or of direct, enlightened statesmanship. After all, the present scene is not wholly without possible portents. Some of the forces I described at the beginning of this book as challenges to the political community and the political way of life—the upthrust of ethnic nationalism, of fundamentalist religion, of the commune, of kinship and localism, and the still-enigmatic role of the multinational corporation, among others—might from a different point of view be thought of as the faint, still amorphous but potentially decisive harbingers of the next age of civilization, one that will contain renewal of the roots of society and culture alike, much as did that age in the West that followed the decline and disintegration of the Roman military-imperial order.

Who can ever be sure in these matters? Prediction of the future is—despite the pretenses of self-styled futurologists—impossible save as expression of intuition, guess, and wish-generated or anxiety-inspired fantasy. No matter how inexorable any given trend may seem, the history of mankind teaches us to be respectful of the impacts of the Prophet, the Genius, the Maniac, and the Random Event.

I do not, in short, know any more about what the future does indeed hold than does anyone else. We can only guess and, on the basis of postulated conditions, describe. What I shall do in this final chapter is indicate a few of the fundamental elements which, on history's evidence, are vital to any real liberation from the kind of power that envelops us at the present time.

THE RECOVERY OF PLURALISM

I begin with the philosophy of pluralism. Everything vital in history reduces itself ultimately to ideas, which are the motive forces. Man *is* what he *thinks!* So might the epigram be restated. He is what he thinks he himself is, what his fellows are, and what the surrounding circumstances are in their deepest reality. Above all, man is what he thinks the transcending moral values are in his life and in the lives of those around him. I know of nothing more absurd than the "realist" position that ideas and ideals do not shape history. What else, in heaven's name, could possibly shape history, lift it above the level of the statistically random or fortuitous? The difference between biological evolution and social evolution consists precisely in the fact that where the former, in its modern scientific statement, is purely statistical, concerned only with "populations" of which we can determine the arithmetic mean and the coefficients of variation from this mean, social evolution is necessarily devoted to the very structures and types which the biological evolutionist is obliged to eschew utterly. Social evolution deals with kinship systems, guilds, communities, churches, schools, universities, economic corporations, political states, and the like. It is inherently and ineradicably "typological" by the standards of the biologist.

Behind each of the structures or types that we deal with in the history of society is, inevitably, a complex pattern of ideas and ideals, for human behavior is nothing if not purposive. They may be ideas based upon cunning, covetousness, avarice, intensification of power and exploitation, or conversely they may be ideas of godliness, redemption, reform, revolution, justice, or freedom; but apart from ideas, however diversely and amorphously, even uncomprehendingly, held, it is absurd to think of either social behavior or social organization.

Insensibly, ideas, ideals, and values form patterns in time, patterns which often, as in the case of religious and philosophical systems, are greater in each case than the sum of the parts. And once human beings become aware more or less directly of these patterns, in whatever sphere, these too operate to inspire and to motivate. Whether it is Buddhism or Islam or Christianity, nationalism, democracy, or socialism, gradualism or revolution, the historical record is plain that human beings do indeed live and die for such things as the "realist" might contemptuously refer to as idealistic abstractions.

Among the greatest needs of our present age is a recrudescence of the whole set of ideas that, for want of better term, we may think of as *pluralism*. It is, as William James wrote, a pluralistic universe we live in, and *that* is the kind of universe one hopes that Margaret Fuller and Thomas Carlyle alike had in mind. And as it is a pluralistic universe, so is it normally a pluralistic society that we inhabit.

One of the most grievous casualties of modern times is the true utopian mentality, the kind of mind we find in Sir Thomas More,

Francis Bacon, in dozens of writers in the eighteenth and early nineteenth centuries including Saint-Simon, Fourier, Comte, Proudhon, and others. This is, or was, a mentality that did not hesitate to try, as realistically as possible, to think out, to plan for, to guide toward, the future. Past and present were indeed respected, but one is not conscious in their extraordinary works of any dogmatic conviction of an inexorable trend that must by its nature reduce human thought to the level of handmaiden or worse. It was, I believe, Marxism, above any other single force in the nineteenth century, that led eventually to the death of the utopian mentality, or else to its inversion, as in the works of Aldous Huxley and George Orwell. No dogma or superstition in any religion yet uncovered by anthropologists is more tyrannizing, and also more intellectually absurd, than that of the historically inevitable or necessary. But it is this dogma nevertheless that has had greatest appeal to several generations of intellectuals bereft of religion and driven thereby into the arms of the waiting church of historical necessity.

The worst aspect of this kind of thinking is its division of the present—basically all we have to observe and to cogitate upon—into the "relevant" and the "irrelevant" present. If one is convinced, by his dogma of the *necessary* future, that progress lies only in the uses of political power, in the sterilization of cultural diversity, the extinction of localism, regionalism, and the whole private sector, and the replacement of all this by something euphemistically called the welfare state, the planned state, whatever, then obviously there is a large realm of the manifest present that can be categorically dismissed as fundamentally irrelevant, as wasteful, as a distraction from achievement of the future, as contemplated by the unitary or monistic mentality. The harshest charge the modern intellectual, so often under the influence of one variation or other of the Marxist mind, has been able to hurl at others is not that their ideas are wrong, immoral, or undesirable, but *unrealistic*, conceived in blindness to what is real and objective in the present.

Given this whole habit of mind, conceived in the union of necessity and politics—the two greatest idols of the modern intellectual mind—it will not be easy for a philosophy of pluralism to reassert itself as it has from time to time in other ages of Western history. And yet I am convinced that it will so assert itself, though I do not know when, if only because the ravages of the social and cultural landscape effected by the political clerisy and its works are bound to become so great, and so visible, that there will be no other way for human beings to turn than to some kind of rebirth of a basically pluralist philosophy. What are the central values of pluralism, either as they may be observed in epochs of substantive pluralism or else imagined for our own future? The following seem to me to be the four constitutive elements of the pluralist philosophy.

Functional autonomy. What characterizes the pluralist view of autonomy can best be thought of in terms of the ability of each major function in the social order to work with the maximum possible freedom to achieve its own distinctive ends. What applies to school or university should apply also to economy, to family, to religion, and to each of the other great spheres of society. Everything must be done to avoid intrusion by some one great institution, such as the political state, into the spheres of other institutions. Perfect autonomy is scarcely possible, or even desirable perhaps, given the needs of unity in some degree in a society. But, as Aristotle observed in his criticism of Plato's communism, there is the kind of unity that comes from harmony, that is articulation of diverse sounds or elements, and there is the kind of unity that comes from mere unison. It is harmony that our society needs above anything else—and I use that word precisely as Aristotle did, and as Althusius, Burke, and Tocqueville later did in their different ways—as the bringing into consonance of elements in the social order the diversity of which is recognized as vital to both freedom and creativeness.

Edmund Burke epitomized this element of pluralism with his characteristic pungency and eloquence:

> The nature of man is intricate; the objects of society are of the greatest possible complexity; and therefore no simple disposition of direction of power can be suitable either to man's nature or to the quality of his affairs. When I hear the simplicity of contrivance aimed at and boasted of in any new political constitutions, I am at no loss to decide that the artificers are grossly ignorant of their trade, or totally negligent of their duty. The simple governments are fundamentally defective, to say no worse of them.

But for the clerisy of power in the West, since at least the time of Hobbes, such words can seem, and have seemed, but the pious exclamations of an irretrievably archaist mind. The managerial revolutions of the twentieth century have been conceived basically by mentalities for whom unity, simplicity, and above all uniformity are not merely desirable values but inevitable values.

Decentralization is the second major element of pluralism. If the functional autonomy of social units is to be respected, if localism, regionalism, and the whole spirit of voluntary association is to flourish, power wielded by government must be distributed into as many hands as possible—not abstract, desocialized *political* hands but those we actually see in the social order, those of workers, enterprisers, professionals, families, and neighborhoods. Centralization, Lamennais wrote, breeds apoplexy at the center and anemia at the extremities. From Aristotle through Aquinas, Althusius, Bodin, Burke, Tocqueville, Durkheim, and Weber, through the whole succession of minds in the West in which respect for social diversity and individual autonomy is to be seen, there has been a profound stress upon the need for decentralization—not merely in political government alone, though there preeminently, but in all large institutions. Few things have more grievously wounded the political community in our time than the kind of centralization that has become virtually a passion in the political clerisy during most of this century and that is increasingly becoming but another word for the Federal government today. Dispersion, division, loosening, and localization of power: these are all vital needs today, and they can be brought about only when weariness with centralization and sickness of its consequences become so great that the philosophy of decentralization will achieve once again the prestige it had among the Founding Fathers.

Hierarchy. I refer of course to the hierarchy that comes from the very functional requirements of the social bond. There is no form of community that is without some form of stratification of function and role. Wherever two or more people associate, there is bound to be some form of hierarchy, no matter how variable, changing from one actor to the other, or how minor. Hierarchy is unavoidable in some degree. Our gravest problem at the present time, in many respects, is the disrepute into which this word, this unavoidable necessity, has fallen as the consequence of the generalized philosophy of equalitarianism I described in the preceding chapter. We have seen institution after institution weakened or crippled in the social order as the result of arbitrary power wielded by one or other regulatory agency in the name of a vain and vapid equality. At the present time the ascendant moral philosophy in the West is that which, as I have noted, takes what is in effect leveling as the desired norm of justice. How welcome would be Burke's words today: "Believe me, Sir, those who attempt to level never equalize."

The philosophy of pluralism is, then, rooted not only in the virtues of functional autonomy and localism but also in frank recognition of the value inherent in hierarchy. This in no sense consigns any ethnic, economic, or regional segment to perpetual servitude. Far from it. Again we may quote Burke:

> Woe to the country which would madly and impiously reject the service of the talents and virtues, civil, military, or religious, that are given to grace and to serve it; and would condemn to obscurity every thing formed to diffuse luster and glory around a state. Woe to that country too, that passing into the opposite extreme considers a low education, a mean contracted view of things, a sordid mercenary oc-

cupation, as a preferable title to command. *Everything ought to be open but not indifferently to every man.* [Italics added.]

We have seen, alas, the appearance of *ressentiment* that Tocqueville and Nietzsche, among others after Burke, predicted: the sense of the greater worthiness of the low, the common, and the debased over what is exceptional distinctive, and rare, and, going hand in hand with this view, the profound sense of guilt—inscribed in the works of the New Equalitarians—at the sight of the latter. Hierarchy in some degree is, as I say, an ineradicable element of the social bond, and, with all respect for equality before the law—which is, of course, utterly vital to free society—it is important that rank, class, and estate in all spheres become once again honored rather than, as is now the case, despised or feared by intellectuals. Certainly, no philosophy of pluralism is conceivable without hierarchy—as open as is humanly possible for it to be but not, in Burke's word, indifferently open.

Tradition is fourth among the central elements of pluralism. I mean reliance upon, in largest possible measure, not formal law, ordinance, or administrative regulation, but use and wont, the uncalculated but effective mechanisms of the social order, custom, folkway, and all the uncountable means of adaptation by which human beings have proved so often to be masters of their destinies in ways governments cannot even comprehend. I shall say more about this adaptational or inventive proclivity shortly. What I have reference to here is the larger matter of maximum possible utilization of tradition in place of law.

At the end of the section on the Romanization of the West above I spoke of the present increasingly broad and committed effort of intellectuals and reformers to bring as much of the economy and the social order within the purview of law, litigation, and the judiciary as possible. Those of revolutionary disposition have, understandably, abandoned the barricade for the courtroom, seeing the manifold accomplishments of the latter in the whole realm of the

New Equalitarianism and the New Despotism that goes with it. Few tendencies in our time are more vivid than that of the conversion of once-traditional, once-autonomous, once-social relationships into those of the law and the courts. The university alone is a superb case history of what I am describing. Within the past quarter of a century we have seen a formerly free and largely autonomous social body reduced in a score of ways to becoming the handmaiden of legislature, law office, regulatory agency, and the courtroom.

Pluralist society is free society exactly in proportion to its ability to protect as large a domain as possible that is governed by the informal, spontaneous, custom-derived, and tradition-sanctioned habits of the mind rather than by the dictates, however rationalized, of government and judiciary. Law is vital—formal, statute law—but when every relationship in society becomes a potentially legal relationship, expressed in adversary fashion, the very juices of the social bond dry up, the social impulse atrophies. The genius of the English common law lies not only in the social and communal roots of this law, as these are to be seen in the history of England during the Middle Ages, but also in its tacit concern, repeatedly expressed in judicial decision, that as little as possible be transferred from the nonlegal, nonpolitical lives of human beings living in a social order to the necessarily legal and political lives of the same human beings conceived as subjects of the sovereign. Nothing, it would seem, so quickly renders a population easy prey for the Watergate mentality of government as the dissolution of those customs and traditions which are the very stuff of morality and, hence, of resistance to oppression and corruption. Again I turn to Burke. What he chose to term prejudice I call here tradition, but the point is the same:

> Prejudice is of ready application in the emergency; it previously engages the mind in a steady course of wisdom and virtue, and does not leave the man hesitating in the moment of decision, skeptical, puzzled, and unresolved. Prejudice renders a man's virtue his habit;

and not a series of unconnected acts. Through just prejudice, his duty becomes a part of his nature.

Of all the consequences of the steady politicization of our social order, of the unending centralization of political power, and of the accelerating invasion of the social order by the adversary mentality of the lawyer, the greatest, in many ways, is the weakening and disappearance of traditions in which authority and liberty alike were anchored. I do not happen to regard present feverish bumbling in connection with celebration of the Bicentennial as the worst of our national afflictions, but the whole spectacle of futility in this instance is a perfect image, it seems to me, of the condition in which we find ourselves. What one celebrates—whether in family, religion, or nation—is tradition, or a set of traditions. The sight of literally thousands of bureaucratic bodies struggling to find something to celebrate, some way of celebrating, the Bicentennial, with little if any help to be had, it must be noted, from press, clergy, or the academic world, is sufficient in itself as a commentary on the role of tradition in our society.

THE REDISCOVERY OF THE SOCIAL

If modern life is to be saved from the monolith of power the state has become, from cultural decadence, and from spreading boredom relieved only by war, spectacle, crusade, or riot, means must be found of restoring the kind of social initiative that springs from the groups, neighborhoods, localities, and voluntary associations within which people so plainly wish to live and indeed do live, at least as far as nationalization of modern society permits.

Of all needs in this age the greatest is, I think, a recovery of the *social*, with its implication of the diversity of social membership that in fact exists in human behavior, and the liberation of the idea of the social from the political. I do not doubt that there are functions in modern society which can be met by the political order alone. The great challenge to the contemporary imagination—unlike the imagination that took shape in the Renaissance—is, however, the identification of functions, processes, and memberships which do *not* belong to the state and whose protection from the state and its bureaucracy should be a first order of business. And not least of the results of our lack of attention to the distinctly social, to the *nonpolitical* areas of human experience, and to means whereby the social can be kept strong, is the seeming inability of the state in our time to manage properly what it can best do: maintain order in the towns and cities, for instance!

We are, it would seem, prisoners in the House of Politics. It is a depressing fact that all the great increases in the theory of political power have come from those who gave the appearance of damning it. Rousseau, father of modern political intellectuals, declared all political government iniquitous, ending up, nevertheless, with that indispensable myth of the totalitarian state, the General Will, with its extermination of all forms of community and association which do not proceed directly from it. Bentham, who made a virtual science of the transformation of social authority into monistic power, loathed politics and government as these existed in an England that was witnessing the rise of modern liberal democracy, but he gave the world his infamous Panopticon Principle. Marx, who yielded to no one in hatred of the bourgeois state and whose condemnations of bureaucracy are among the most eloquent anywhere, yet was the author of that politicization, that totalitarianism indeed, which socialism came increasingly to know thereafter. So it goes: hate politics and love power—provided only that the cosmetics of humanitarianism, of equality, rights, and freedom are liberally applied to it.

To identify any act or structure of government, however blatantly bureaucratic it may be, however destructively it deals with the natural communities of human beings, however closely it binds the individual to itself at the expense of older and deeper loyalties, as *social* is, of course, to endow it with a luster it would not and could not have were it to be advertised for what it is in fact: political and bureaucratic. The adjective *social* is the tribute politics pays to those still-remaining wisdoms and apprehensions in the popular mind which recognize and properly fear the never-ending invasion of the political state in the social sphere. In an earlier chapter I noted the appalling corruption of language in our time, a corruption caused chiefly, as George Orwell stressed, by the political mind and, more often than not, the left political mind. Of all such corruptions none seems to be greater in effect than that which buries the *social* in the *political;* which, in its more ignorant and arrogant forms, actually denies any difference between the two, declaring that the political is simply the summation of all that has ever historically been involved in the social and moral structures.

But even leaving aside here the practical question of whether there is any alternative to the nearly total domination of the social and moral orders by the political state, it is at least disingenuous, at worst dishonest and deceptive, to blur the difference between the political and the social and also between the separate traditions in Western thought which express the two.

I offer the guess that 90 percent of what passes for "social thought" in the textbook histories written during the past century is either political thought in fact or else presented with a strongly political thrust. The divisions and stages which we create in our history-writing are overwhelmingly political, reflecting the dominance of the West since the Renaissance at least by largely political values. That overweening attention to the political and the military which a few social and cultural historians complained about in the nineteenth century in their efforts to get the social lives of human beings more nearly center stage in historical writing had its full effect upon those who, starting about the end of the nineteenth century, began to deal with the history of social, cultural, and intellectual materials. Such historians took over, and still do in large degree, the categories of Renaissance, Reformation, Age of Reason,

Enlightenment, Age of Revolution, Democracy, Welfare State, among others, all originally conceived by minds concerned foremost with political matters.

But this practice is awkward to say the least, often downright delusive. The distinguished historian of science Herbert Butterfield has written that for purposes of the history of science in the West the cherished historiographic categories of Renaissance and Reformation can simply be disregarded. As categories or epochs, Butterfield writes, they contribute nothing of substance to any understanding of either the central periods or central processes involved in the rise of modern science. I would suggest that from the point of view of social, cultural, and intellectual history we would be well advised to abandon, or at least significantly reduce dependence upon, these two, and other constructed time-periods brought into being initially, as I have noted, in the terms of an overwhelmingly political orientation toward Western history.

If we are concerned with periods of rise and fall, of prosperity and depression, in the realm of social institutions such as property, local community, neighborhood, guild, and family, we discover that it is precisely in some of the most celebrated of ages—such as Renaissance and Enlightenment—that these institutions underwent significant erosion or dislocation. Much the same, it might be observed in passing, holds true in the history of certain notable intellectual areas as well. What Butterfield has pointed out with respect to science is equally true of philosophy. Despite the widespread conviction that the Italian Renaissance was an illustrious age of philosophy, it was in fact as sterile in this regard as it was in science. I know of no other epoch in Western history that has been the beneficiary of historiographic inflation to the degree that the Renaissance has—*the* Renaissance, as we are prone to refer to it, as though there were no other renaissances in Western and also world history.

We may truthfully say that the Renaissance was the period in which worship of political power and of ethically unlimited warfare made its entrance. Within a century after Renaissance humanist writings, overwhelmingly consecrated to political power in their hatred of church, had appeared on the scene, the momentous theory of the modern national, collective state had been brought into existence. Socially, however, the Renaissance was in large degree a time of institutional dislocation, breakdown, and collapse.

There have been two great traditions in Western social and political thought, and these have little to do with conventional distinctions between "liberal" and "absolutist." In the first, which begins with Plato, the political state is given an emphasis that virtually extinguishes other forms of association. Hobbes, Rousseau, Bentham, Michelet, Fichte, Treitschke are among principals in this tradition which includes, of course, the numberless members of the political clerisy of our own day. Distinction between state and society is either denied in this succession of thinkers or else the social sphere is deemed to be so inherently ridden with conflict and corruption that only through the most stringent uses of political power may the individual be saved. Such groups as family, locality, neighborhood, church, and other autonomous associations are almost uniformly reduced to their individual atoms, made into unities dependent upon concession of existence by the state, or in some other way significantly degraded.

The second tradition is far more interesting and also valuable, I would argue, so far as the actual history of Western society is concerned. This tradition begins, really, with Aristotle, in his famous criticisms of Plato's unitary state, and it includes among its most illustrious figures Cicero, Thomas Aquinas, Bodin, Althusius, Burke, Tocqueville, Proudhon, and some of the members of the lamentably short-lived school of modern English and French pluralists. Basic to this tradition is the clear distinction between social institutions and the political state and the insistence that true freedom in any society proceeds less from what the actual constitution of the political order proper may prescribe than from the relationship that exists between political state, whatever its form of government, and the several institutions of the social sphere. A political government may be nominally democratic or republican, but it cannot be a genuinely free government if the powers of the state have reached out to encompass all spheres of social, moral, economic, and intellectual existence. Conversely a government monarchical or oligarchical in structure can be a free government if—as has been the case many times in history—it respects the other institutions of society and permits autonomies accordingly in the social and economic spheres.

I believe this second tradition, stretching, as I say, from Aristotle down to Burke, Tocqueville, Acton, and to some of the anarchists of the nineteenth century, is by far the more relevant to the needs of our own time. No doubt there are ages and societies in which affirmation of the centralized power of the state is valuable, and I do not argue that any utopian abandonment of the sovereignty of the political state is worth much reflection even today. But we live nevertheless in a time of saturation of social order by political power, and I suggest that it would require a great deal of political retreat from the social sphere before anything resembling a crisis in this respect would be likely.

There are two separate and distinctive manifestations in the nineteenth century of this second, social, tradition of Western thought. The first is conservative, the second is radical, but what they have in common is profound belief in the necessity of protection of the social from the political. Whether it is Burke and von Haller among conservatives, or Proudhon and Kropotkin among radicals, there is identical emphasis upon the values of localism, regionalism, voluntary association, decentralization of authority, and also identical fear of the political state, whether monarchical or republican in character.

It was the French Revolution that formed the background of both bodies of thought. Burke's famous attack on revolutionary centralization and collectivization of power is the starting-point. During the quarter-century that followed publication of his *Reflec-*

tions a veritable renascence of conservatism took place in the
West—to be seen in the works of Bonald and Maistre and the
young Lamennais in France; in Haller in Switzerland; Hegel in
Germany; Balmes and Donoso y Cortes in Spain; and in Southey
and Coleridge in England. The central thrust of each of these
minds was, irrespective of base, against the revolutionary-Jacobin
conception of a quasi-totalitarian state in which all authority is
made the monopoly of political government. It is in this tradition
that kinship, guild, locality, region, parish, and voluntary association became once again ascendant in Western thought after the long
period of adoration of the sovereign political state that had begun in
the Renaissance. However harsh the religious ideas of, say, a Bonald or Maistre might be, there is nevertheless a clear vein of pluralism to be seen in their writings as in those of the other conservatives.

But if the conservative reaction began the rediscovery of society
and of social values, there were other groups, in no way conservative, to continue and to develop the reaction against political mon-
ism. Among liberals there were Lacordaire, Montalembert, Tocqueville, Wilhelm von Humboldt, Mill, and Acton, all of whom
were manifestly influenced by the conservative recovery of the
social, of the local, voluntary, and decentralized, that had begun
with Burke.

In many ways the most interesting of all such groups in the nineteenth century is that which has come to be called the anarchist.
There is a world of difference between the radicalism of the anarchists, as stated brilliantly by such minds as Proudhon and Ba-
kunin and Kropotkin, and the radicalism of the Marxists and of
other elements that made centralization of power, dictatorship of
working class, even the national state itself the contexts of their war
against capitalism. The hostility that can be seen to this day between Marxists of the main line and radicals of anarchist persuasion
has its roots in the bitterness that developed early on between Marx
and Proudhon in the late 1840s. For the smaller patriotisms of fam-

ily, guild, parish, and cooperative association Marx and his disciples had only contempt; such groups were consigned by Marxists, in accord with an iron determinism of philosophy of history, into the dustbin of history. But in the works of the anarchists, from Proudhon's day to ours, and nowhere stated more profoundly and encompassingly than in Kropotkin's *Mutual Aid* and *Fields, Factories and Workshops*, it is precisely on the foundation of such groups, each with maximum autonomy of function and authority, that the edifice of the free society is to be built.

I do not for a moment question the major differences of emphasis which are to be found between nineteenth-century conservatives in the Burke tradition and anarchists molded by Proudhon. But I do not hesitate to say that there is a great deal more in common, so far as fundamental perspective is concerned, between a Burke and a Proudhon than there is between the former and some of those who today style themselves conservatives and between the latter and the vast majority of radicals, overwhelmingly dominated by Marx, in the late nineteenth and the twentieth centuries. In what I here term the recovery of the pluralist and the social, there is as much to be learned at the present time from the classical anarchists as from the classical conservatives.

There are others in the nineteenth and early twentieth centuries from whom there is much to be learned at this juncture in history. I think of the founders of the cooperative movement, consumer and producer, of the labor unions before they chose to enter the political lists, as they have in recent times, and also the guild socialists and the so-called political pluralists, the latter including such illustrious minds as J. N. Figgis, F. W. Maitland, Otto von Gierke, and Léon Duguit. It is one of the tragedies of the twentieth century that, in such large part as the intellectual consequence of World War I and its bizarre but momentous combination of so many creeds from the left, right, and center into the unitary, collectivist nationalism that has been a byword for political thought and planning ever since, we have lost for all practical purposes both the content and the buoyancy of the pluralism and devotion to the social which flourished in so many spheres in the decades following the French Revolution.

It is worth noting here also that what are today called the social sciences had their origins in the same currents of thought I have been writing of. Those minds in the very late eighteenth and the early nineteenth centuries which are by common assent the founders of the social sciences were for the most part extremely skeptical of the role of the state and apprehensive of the centralization its administering of power had already made a dominant fact in Western Europe. Such thinkers as Adam Smith, David Ricardo, Auguste Comte, Haller, Mill, and Maine, down through Le Play, Durkheim, Geddes, Weber, Spencer, and Sumner—one and all concerned with putting the study of social behavior and of institutions on a scientific basis—were far from envisaging social reconstruction and the conduct of society's institutions in the narrow terms of nationalist politics and administration. In reaction to the long tradition, the unitary tradition, that stretched from Renaissance to the bureaucratized monarchies of the eighteenth century, that reached very high apogee in the Jacobin centralization of the Revolution, these minds set themselves to discover the mechanisms, processes, and structures in society that proved that man was *not* dependent upon the political state as the unitary tradition argued—and continues to argue in our own day.

Behold how we have fallen! I mean in the social sciences. There are distinguished exceptions in our day, but for the most part the ideas and proposals of self-styled social scientists should require that the social sciences be termed for what they so largely are: the *political* sciences. It is the national state and its centralized power that is the be-all and end-all in the minds of the vast majority of social scientists in our time. The discovery of the free market and its self-regulating processes in the economy was—though our histories of social thought rarely reveal this fact—matched in the nineteenth century by the discovery of comparable processes in the whole social realm: in kinship, local community, voluntary association, and other forms of social life. Such discovery was, as I say, the overwhelming objective, and triumph, of the titans of social science. However different a Comte may have been from a Spencer, a Morgan from a Tylor, a Wundt from a William James, there was common belief in the reality of social and psychological processes which separated man from the pawn-like, robot-like position in which the philosophy of centralized, unitary sovereignty had put him ever since Hobbes.

For a time just after World War II there seemed to be a reversal of the drive toward politicization of mind that had dominated most of the twentieth century. There was the New Conservatism that had so much to do with restoring both Burke and Tocqueville to rightful place. In sociology and anthropology, and certain other small areas also, the ideas of functionalism were ascendant, ideas which went straight back to classical preoccupations with the nature of the social bond, those of the early and late nineteenth century, those which were mediated by such minds as Weber and Durkheim. In economics the now-historic Chicago school, chiefly under the intellectual leadership of Milton Friedman, flourished— indeed still does—and radiated an influence that had not been dreamed of since Keynes exerted his power over the economic mind in the 1930s. Then came, albeit in very different guise, the New Left, which also spurned, at least in the beginning, the political centralization and bureaucratization which had become hallmarks of the left up to that point. Not Marx but Proudhon was king; or if Marx it was the "humanistic" Marx of the Paris years that the New Left welcomed, not the Marx of *Capital* or *Criticism of the Gotha Program*.

But few if any of these movements would appear to have retained their luster. Emerging conservatism was dealt a possibly fatal hammer blow by the right that culminated in Nixon's Watergate; the new radicalism dissolved into intellectual inanity and vandalism on the campus. And the movements in the social sciences I mentioned above, particularly functionalism, are scarcely to be seen now. None of them has been proof against the political clerisy that governs, in effect, the modern social sciences as it does so many other areas of life and thought.

THE PUBLIC AND PRIVATE

I shall be brief here, for the point I wish to stress has already been set forth, though in different perspective and terminology, in the two preceding sections. If there is to be an efflorescence of a truly free and also stable society, there must be a revival of the prestige of the private, as contrasted with the public. Perhaps this revival is under way now in some degree, the result of the horrifying invasions of personal life which we have discovered to be endemic in modern democratic government, especially since Woodrow Wilson's America of World War I, since Roosevelt's New Deal, and most recently since the administrations of Kennedy, Johnson, and Nixon. True, the anguish over such invasions tends to be limited to the invasions of bugging, reading of mail, and other forms of governmental penetration to the innermost lives of individuals; it is not as often manifest in the kinds of invasion we see in the economy as the result of a host of regulatory agencies, or in the professions and in the universities and schools as the result of HEW's massive and ever-suspicious bureaus and offices. It is, as we know, difficult for the modern liberal to believe that the two kinds of invasion of personal privacy are closely related, that invasion which begins in the name of Plato or Rousseau commonly winds up as invasion in the name of CIA and FBI.

The main point here, though, is reversal, so far as possible, of the whole tendency in political and social philosophy that has, ever since the early nineteenth century, made the "public" ethically superior to the "private." It is Rousseau in the first instance, with his doctrine of the General Will, and then Bentham, with his hatred of all traditional privacies, his veneration of the collective, who are chiefly responsible, I believe, for the conviction that what is public is inherently better in the moral sense than what is private.

Insensibly in the nineteenth century the idea began to spread that what could be justified only in terms of private property, personal reward, economic position, or the like was inherently inferior, from the point of view of ethics, to what could be justified in the name of "public." The immense upsurge of national patriotism that I wrote of in the first chapter was bound, of course, to accelerate veneration for the public in contrast to the private, even though for a long time private enterprise in all spheres managed to prosper.

The result of all this has been that actions by individuals in the realm of the private which have been roundly condemned as immoral or antisocial by our political clerisy have managed until recently to escape censure if only service to the public could somehow be pleaded. To be aggressive and rapacious in the name of one's family, job, or business is by definition evil; but to be aggressive and rapacious in the name, say, of HEW or IRS, or, as we have learned in such nauseating detail, of the White House, carries a different evaluation in the mind of the political intellectual.

This, however, may well be changing. What began as dismay and revulsion over Watergate has possibly acquired a momentum that will come to include those regulatory agencies in Washington—and there are by now dozens of them—which invade every intimate, personal detail of our educational, intellectual, moral, medical, as well as our economic lives. There is no need to repeat here what I said above about the shape of the New Despotism. But it is worthwhile to insist that until the Private has become once again as honorable a concept as the Public—and this in *all* areas—we are not likely to know freedom.

THE RENASCENCE OF KINSHIP

As I suggested at the beginning of this book, strange shapes are to be discerned among the mists which envelop the historic political community, among them those of revived religion, ethnicity, kinship, localism, and voluntary association. I shall concern myself here only with the last three.

There is no doubt that family and kindred hold a very different place in both intellectual and popular consciousness from what they held even a generation ago. Then the heritage of the rationalist Enlightenment was almost entirely unchallenged, and there was little place in this heritage for a group as ancient and freighted with traditionalism as the family. A great many minds earlier in this century would have agreed with Rousseau and Bentham that kinship was both obsolete and a barrier to individual freedom. That is plainly not the situation today. A steady succession of studies has made clear the vital place the family holds in individual motivation toward education, reason, and achievement generally. In society in large there would appear to be forces germinating in support of not only the conjugal family but also, more important in some ways, kindred. Very possibly the popularity of "kin groups" among the young is some kind of augury.

The great contributions of kinship to society are, on the one hand, the sense of membership in and continuity of the social order, generation after generation; and on the other, the spur to individual achievement, in all areas, that the intimacy of the family alone seems able to effect. These are the essential psychological functions of family, and may be seen as the sources of the desire for autonomy and freedom of the household and kindred which has for many millennia been the strongest force against the kind of military or political power that atomizes a social order. Between family and state there has been everywhere, throughout history, an inverse relation so far as the influence of each on society is concerned.

More than any other social scientist, it was Frederick Le Play in the last century who first saw clearly and systematically the close relation between what he called the "stem" family—*la famille souche*—and the general creative prosperity of the surrounding social order. The "stem" family Le Play found among the Jews, ancient Greeks, pre-Imperial Romans, and most of the European peoples prior to the advent of the national state and its increasingly atomizing effect upon kindred, clan, and household. It was a type of family, Le Play observed, that combined communality and opportunity for individual expression in a way that avoided the corporatism of the ancient patriarchal type of family on the one hand and the egoistic particularism of modernity on the other. Le Play thought revival of the family, for purposes of both mutual aid and individual enterprise in all spheres, the sovereign need of a Western Europe that was fast becoming straitjacketed by national centralization and bureaucracy.

Every great age, and every great people, Le Play discovered, is characterized at bottom by the strength of the kinship principle. We can, he argued, use the family as an almost infallible touchstone of the material and cultural prosperity of a people. When it is strong, closely linked with private property, treated as the essential context of education in society, and its sanctity recognized by law and custom, the probability is extremely high that we shall find the rest of the social order characterized by that subtle but puissant fusion of stability and individual mobility which is the hallmark of great ages.

I believe that by common assent the Greeks, Jews, and Chinese are the three most creative peoples in history of whom we have substantial record. There is not much of high quality in Western civilization that is not the product of thought processes emanating within from the first two and from thought processes diffused to the West from China. Naturally, fusion in complex and often subtle ways of these thought processes has been a vital aspect of the record. Observe in all three of these peoples, especially during periods of their greatest creative fertility, the immense strength of the family tie. Family has been more than the nidus of cohesion and of continuity; it has been visibly the source of themes in ethics, literature, and art which have been among the very brightest and most durable in the history of civilization. Merely to study the great fifth century B.C. in ancient Greece is to be struck repeatedly by the power that kinship and its multifold themes exerted upon tragedy and comedy alike, upon religion, and also upon philosophy. Nor was the matter very different in England's Age of Elizabeth, not very far in quality and intensity from the Athens of Pericles. Here too we are struck by endemic fascination with family, descent, lineage, and all the vices as well as virtues inseparable from the bond of kinship. It is pretty much the same, I believe, in all the greater ages of culture. Granted, as I shall stress in the next section, that localism is also vital, family yet remains the greatest single element of a creative culture—that is, so far as social contexts are concerned.

I am aware that more than simple family allegiance is involved in such ages. Using literature as an example, there is almost invariably to be seen the unleashing of passions, emotions, and moral evils which can properly be regarded as signs of disintegration of family, of conflicts often too great to be contained within a single kindship community. But such observation in no way negates the social and psychological importance of the kinship principle. Only the naivest would ever define or conceive of family as a synonym for unadulterated love and tranquility.

Almost certainly it is the form and significance of the family tie rather than racial or genetic stock that explains individual achievement in history. That variations of genetic quality exist among population groups, as among individuals, is scarcely to be denied. But, as Tocqueville declared, almost passionately, in his interchange of views on race with Gobineau, it is unlikely that we shall ever be able to so isolate and hold constant non-genetic factors as to assess usefully the role of the biological—the actual, operational function of the genetic—in the appearance of genius.

It was Sir Francis Galton among modern scholars who first called attention to the striking relationship between individual achievement and family line. He did not err in seeing the whole issue in terms of family—conceived as a unity in time as well as of place. Where Galton unfortunately did err was in his assumption that what is crucial in family is *genetic*. It was to the biological element, basically, that Galton was referring in his notable concept—and it is only a hypothesis, we must remember, in Galton—of "genius." Why are certain individuals great? Because, Galton tells us, of their "genius"; that is, their superior biological aptitude transmitted through the family line.

What Galton neglected in kinship was the important *social* aspect of norms, roles, statuses, and traditions transmitted from generation to generation. That talented individuals so frequently are found to have talented, or at least extraordinary, fathers or mothers and even more distant forebears and relatives may and probably does argue something in behalf of genetic transmission, but it much more visibly and incontestably argues something in the way of continuity of cultural patterns: patterns of incentive—recorded achievement to serve as example; of the kind of training and instruction that can come only from someone who is emotionally close, indeed persistingly close; and of the discipline, encouragement, and emulation which are so vital in the formation of personalities, good or bad, gifted or sterile.

In his superb *The Art of Teaching*, the classical scholar Gilbert Highet has given special attention to the father as teacher in history. Rightly does Highet write: "It would be interesting to write a book on the fathers of great men: those who educated their sons by neglecting them, those who educated their sons by bullying and thwarting them, those who educated their sons by being their friends." Precisely! Let us have no nonsense about love and unremitting devotion—among the most evanescent and rare of qualities, surely, in the total picture of the family that history reveals; for, paradoxical as it may seem, it is not love—least of all sexual passion—that the family has been built around historically, but, rather, duty and obligation. And these, obviously, may or may not coexist with love and affection.

This is why, as Durkheim pointed out in several of his lectures and essays on morality, the conjugal family—so single-mindedly stressed in modern culture—is the last important aspect of the kinship institution save only in respect to its procreative function. As we know, not many peoples apparently have allowed even the conjugal tie to rest upon something so fragile as the emotion of love; but even if we assume that in most places at most times a majority of spouses knew something akin to passionate love, however fleetingly, the great strength of the family has everywhere been consanguineal rather than conjugal. And here, not affection, but duty, obligation, honor, mutual aid, and protection have been the key elements.

And yet, all of this kept in mind, we would be blind were we to neglect the countless instances in the biographies of the great where the kindly if not affectionate devotion of a parent or grandparent or collateral relative proved to be the decisive factor in the subsequent development of the individual concerned. Granted, as Highet points out, that Beethoven's father was a drunk and often a bully, with Beethoven's own revolt against his father a paramount aspect of his life, the father yet taught Beethoven at the age of four both violin and clavier. And there is much reason to suppose that the relationships that existed between Mozart and his father, within the Bach family as a whole, or, changing our field of illustration, between Aristotle and his biologist-physician father or St. Augustine and his Christian mother and pagan father, have been by far more characteristic of the emergence of genius or great talent.

Quite as important, though, as the direct relation between two or more family members of different generations is the tradition that can develop within a family line over a succession of generations. No prescription can be infallible in such complex matters as these, but one is almost tempted to recommend a minimum of three sequential generations of cultural quality within a single family line for the production of truly high talent. Heaven knows, exceptions abound of every kind, and the last thing I would claim for this section is the secret of genius, which will no doubt be a well kept one for a long time. And yet the continuity of these intellectual and cultural elements of high quality in a family line in which unity of property has a powerful constraining effect is surely of inestimable value. As I say, Galton did not err in pointing to genealogical continuity, only in assuming that biological stock was alone vital in this. Far more important, it would seem to me, in the eventual emergence of a Charles Darwin was exposure to the legacy of a grandfather like Erasmus, no less fascinated than his grandson with fauna and flora and the complex relations in time and space to be found among them. For such a legacy cannot help but create an ambience of striking value and stimulus. Nor was Charles Darwin without other family relationships, on both sides, which must have had cumulative effect in the creation of a fertile tradition.

Emulation is a most important element of the creative process. The Roman Velleius Paterculus, among the first to speculate on the spasmodic appearance of genius and great talent in history, using the drama as his primary example of thought, concluded that emulation was the vital factor. Naturally, it need not be emulation solely or even at all of a parent or other relative, but clearly kinship is the commonest field of emulation.

There are, of course, surrogate fathers. I mean the kind of teacher or "father" of whom Socrates will always remain the most luminous example in Western thought. Here instruction is vastly more than what is ordinarily conveyed by that word. There is the whole range of ties, from explicit coercion and discipline to affection and devotion, that makes the teaching-learning process almost indistinguishable from what might be found in the kinship context. What Alfred North Whitehead called "the habitual vision of greatness" is without any question crucial in the life of the pupil—be he child of parent or child of great teacher. There could not be very many truly creative minds in history which lacked altogether in their formative priods "the habitual vision of greatness," whether this was experienced in family or, *in loco parentis*, in a Socrates-Plato relation or, as the American educational idiom has it, with Mark Hopkins at one end of a log and a pupil at the other.

Heredity, then, is immensely important to any society that prizes genius and talent. But it is an error of vast proportion to limit this word to what is transmitted by the germ plasm. Social and cultural and moral heredity are equally real within any family line.

For a long time it was a cardinal proposition of the democratic dogma—one derived chiefly from Rousseau—that what had been accomplished by kinship for so many millennia in history could be accomplished in equal, if not superior, degree by other structures, such as the public school. Given the stress upon equalitarianism in the Rousseauian and populist traditions of democracy, animus toward the family might be expected. Rousseau, as we have noted, saw the state as the means of saving the children from the prejudices of their parents, and like all others who have made the state the sacred object of their aspirations, he saw it as the indispensable instrument of the kind of equality to which kinship, when active and buoyant, must forever be a barrier.

We have discovered that the school, for all the vast sums of money spent on it in American society, is not, by itself, particularly effective. That it is indispensable to any society such as ours is evident enough; the technical demands of modern society make school and college imperative. But, as countless studies—the most important and exhaustive being the now famous Coleman report—have suggested, the effectiveness of the school is greatest when it is united in a pupil's life with family. We know of great peoples and ages of history where a strong family system, together with deliberately created surrogates for the family and its roles, has existed in the total absence of institutions comparable to our by now almost hopelessly formalized and bureaucratized schools and colleges. But we have not yet seen a great people or great age of history resting on the school or college to the exclusion of those ties and motivations which are inseparable from kinship.

It should be obvious that family, not the individual, is the real molecule of society, the key link of the social chain of being. It is inconceivable to me that either intellectual growth or social order or the roots of liberty can possibly be maintained among a people unless the kinship tie is strong and has both functional significance and symbolic authority. On no single institution has the modern political state rested with more destructive weight than on the family. From Plato's obliteration of the family in his *Republic*, through Hobbes, Rousseau, Bentham, and Marx, hostility to family has been an abiding element of the West's political clerisy.

THE REVIVAL OF LOCALISM

Along with the apparent beginnings of a renascence of the kinship tie are those of revival of the sense of locality and neighborhood. There is, of course, close affinity between the two types of social attachment, and there has been ever since the local community came into being, with the rise of the agricultural arts, approximately ten thousand years ago. The toll exacted from both social unities by modern forces of collectivization and centralization has been great.

Recent events in both the totalitarian countries and the democracies make evident how deeply rooted the local tie, like kinship, remains in the human spirit. Extreme measures taken during the past several years by the Chinese government suggest how resistant to national collectivization village and regional allegiances remain. In Soviet Russia even after a half century of continuous official assault upon these allegiances, we learn that they continue to exist and, at times, to make difficult the life of the bureaucrat in Moscow.

In the United States conflict between national government and the smaller regional and local ties has been evident from the beginning, with nationalism on the whole winning out. Even so the emotional roots of local loyalties remain strong. The results in this country of the government effort to achieve racial balance in the schools is some indication of how profound are human loyalties to neighborhood and local community. I do not doubt that some of the resistance to busing is racist in origins. But by this time agreement is quite general that the greater part of the opposition to such busing springs directly from pride in and sense of attachment to neighborhood.

Nor are expressions of such attachment confined to opposition to integration quotas. We could have taken some counsel from the bitter reactions beginning in the late 1940s, perhaps even earlier, to urban renewal and to the depredations of what has so well been called "the Federal bulldozer." Jane Jacobs is only the most eloquent of experts on town and city planning to register dismay at the callous destruction in the larger cities of old and tightly constituted communities, some ethnic, some occupational, most merely local, under the spur of Federal programs of urban reconstruction. It could well be that the greatest and most valuable single consequence of such nationalizing programs is the counteracting awareness on the part of individuals of how much locality means in their lives.

The fault is by no means lodged in Federal government alone. Great industries, trade unions, and other elements of American society have not infrequently shown—and often lived to regret—comparable insensitivity to local allegiances. We have seen, during the past two or three decades, small businesses, branches of large business, and union locals react with extreme passion to centralizing, nationalizing programs of great industrial and labor organizations. The situation is hardly different in the university. It would be difficult to list accurately all of the once-small, once-local colleges and schools which, after World War II, were swept into large, unified, centralized systems of university administration in the various states, all in the name of educational progress and efficiency.

Many years ago, in his *School for Dictators*, Ignazio Silone wrote:

> The first test to be applied in judging an alleged democracy is the degree of self-governing of its local institutions. If the master's rule in the factories is absolute, if the trade unions are controlled by bureaucracies, if the province is governed by representatives of the central government, there can be no true and complete democracy. Only local government can accustom men to responsibility and independence, and enable them to take part in the wider life of the state.

Silone gives modern expression to a very old theme in Western writing on freedom. Aristotle knew how important, even with the culmination of social evolution in the political state, the local community and its prosperity were, and his criticisms of Plato's centralized, unitary state rest upon defense of localism as much as any other form of social attachment. Similarly, the names of St. Benedict, Thomas More, Althusius, Burke, Tocqueville, Le Play, W. H. Riehl, and, in our century, Patrick Geddes and Victor Branford in England and Lewis Mumford in this country are properly associated with awareness of the importance of local ties in a genuinely stable and free society.

Unfortunately the tradition they represent has been overshadowed, especially in modern times, by that which is devoted to the homogeneous national state and to centralization of power. Plato had no more affection for local autonomies within his ideal political order than he did for any other distractions from its unity. And from Plato through the Roman Lawyers, Marsiglio, Machiavelli, Hobbes, Rousseau, and Bentham, down to our own clerisy of power today, there has been scant regard for the values of localism and regionalism. Progress was escape from localism. Mumford writes that in the eighteenth century the *philosophes* and others of like devotion to the uses of central power would in drawing a burgomaster commonly give him the head of a donkey. In England

Bentham and other Philosophical Radicals, committed as they were to a nationalized civil service with power focused in the national capital, did everything in their capacity to weaken the traditional liberties and functions of the villages and towns, in which Bentham saw only the dead hand of the past.

There is no more affection for the values of localism in Marx and Engels. Marx, as I have noted, even endorsed English depredations in India on the ground that these would hasten Indian emancipation from the village. "The idiocy of rural life" is the phrase in the *Manifesto* that faithfully reflects Marx's attitude toward local allegiances, and his own hatred was continued in that of the Bolsheviks for the *mir* and other traditional unities of place in Russia.

Such, however, was the depth of regard in Russia for local attachments that the Bolsheviks were forced, in their bid for power, to support a high degree of local autonomy. Hannah Arendt in *On Revolution* writes that the most popular, and undoubtedly crucial, of all Bolshevik proposals in 1917, second only to bread, was the idea of the *soviet,* which was in principle a local articulation of economic, social, cultural, and political functions. "All power to the soviets" was, as every student of the Russian Revolution knows, one of the most popular slogans, and it was only after several of the peoples' soviets had been put down bloodily by Bolshevik forces in the interests of party rule and Communist centralization that it became evident how hollow Lenin's promises regarding the soviets actually were. To this day the use of the word "soviet" in the official name of the Russian nation is some testimony to the continuing appeal of the idea of the soviets. Their existence is, however, purely nominal and has been since the earliest days of the Revolution. It was discovery of that fact, almost above anything else, that turned such previously eager minds as Emma Goldman, Alexander Berkman, and Peter Kropotkin away in deep disillusionment from the Russian Revolution.

It is interesting to discover that prior to about World War I, the principle of localism had become a powerful one in a good many

Western circles. In England the first major book of Sidney and Beatrice Webb was on the history of local government in England, and the story of the Webbs' life can be told pretty much in the tragic evolution we see from their early interest in localism and pluralism to their notorious whitewash of Stalinist government in the 1930s. Along with the early Webbs there were the Fabians and the Guild Socialists in England. On the continent the syndicalists and cooperationists were strong. In all of these, under whatever name, there was deep recognition of the vital importance of the local community. In the social philosophy of the great town planning movements associated with Riehl, Le Play, Geddes, and Branford in Europe and with Ralph Adams Cram in this country, the local community and its development was foremost. Socialist thought in this country—never extensive, to be sure—was strongly tinctured by values at once utopian and local. The increasingly nationalized socialism of such a country as Germany was utterly foreign to socialist thought in America.

World War I is, I think, the sharp dividing line. Afterward interest in local community did not attain its earlier intensity, flavor, and eloquence. The influence of Woodrow Wilson and his New Freedom in this country and of Lenin in European radical thought had a great deal to do with turning revolutionary and progressive thought away from its concern with locality or, for that matter, any of the smaller unities. The nation, the centralized nation freed of local regional encrustations, seemed to an ever larger number of intellectuals the true repository of the spirit of progress. Suddenly the local community became the symbol of reaction, dullness, mediocrity, and oppression of mind. Sinclair Lewis's *Main Street, Babbitt*, and other novels were only the most popular of a literature in the 1920s that satirized, caricatured, and pilloried the village or small town. And such rendering of local roots was in keeping with the increasing nationalism to be seen in the social sciences, in education, and in government policy from World War I on.

Schools and colleges were particularly hurt by it. So much of their genius and effectiveness had been precisely their close relation to locality and region, making possible an unrivaled diversity and opportunity for experiment in American education, as contrasted with European. But increasingly, from one side of the country to the other, national models began to prevail. Universities like Harvard sought to broadcast the image of a "national" rather than local or regional university; and what Harvard began, and managed to do with some distinction, other universities in all parts of the country sought to emulate, often taking Harvard as the model but failing for the most part to achieve comparable distinction—and losing much of what had been distinctive and potentially creative in their regional flavor.

As I say, all that may be about to reverse itself. Certainly, there is a manifest reaffirmation of the tie of neighborhood, whether in city or suburb, some of it—though not all, by any means—in reaction to integration-based busing operations. But there is more, I suspect, to this beginning of local renascence than reaction to busing or to urban renewal projects emanating from Washington. The weakened position of nationalism on the world scene, the growing acceptance of transnational economic and political authorities, bespeak a certain universalism that harmonizes very nicely with localism in any given country. This point needs brief expansion.

Despite a widespread misunderstanding, the era of the national state has been as disruptive of an earlier universalism in the West as it has of an earlier localism. There is nothing paradoxical in the fact that in medieval society, when local roots were strong, one could make his way—as so many traders, merchants, students, and others did regularly—throughout Western society without the slightest thought of passports, visas, or other restrictions upon travel. It was, as only a few historians have adequately realized, the absence then of the national state in any significant form that made possible economic and intellectual universality, as well as the vigorous town and village life of the Middle Ages. Such remarkable instances of universalism as the various leagues of cities—Hanseatic,

Rhenish, and other—could only have been present in a society largely free of centralized national sovereignty. And that fact is evidenced strongly by the almost instant disappearance of the leagues of cities and towns during the period when national states were becoming powerful. I think it entirely possible that in the years ahead, if national sovereignty should continue to weaken, if the more universal types of economic and political organization continue to increase on the world scene, that the local community everywhere will flourish. We shall then have a chance to see how constrictive, how suffocating, the modern national state has been in its impact upon regional and local diversity.

It is possible that we shall also see a great recovery of culture, high culture, a possible liberation, or the beginning of it, from the twin forces of triviality and subjectivism which have been so long ascendant in Western imaginative writing and art. It is impossible to be certain in such matters, but the historic roots of the greater ages have lain in diverse, varied, relatively small areas rather than in the atmosphere that goes with bigness, impersonality, and standardization. We refer properly, of course, to *American* literature, but looking back on its more resplendent periods of creativity, it is impossible to overlook locality and region. What Van Wyck Brooks and others have referred to as the flowering of New England took place in a strikingly small geographic sector; so did those other efflorescences we identify with New York at the turn of the century, San Francisco, Chicago, and a few other places. It has not been different, really, throughout the history of the creative mind, and this seems to be as true of the sciences, including technology, as of the arts. "The glory that was Greece" was really the achievement of a tiny part of Greece— Athens—in a very short period of time. Rome was, by modern standards, a small town when Vergil and Lucretius flourished. The remarkable developments in the arts and sciences which we find in the twelfth and thirteenth centuries are all tied closely to highly individualized towns; and this role of the locality remains in substantial degree right down to the present century. We take nothing away from the vital, indispensable role of the city in the history of creativity and intellectual freedom in noting all this, for, prior to the metropolitan giants in this century, cities have always possessed, despite their relative size, a tightness and a sense of enclosure that, as is only too obvious now, have disappeared or weakened.

There is also the fact of neighborhood in the city, seemingly as important to the creative mind as to the rest of us. Even on present evidence, artists, writers, and others engaged in analogous pursuits seem to like a certain degree of propinquity. If the modern city as a whole has become too large to serve as did a medieval Florence, Bologna, Oxford, Paris, or a more modern London, Boston, and New York as the effective context of intellectual labor, there is no reason why, within our swollen cities today, there cannot be local influences, as in neighborhoods. Even in a city like New York, there is far more neighborhood community than we commonly give it credit for in the country at large. The tragedy is the lack of recognition in so much national and state policy of the role of neighborhood. When the local-ethnic sentiment began a few years ago to manifest itself in school matters, reaction against it from school systems, urban government, and the Federal bureaucracy was for the most part very strong. No one aware of what happened, what continues to happen, will deny that mistakes have been made, sometimes with serious lowering of academic standards, but it would be wise policy to encourage, aid, and reinforce such local sentiment. Only when education—and art and thought and leadership—can be seen and undertood in genuinely local terms is efflorescence likely. It has always been this way.

By comparison the tie of nationalism in the modern West has been singularly ineffective in promoting intellectual works of high order. I think it is possible to see a certain impetus in the beginning when nationalization takes command, as in England and France in the sixteenth and seventeenth centuries, in Germany in the late nineteenth, and in the United States after the Revolutionary War. I have noted above the coincidence of creative ages and a high degree of politicization, but this coincidence is almost always of very short duration. Alas, what happens after the scintillating presence of a Pericles, Julius Caesar, Frederick II, or like figure in political history is the routinization of politics and a consequent drying up of stimulus.

And in the world we have known since about the middle of the nineteenth century, the spirit of nationalism—so often a deliberately manufactured spirit—has rarely if at all entered into great creative performance. The art, the letters, the music, and the architecture we associate with celebration of the nation as a whole and of its capital is almost always deadly. We see such work at its worst when the nationalist mind is seized by war and its passions. This state of mind can be very destructive of art and thought, as in its depredations on works thought to be favorable to the enemy (the tearing out of German songs from American songbooks during World War I will serve as an example here), and its record of constructive achievement is dismal and frightening.

Any release, though, from the hold of nationalism in all areas is not likely to come easily or soon. I noted in the first chapter the signal decline of the tie of patriotism in each of the Western countries, but it will not do to see in that decline the weakening also of the spirit of nationalism. For that spirit is sustained largely by centralization and collectivization of power, qualities which, as we have seen, continue to loom large in the conventional wisdom of the political clerisy. A whole philosophy of history—false, as I believe, but not the less powerful in its hold on the intellectual mind—tells us that progress has consisted in mankind's liberation from the smaller unities of village, town, and region, and in mobilization at the national level of loyalties which once went directly to them. To think, dream, plan, and hope in terms of the entire nation has been for a long time the mark of the political intellectual in whatever area he works—economy, education, or the arts and sciences. What Tocqueville wrote on the subject remains pertinent:

> I am of the opinion that, in the democratic ages which are opening upon us, individual independence and local liberties will ever be the products of art; that centralization will be the natural government.

VOLUNTARY ASSOCIATION

Despite the American creed of individualism, which locates motivation and achievement in the recesses of the individual mind and character, human accomplishment in almost any form is the product of association, usually in small and informal structures whose essence is a high degree of autonomy. This is in no way to obliterate the fact of individuality, to deny the superlative powers which lie in certain individuals in all realms of culture and society; it is simply to call attention to the contexts in which individuals, even the greatest, thrive. What John Dewey wrote many years ago is eloquent and correct:

> Individuals who are not bound together in associations, whether domestic, economic, religious, political, artistic or educational, are monstrosities. It is absurd to suppose that the ties which hold them together are merely external and do not react into mentality and character, producing the framework of personal disposition.

It is only under the spell of the romantic individualism we have known for two centuries in the West that the myth of purely individual achievement—reflected in the enormous number of biographies written during the last hundred years or more—has achieved the commanding importance it so plainly has even at the present time. Only in the best of these, and even then the going can be difficult, do we come to sense the crucial importance in the life of even the most gifted creator or innovator of the tiny network of human attachments which is the true field of the creative impulse. Over and over, whether in literature, art, science, politics, economic enterprise, or technology, what we discover if we look carefully is not the lone individual obeying inner impulses but the human being who at some crucial point in his development has known, commonly in the most intimate and spontaneous of ways, a circle of other human beings brought together by common interests. That statement is as true of Darwin and Einstein as it is of Cézanne and Picasso. There is not a hint of social determinism in it; only recognition of the fact that it is in association—intimate, relevant, and free association—that individual energies become stimulated, strengthened, and, finally, focused.

Crucial are the *voluntary* groups and associations. It is the element of the spontaneous, of untrammeled, unforced volition, that is undoubtedly vital to creative relationships among individuals. Such associations have figured prominently throughout history, and we should no doubt know a great deal more than we do about them were it not for a historiography in the West that has been anchored for so long in the political state on the one hand and the individual on the other. Every city, every large, formal organization, when carefully examined, turns out to be a network of small, informal, voluntary associations. If cafes, taverns, and similar establishments have assumed importance in the history of culture, along with forums and town squares, it is because these are such natural environments for autonomous groups. It would be interesting to know whether, as the result of urban planning and contemporary styles of architecture, and also of skyrocketing of land values, there are as many such natural environments as there once were. I am inclined to believe that there are not, a fact that is bound to affect the nature of personality and the whole creative process.

But voluntary associations have an importance well beyond what they do directly for their individual members. Most of the functions which are today lodged either in the state or in great formal organizations came into existence in the first place in the context of largely voluntary association. This is true of mutual aid in all of its forms—education, socialization, social security, recreation, and the like. To say, as is so often said, that responsibility has passed from the *individual* to the state is a half-truth. It is much truer to say that responsibility has passed to the state from what were once voluntary associations. It is in the context of such association, in short, that most steps in social progress have taken place. To compare our bureaucratized, politicized age with some age in the past when individuals were obliged to look out for themselves, singly or in small households, is mere fantasy. Once we look carefully into the matter we are surprised by how many social groups, associations, and communities there actually were through which the fragility and precariousness of individual and family life were moderated.

It is impossible not to conclude that the impulse to form spontaneous and voluntary associations, of all sizes, has diminished in recent times. How could it not have? The whole thrust of modern society toward a politically managed social order; the well-recorded jealousy of governments, even democratic ones, toward such associations; and the incredible network of ordinances, zoning regulations, legal preemptions, and other emanations of the political order which hamstring the associative ethic—all these and other forces make voluntary association difficult indeed in our age, especially, it should be noted, when such association tries to deal with really significant social and economic problems.

There is a curious paradox in the legal position of voluntary associations today. In one sense they have a constitutional status they lacked in the past in this country. Yet is is not difficult to show that for political reasons their actual autonomy and mobility are less than in the past. Strangely, and regrettably, the Founding Fathers said nothing about freedom of association in their Constitution; the right to petition and freedom of assembly are very different from freedom of association. One can only conclude that the reigning political minds in this country were as uneasy at the thought of internal, private associations as were many European thinkers, *philosophes* included. The prized unity of the state, ideally resting on the people considered as a whole rather than as an assemblage of possibly discordant groups, made such associations unwelcome; for they all too easily become, it was thought on both sides of the Atlantic, conspiracies. Secret societies, even those in the form of lodges, were for a long time suspect on the ground of possible conspiracy. Very probably the law of conspiracy, to this day a powerful and enveloping law, has discouraged a great deal of voluntary association. An act that is relatively venial in individual conduct can become felonious when engaged in by two or more persons. Such is the state's fear of internal association, going back deep in modern political history.

In 1958 the Supreme Court in effect brought freedom of association up to constitutional level by affirming the right of the NAACP to carry on its regular activities in Alabama. According to Charles E. Rice, whose study of the relation of law to associations is seminal, this decision was the first in American history to give constitutional status to a freedom that has been widespread in America almost from the beginning.

Even so, one could wish for a specific, detailed amendment to the Constitution granting this intellectually and politically vital freedom. For, however welcome the Supreme Court decision is, it has to be seen among a whole thicket of other decisions, laws, and ordinances which by this time in our history make the actual act of voluntary association difficult. The paradox I mentioned above consists in the fact that while we do live now in the afterglow of a salutary Supreme Court decision, still the general combination of politicization of society, increasing recourse to bureaucracy and formal organization, and the predictably hostile attitude of the clerisy of power makes any really substantive freedom of association seem tenuous.

In the past freedom of association in this country was far from tenuous. Lack of constitutional sanction notwithstanding, proliferation of voluntary groups, associations, and societies was great throughout the nineteenth century, down, indeed, to World War I. Nothing seems to have impressed Tocqueville, and then later Lord Bryce in his own study of American democracy, more than did the great wealth of associations, constructed around a large variety of objectives and interests. Tocqueville well knew the status of such associations in France, a status that went back to the *ancien régime* and that had been given heavy confirmation by the Revolutionary law of 1791 which in effect forbade all voluntary associations. He knew too that nothing in the American Constitution specifically granted Americans this form of freedom, one that Tocqueville admired. He had already formed a strong opinion of the necessity of free voluntary associations to any free society, especially when that society is a democracy. He was as sensitive as Lamennais, Lacordaire, and Montalembert to the insufficiency of a merely individual freedom in the modern mass state. His firm belief in autonomous association, along with localism and decentralization, carried through indeed to his work on the Constitutional Commission in the Revolution of 1848, where, with Lamennais (whom he did not much like), he made every possible effort to embed these principles in the constitution.

It is of course in *Democracy in America* that we have the most eloquent and penetrating account of the value of voluntary association. There Tocqueville sets forth this value in political, social, and also psychological terms. Voluntary political associations are, of course, political parties, and Tocqueville, recognizing and lamenting somewhat the "decline" of great parties in the United States, declares political parties indispensable to the stability and the freedom of democratic life. Few things, he tells us, are more misunderstood by the sovereigns of Europe than the contributions that could and would be made to the stability of their kingdoms and republics by profuse political association. Political parties not only provide the seed ground for new and necessary legislation; they are also vital structures of opinion and sentiment which would otherwise become mere dust. The occasional danger that a political association may prove to be a conspiracy rather than a party is small by comparison with the dangers which ensue when there are no such associations.

It was, however, in the social, economic, and cultural realms that Tocqueville was most impressed by the remarkable proliferation of associations in American life. Here, in self-help, mutual-aid, and assurance associations, in organizations directed toward the accomplishment of some moral or spiritual end, and in the multitude of little societies for the furtherance of mind and taste, was a whole body of membership and behavior that Tocqueville thought utterly vital to freedom in a democracy. In earlier monarchical-aristocratic society, he tells us, the need for such associations was not so great, for in these the principle of social class, particularly of the aristocracy itself, along with the kind of local diversity that existed, went a long way toward providing society with that variegation and context of autonomy that was required by freedom. In modern democracy, however, the sheer weight of authority that is placed upon the people as a whole, the atomizing effects of democratic sovereignty upon traditional, especially class, distinctions, and the constant threat of public opinion limiting true individual freedom, all give special importance to the preservation of voluntary association. Each such association is a nursery of freedom, if only because it is built around a value or idea that men wish to be free to espouse. Voluntary associations are buffers between individual and state.

"Among the laws that rule human societies," Tocqueville wrote, "there is one which seems to me more precise and clear than all others. If men are to remain civilized or to become so, the art of associating together must grow and improve in the same ratio in which equality of conditions is increased."

I said above that the impulse to significant voluntary association in Western society has withered in recent times. Yet as I write there are also faint signs of a possible resurgence of this impulse—to be seen among the varied reactions today to the failure of the political community in so many areas. The same pattern of forces that includes renewals of religion in certain manifestations, of ethnic loyalties, and of cooperative relationships in the smaller spheres of living, includes also, I think, a recrudescence of the spirit of voluntary association. It is noteworthy that more and more studies of the phenomenon are beginning to appear, that increased interest is clearly manifest among the younger age groups, and that objectives which only a decade or two ago would have been made the subjects of political action are at the present time nuclei of voluntary association. What would be immensely beneficial is the development of a clear philosophy of voluntary association that could take its place alongside philosophies—also to be hoped for—of the local community and of decentralization. Any such philosophy will, however, have to face the political clerisy's deeply seated aversion to any form of social pluralism. The Renaissance-born, revolution-developed fondness for the unitary state based on an undifferentiated mass of citizens, availing itself of every possible technique of centralized power applied in nationalist-collectivist terms, will not disappear easily. To the mind of the political intellectual today, as in the age of the Italian humanists and in that of the Jacobins, nothing must seem more absurd, more reactionary, more at odds with the locomotive of history than what is private, voluntary, and social.

But one need only scan the pages of comparative social and cultural histories to be made aware of how often human societies have been rescued from political paralysis, from the boredom and apathy which go with homogeneity of life, and from the subjectivism that in time becomes the death of culture, by processes which are, at bottom, those of voluntary association turning itself imaginatively to new ways of life and thought.

A NEW LAISSEZ-FAIRE

Basically, the problem is not one of any single type of group, community, or association. The essential problem to be met, whether by legislative and judicial design or by the forces of history, is that of creating a setting in which the social impulse will flourish. I mean the impulse to form associations of whatever kind in which significant function or role in the larger society can be combined with the sense of the social bond, of social authority, that is so fundamental to freedom in any of its significant forms. I have argued at length in this book that the greatest need in our age is that of somehow redressing the balance between political-military power on the one hand and the structure of authority that lies in human groups such as neighborhood, family, labor union, profession, and voluntary association.

What is required, obviously, is a form of laissez-faire that has for its object, not the abstract individual, whether economic man or political man, but rather the social group or association. I argued this a quarter of a century ago, although briefly, in *The Quest for Community*, suggesting there that only through such laissez-faire could the human need for community be met through ways other than politics—political action, political crusade, political Leviathan.

Nothing that has happened in twenty-five years indicates that the need for this kind of laissez-faire is anything but greater than ever. In an era of prosperity and opulence that could hardly have been imagined in 1950 we have seen the powers of government and bureaucracy steadily increase, to the corresponding moribundity of the social order. Mere economic affluence, we have discovered, can indeed be a virtual recipe for the widespread turning of responsibilities over to the ever-flowing revenue powers of government and for the consequent divorce between human beings and their ordinary, natural impulses toward social initiative.

What is required and what, on the evidence of history, periodically occurs is the establishment of a scene in which there is profound incentive to form, and to live in and by, associations or groups which are distinct from political government. It is absurd to say that such a scene exists at the present time. In countless ways, as I have indicated in the preceding sections, government, and also a whole attitude of mind supported by the political clerisy, discourages or makes difficult such associations. The police-sniffing in the name of conspiracy that goes on constantly is well accompanied by the kind of sniffing in disdain we find in the ranks of political intellectuals for whom anything worth doing is only worth doing through the political government. The blunt fact is, a large number of obstacles, starting with the mentality of the political clerisy, exist today so far as groups and communities are concerned, just as a large number of obstacles could be seen at the time Adam Smith, Turgot, and Ricardo proposed, in effect, a laissez-faire for individuals. I consider it just as important today as it was in these philosophers' time to stimulate through every possible means the liberty and creativeness of individuals. But our age is very different from theirs in the degree of strength that then existed, but now does not exist, in the social sphere.

It is not necessary to repeat what I have said in several connections in this book: that individual initiative and talent are rarely to be found outside the framework of some kind of moral and intellectual community. The point is simply that where an Adam Smith could rightly see in the sometimes too-abundant strength of the traditional social order occasional oppression of individual talent, in our own day the problem is that of finding the means of generating a social order within which the individual can live and derive a spirit of initiative. Nowhere, not in economy, state, or culture in any of its forms, do we in fact find aggregates of "individuals." What we find are human beings bound, in one or other degree, by ties of work, friendship, recreation, learning, faith, love, and mutual aid. That such ties can on occasion become constricting is not to be questioned. There are indeed ages, as I have noted, which are too strong in the social ties which in our own age in the West have grown so weak and attenuated. Nor do I doubt that there are a few individuals, by no means pathological, who, far more than most of us, desire solitude and liberation from the social bond in any form. Such individuals are not, however, elements of the problem we face at the present time.

Clearly, in an epoch of massive politicization, and with this of atomization of not merely numerous forms of association but also of the social impulse itself, we are in need of the creation, or re-creation, of *intermediate* associations, of groups and communities which lie intermediate to individual and state and whose autonomy from either state or the political mentality is some measure of the allegiance they command in their members' lives. With such inter-mediate associations, those which exist normally in society, or those which might be created through legislation along lines both Emile Durkheim and Lord Keynes separately proposed, with max-imum autonomy of operation once brought into being, a great deal of administration would be possible that would not be mired in the vast, imperial bureaucracies which now fill the political landscape. What has long been known as *indirect* administration would be pos-sible in far higher proportion than exists at the present time. Of all the tragedies which have attended the effort to spread democracy without, however, altering the essentially Romanist form of the state that came into being in the Renaissance, the greatest, I am inclined to think, is the systematic flouting by government of the richly varied groups and institutions in the social order which could so easily become themselves the channels or instruments of governmental funding when this becomes necessary in time of cri-sis.

A single illustration will serve here: that embodied in Milton Friedman's celebrated plan for a negative income tax on the one hand and educational vouchers on the other. From what labyrinths of bureaucracy we would be saved in the grim worlds of social workers and educational administrators had there been instituted in the beginning a system whereby a natural, already-existing social group—the household—would be the means of distributing public funds for welfare and for education. What better way of encourag-ing initiative in both family and in individual than through use of family as an indirect means of administration. Other organizations come to mind which, in appropriate circumstances, might also become such means or channels: private schools (so notably less expensive and more efficient than public schools), even churches, labor unions, cooperatives, neighborhoods, and so on.

There is nothing fanciful in this. The fact is that in some—now, alas, slight—degree we already engage in indirect administration. Nor should we forget the civilizations and the long ages in which, as in the cases of traditional China and the Western Middle Ages, the vastly greater part of administration was through kinship, guild, and other local groups. The proper way of distinguishing states in human history is not so much by the forms of manifest government as by the relationships which exist between government and the social order. Plainly, a government can be ostensibly "absolute" in its structure and yet, through broad and deep delegation of authorities to existing social groups, or through utilization of these in its administrative operations, be in substance a free government, or at least free society.

But the overriding objective of a new policy of laissez-faire would be that of stimulating *social inventions*. Since this idea is relatively unfamiliar, I must expand briefly on it.

All progress in civilization comes from inventions. It is wholly inadequate to make the word "invention" serve only the material and technological areas. There are also cultural inventions such as the epic poem, the tragedy and comedy, the novel, the essay, the painting, fugue, ballet, and symphony. We are prone to say these are outcomes of "cultural growth," but that is an evasion. Each is an invention. We invent forms of art just as we do mechanical things.

So are there social inventions: creations of structures which become elements of the social bond; some minute, others very large and widely diffused. I do not know why more attention is not paid in the larger study of change to this fact. The history of the social order is not some vague and continuous growth in time, analogous to the growths of plants and organisms, though there is of course a vast inherited symbolism to suggest that such growth is the very essence of society. Nor is the social order a mere emanation from man's biological, instinctual nature. Both the metaphor of growth and the extrapolation of instinct have done infinite harm to the understanding of the social order. We are prone to take something as complex as, say, primitive kinship systems and, because these involve sexual and procreative activities, assume that kinship structure is some kind of evolutionary exfoliation of biological instincts. No mistake could be greater. The origins of kinship in man's history are of course lost, but we would do better to conjure up a vision of some primitive Solon than of mere instinct in the fashioning of structures as ingeniously designed as clan, moiety, and tribe, with their complex requirements of endogamy and exogamy, and their delicate balancings of authority and responsibility.

If mankind's earliest social inventiveness is to be seen in kinship, the discovery of the agricultural and metallurgical arts about ten thousand years ago made possible a large number of other social inventions that in their entirety form what we call the social and economic and political orders. In every legitimate sense of the word the local community, with its often complex functions and roles, was a social invention. So, in due time, was the walled town and then, in rising occurrence, the guild, the trade fair, the marketplace, and the host of other social devices which were hit upon to facilitate handicraft and trade. It is impossible, and also needless, to list in any detail the social inventions which have made their appearances over the past few millennia. Suffice it to say that among them are the monastery, the university, the studio, the trading company, the mutual aid association, the labor union, and the economic corporation. The history of social organization comes down, basically, to the history of the rise and spread of social inventions— relationships among individuals which, once found useful and accepted, have in many cases gone on for thousands of years in a variety of civilizations.

History from this point of view is as checkered as the history of culture or any other area of human life. There have been periods of relative dearth of such inventions and other periods of relative fertility. If we look at the historical record in terms of efflorescence of social inventions we find certain ages very rich which we are often prone to think of as the opposite. Thus the Middle Ages—so long consigned to darkness by historians who took their cues from the Italian humanists or the French *philosophes*—is rich in social inventions, quite as rich indeed as we have discovered it to be in technological inventions. Monastery (in its distinctive Western form), village community, manor, fief, guild, university, parish: these are some of the more notable inventions—"developments" as we are more likely to say—of the medieval period. By comparison the following ages of Renaissance and Reformation were sterile as producers of social forms.

But there have been other periods of richness along these lines, such as the seventeenth century, with its creation of institutes and academies in the arts, letters, and sciences, all admirable as means of uniting the creative impulses of individuals in the areas represented. The eighteenth century is probably best thought of as a period of lull in social respects. This was, after all, the supreme century of development of the idea of the state from its absolutist to its popular form.

The nineteenth century, coming hard on the heels of the great political revolutions of the preceding century, confronted with the challenge of industrialism and its wrenching of so many human beings from the ancient ties of kindred and village, is also relatively rich in social inventions. The mutual aid society in new forms, the consumers' and producers' cooperatives, the assurance societies, the labor unions, and the business corporations were all without exception ingenious adaptations to problems presented by a new economic age. As I have noted, much conservative and radical thought alike saw in some of these structures the bases of a society that would not become devoured by militarism and political power. Nor should we overlook in this century the great wave of anarchist utopias, especially to be seen in the United States. On the frontier there were numerous adaptations along these lines: the storied logging and quilting bees, for example, only two of a significant number of social arrangements whereby the individual was rescued from ineffectuality or insecurity. We exaggerate the "individualism" of the frontier. It was in fact rich in social inventions, all of which were necessary to progress and protection.

I think the twentieth century has been singularly weak on the whole in social respects, and for reasons I have already given. The atmosphere of nationalism, of creeping bureaucratization of social life by the state, the political clerisy's adoration of those things which are done by the state alone have inevitably had a suffocating effect upon the desire to create in social as well as cultural ways.

Is a change becoming evident? I think it is, although it is too soon to be certain. Along with recrudescence of kinship, neighborhood, and local community, there are surely to be seen occasional signs of an inventiveness in social matters that reflects disenchantment with the state. The contemporary commune is, without question, one such sign. It is said that there are at present more than ten thousand communes. If so, there is much significance in that movement. Not very many years ago there were none except the outrightly religious ones, the monasteries. It is quite possible that other social inventions are to be seen coming into existence if we but look closely enough. In large degree social inventiveness and voluntary association are the same, but they should nonetheless be distinguished—such is the potential importance of each considered separately.

Intermediate association, indirect administration, and social invention are in no sense utopian fantasies; history, properly read, is filled with examples of all three. I not only think them worthy of deepest consideration as important avenues of calculated social policy; I believe that such is the widening in our time of the perceived impotence of political government in the scores of social, cultural and economic areas to which it has addressed itself during the past few decades that we are almost certain to see these ideas, along with revived localism, kinship, and voluntary association, being applied in human lives. Just as twilight ages are a recurrent phenomenon of Western history, so are ages of social replenishment, of reinvigoration of social roots, though less distinctly in our history as it is written. Human beings cannot long stand a vacuum of allegiance, and if, as seems evident enough, the political state in its present national, collective, and centralized form is no longer capable of fulfilling expectations and supplying incentives, human beings will surely turn, as they have before in history, to alternative values and relationships.

I do not, I think, underestimate the opposition that will be mobilized on every possible ideological ground against such an eventuality. The voices of the present political order are clamant and often powerful. But I believe they will be revealed, and perhaps before the end of this century, to be as ineffectual as the voices of another once-powerful clerisy in Western history, that of the Roman Catholic Church, proved to be in the fifteenth century.

I hope so. The drive of both clerisies is, and always has been, toward universality with its overtones of homogeneity, toward unity with its inevitable degeneration into uniformity, and toward authority that shortly degenerates into monistic power. Ideas do not entirely make history; social, economic, and military forces are required. But no force ever becomes ascendant apart from an idea or philosophy that gives it legitimacy and intelligibility.

THE IMAGE OF CITIZENSHIP

In the end it all comes down, I suggest, to the way in which we conceive the nature of the citizen. In the Middle Ages the essence of citizenship was urban man's freedom from the exactions of obedience which existed in the more feudal countryside. One was a citizen by virtue of free association in the town, and although individual identity certainly existed in the towns and cities, there were nevertheless substantial contexts of kinship, occupation, religion, and other association which in effect put the individual at the center of a series of concentric circles. There was a great difference between the status of citizen and that of subject. The medieval expression "the city makes free" was apt description of the status, for the most part, of the citizen.

Over the centuries, however, the concept of citizen tended to become increasingly merged with that of political subject. In Hobbes' *Leviathan* and also his *Behemoth* one can see vividly the transition that takes place. The suspicious, even surly, view that Hobbes gives the claimed rights of citizens is part and parcel of the identical view he gives the historic corporate liberties of city, university, borough, and nobility. In Rousseau's *Social Contract* the whole matter is resolved by the absolute destruction of any individual or associative rights whatever and the assimilation of both into the monolithic General Will. In the French Revolution the title *citizen* became the highest possible form of address, replacing such ancient and honorable titles as *father*, *magistrate*, *scholar*, *priest*, and *lord*. Patriotism was now anchored in the state *une et indivisible*. The Revolution achieved what absolute monarchy had never been able to achieve; it swept with "gigantic broom," in Marx's words, all the smaller patriotisms away, leaving individual and national state as the two ascendant realities. The new citizenship, far from being based upon, rooted in, the social groups in which human beings actually live, was now the exclusive property of the unitary national state.

In substantial degree it has been this way ever since. Not, to be sure, in the United States for a long time, where a constitution recognized and guaranteed divisions of power, a hierarchy of authority, and local and regional contexts of citizenship which were almost feudal in certain respects. But, as I have suggested, the Civil War altered this in considerable degree, and World War I, with its war-based, totalitarian enthusiasm, its almost fanatic patriotism, did a great deal more to transform the nature of both loyalty and citizenship. Gradually the claims of locality and region waned. Add to this the popularity of the "melting pot" concept, with its inevitable derogation of regional as well as ethnic identities, and much the same flame of citizenship began to burn in this country that had burned so brightly in France at the time of the Revolution and had succeeded in melting so many of the ancient ties of association.

But that conception of citizenship is by now as obsolete, as moribund, as the kind of political state that gave it birth. We live, as is evident enough, in a world in which the ties of nationalism and patriotism threaten to be like museum pieces, in the West at least; in which the upthrusts of ethnicity, localism, regionalism, religion, and kinship, small and scattered though they yet are, loom up as signposts to the future; in which the single most radical expression of youth is not political creed or crusade but communal retreat from politics. No doubt the conventional wisdom of the political clerisy sees the matter quite differently. The dream of the right President surrounded by the right aides, governing the right Congress, promulgating all the right laws, ordinances, regulations, and decrees, to take effect in all sectors of society, with a now disenchanted multitude converted overnight into a militant and centralized democracy of eager citizens—this dream is presumably an ineradicable one. But as the Reformation taught the West the expendability of one kind of clerisy, so, it seems evident, will this twilight of authority we are living in teach us the expendability of the political clerisy. In simple, blunt truth, the political intellectual is as obsolete as his religious prototype had become by the sixteenth century.

If citizenship is to be restored in any form at all in the Western nations it will be through the processes and structures I have described in the preceding sections of this chapter. Every voting study has shown us that the impulse to participate in politics, to the degree that it exists at all, is closely dependent *not* upon primarily political values and objectives but upon economic, social, and cultural ones. If there is to be a citizenship in the useful and creative sense of that word, it must have its footings in the groups, associations, and localities in which we actually spend our lives—not in the abstract and now bankrupt idea of *patrie*, as conceived by the Jacobins and their descendants.

There are two traditions of citizenship in the West and there have been since Plato and Aristotle. The one draws from the unitary state Plato so adored, with all loyalties other than that to state extenguished in the interest of the state. From Plato to Hobbes and Rousseau to the contemporary political clerisy, that tradition of citizenship has been a powerful one. I would not go so far as to declare it totally wrong, given certain historical circumstances, given times and places where ties of caste, occupation, and church may become oppressive with only the central government a means of some degree of individual liberation. Such conditions are, however, the very opposite of the dominant ones in the West at the present time, when the state in the form of Leviathan has become the overriding form of oppression and exploitation.

The second tradition of citizenship begins in Aristotle's notable criticism of Plato and the unitary communism of *The Republic*. Its essence is Aristotle's pluralist envisagement of the good society. He writes:

> The error of Socrates must be attributed to the false notion of unity from which he starts. Unity there should be, both of family and state, but in some respects only. For there is a point at which a state may attain such a degree of unity as to be no longer a state, or at which without actually ceasing to exist, it will become an inferior state, like harmony passing into unison, or rhythm which has been reduced to a single foot.

This is the tradition of citizenship that became in time the cornerstone of Burke's philosophy of government, but also of the philosophies of such disparate minds as Hegel, Tocqueville, Burckhardt, and Kropotkin—minds one and all committed to the view that citizenship must be rooted in the groups and communities within which human beings actually live. It was Burke who gave this view of citizenship its greatest expression. We find it toward the end of *Reflections on the Revolution in France* where he is commenting on the "geometrical" system of the Jacobins, on their effort to destroy all allegiances in any way competitive with the state, and their determination to replace social diversity with a political monolith of virtue. Burke writes:

> We begin our public affections in families. No cold relation is the zealous citizen. We pass on to our neighborhoods and our provincial connections. These are our inns and resting places. Such division of our country as have been formed by habit and not by a sudden jerk of authority are so many little images of the great country in which the heart has found something it could fill. The love to the whole is not extinguished by this subordinate partiality.

I cannot help thinking that any political society committed to that concept of citizenship, and to the structure of government and society, the plural structure, that must necessarily surround the concept, would find that crises, even those of war, could occur occasionally without fatally wounding the political community and the larger social bond of which it is a part.